TWO VISITS TO THE TEA COUNTRIES OF CHINA AND THE BRITISH TEA PLANTATIONS IN THE HIMALAYA

TWO VISITS TO THE TEA COUNTRIES OF CHINA AND THE BRITISH TEA PLANTATIONS IN THE HIMALAYA

ROBERT FORTUNE

GYAN

Published by

GYAN

Gyan Publishing House
5, Ansari Road
Daryaganj, New Delhi-110002
Phone: 011-47034999, 9811692060
E-mail: books@gyanbooks.com

Distribution Network
gyanbooks.com
India, USA, Canada, UK, Australia

ISBN: 978-93-7225-049-7 (PB)

First Published, 1913

2nd Impression 2026

Printed at: Gyan Press, Delhi.

TWO VISITS TO THE TEA COUNTRIES OF CHINA AND THE BRITISH TEA PLANTATIONS IN THE HIMALAYA
Author: ROBERT FORTUNE

Curious mode of gathering the Ling (Trapa bicornis).

Vol. ii. p. 11.

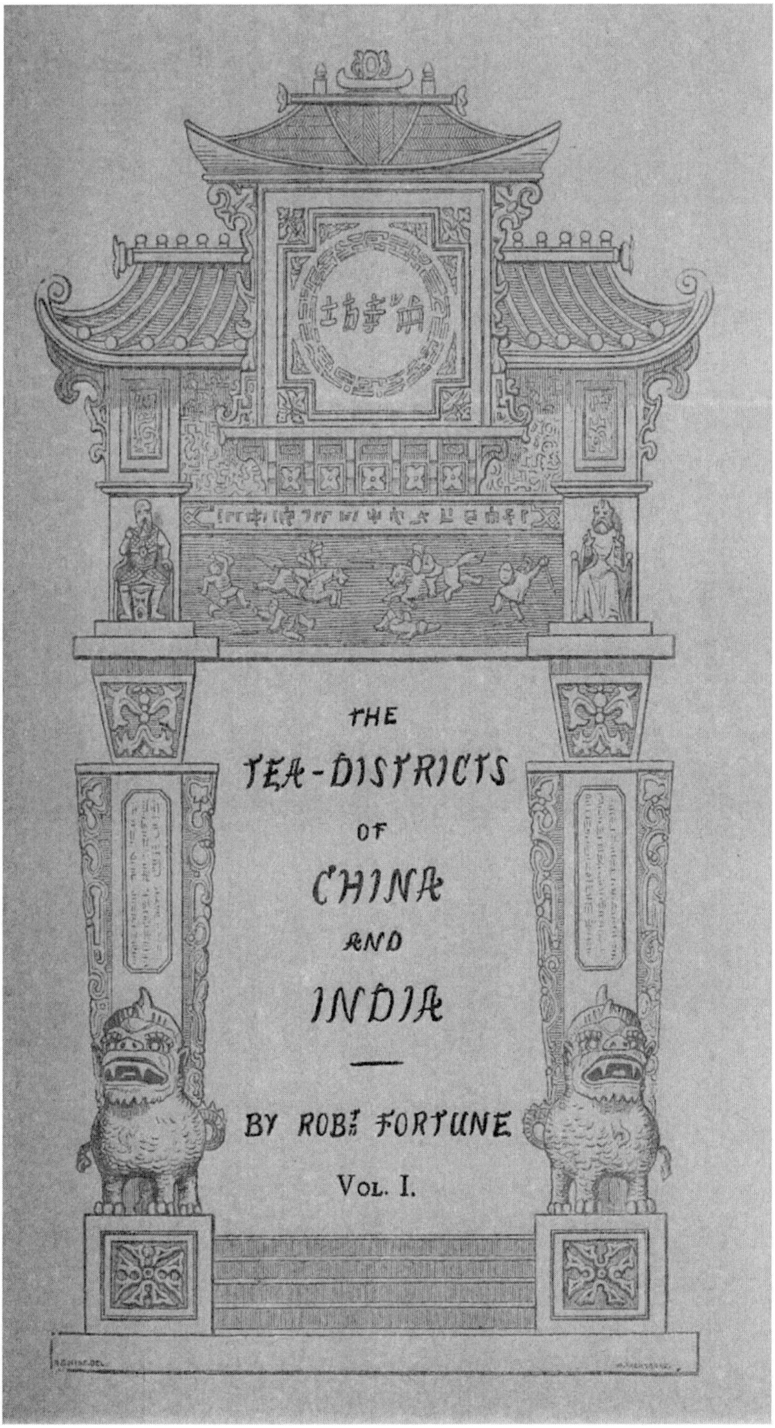
THE
TEA-DISTRICTS
OF
CHINA
AND
INDIA
BY ROBT FORTUNE
VOL. I.

TWO VISITS

TO THE

TEA COUNTRIES OF CHINA

AND THE

BRITISH TEA PLANTATIONS IN THE HIMALAYA;

WITH A NARRATIVE OF ADVENTURES, AND A FULL DESCRIPTION OF THE CULTURE OF THE TEA PLANT, THE AGRICULTURE, HORTICULTURE, AND BOTANY OF CHINA.

BY ROBERT FORTUNE,

FORMERLY BOTANICAL COLLECTOR TO THE HORTICULTURAL SOCIETY OF LONDON, AND NOW IN THE SERVICE OF THE HON. EAST INDIA COMPANY IN CHINA.

IN TWO VOLUMES.—VOL. I.

Third Edition.

WITH MAP AND ILLUSTRATIONS.

LONDON:
JOHN MURRAY, ALBEMARLE STREET.
1853.

PREFACE TO THIRD EDITION.

It is now about ten years since I paid my first visit to the Celestial Empire in the capacity of Botanical Collector to the Horticultural Society of London. On my return to this country in 1846 I ventured to publish an account of my travels in a volume entitled *Three Years' Wanderings in the Northern Provinces of China.* This work was very favourably received by the public, and a second edition was called for soon after the publication of the first. In 1848 I was deputed by the Court of Directors of the East India Company to re-visit China for the purpose of obtaining some tea manufacturers' implements, and a large collection of tea-plants and seeds, from those northern or central districts of the empire where the finest descriptions of teas are made for the European and American markets. A few months ago I returned to England, having accomplished the object of my mission, and submitted to the public an account of my *Journey to the Tea Countries.* My object, as stated in the Preface to that work, was to give the reader "a peep into the Celestial Empire; to show its strange hills and romantic valleys; its rivers and canals; its natural productions, whether in the field, on the hill-side, or in the garden; and its strange and interesting people, as they were seen by me in their every-day life." And I expressed a hope that the public would receive the work in the same kind spirit, and with the same indulgence and favour, that were shown to my first "Wanderings."

My wishes have been fully realized. The *Journey to the Tea Countries* has been received with great favour, both by the public and the press; and, while I gladly take this opportunity of expressing my thanks, I need scarcely say I have been highly gratified.

As the style in which these works were brought out did not admit of their being sold at a price within the means of the great mass of the people, who are no doubt much interested in a country like China, and in the cultivation and manufacture of Tea, a beverage which is now indispensable to the poor as well as to the rich,—"that cheers but not inebriates,"—Mr. Murray is of opinion that an edition slightly abridged will be acceptable; one which, while nothing is left out of importance to the general reader, will enable the work to be brought out at a smaller cost. I have, therefore, gone carefully over the two volumes, and have struck out some things in the first which experience taught me to improve in the second. I have also omitted some meteorological observations and dry botanical details, which, although most acceptable to the scientific and learned, are not very interesting to the general reader. Nothing, however, has been omitted which I believe of general interest. My adventures amongst the most remarkable and least-known people in the world, their manners and customs, the natural productions of the country in so far as they are of importance to man, and, above all, the mode of cultivating and making our favourite beverage, tea, have all been left as originally written in the country itself, unless where my earlier observations have been corrected by more experience. My encounter with a fleet of pirates on the coast of Fokien, which at one time was considered a "traveller's story" by those who were wiser than the traveller, will now, when people have more knowledge of the Chinese, be more easily credited, particularly by the members of missionary societies in Europe and America, who have to deplore the loss of several of their most promising labourers, who have been cruelly murdered by these lawless savages.

London, December, 1852.

CONTENTS OF VOL. I.

CHAPTER I.

CHAPTER II.

CHAPTER III.

CHAPTER IV.

CHAPTER V.

CHAPTER VI.

CHAPTER VII.

CHAPTER VIII.

CHAPTER IX.

CHAPTER X.

CHAPTER XI.

CHAPTER XII.

CHAPTER XIII.

CHAPTER XIV.

CHAPTER XV.

CHAPTER XVI.

CHAPTER XVII.

CHAPTER XVIII.

LIST OF ILLUSTRATIONS.

VOL. I.

WANDERINGS IN CHINA.

FIRST JOURNEY.

CHAPTER I.

First View of China, and the Impressions produced — Land at Hong-kong — Description of its Harbour — Town of Victoria — Chinese Towns, Stanley and Aberdeen — Description of the Island — Effects of Rains — "Happy Valley" noticed — Chinese mode of "Stopping the Supplies" — Views from the Tops of Mountains — Climate — Botany of the Island — Few Animals indigenous — Unhealthiness of the Settlement — Character of the Chinese Population — Mixed Character of Foreigners — Remarks on the Settlement as a Place of Trade.

On the sixth of July, 1843, after a passage of four months from England, I had the first view of the shores of China: and although I had often heard of the bare and unproductive hills of this celebrated country, I certainly was not prepared to find them so barren as they really are. Viewed from the sea, they have everywhere a scorched appearance, with rocks of granite and red clay showing all over their surface: the trees are few, and stunted in their growth, being perfectly useless for anything but fire-wood, the purpose to which they are generally applied in this part of the country. A kind of fir-tree (*Pinus sinensis*) seems to struggle hard for existence, and is found in great quantities all over the hill sides; but, what with the barren nature of the soil, and the Chinese practice of lopping off its branches for fuel, it never attains any size, but is merely a stunted bush. Was this, then, the "flowery land," the land of camellias, azaleas, and roses, of which I had heard so much in England?

After a few hours' pleasant sailing amongst the islands, we at last reached the beautiful bay of Hong-kong, and anchored opposite to the new town of Victoria. Hong-kong bay is one of the finest which I have ever seen; it is eight or ten miles in length, and irregular in breadth; in some places two, and in others six miles wide, having excellent anchorage all over it, and perfectly free from hidden dangers. It is completely sheltered by the mountains of Hong-kong on the south, and by those of the main land of China on the opposite shore; land-locked, in fact, on all sides; so that the shipping can ride out the heaviest gales with perfect safety.

The new town of Victoria is situated on the north side of the island, along the shores of this splendid bay, with the mountain chain rising precipitously and majestically behind it. When viewed from the sea it has a curious and irregular appearance; but as the plan of the town becomes more developed, and better houses are built, it will really be a very pretty little place. When I left China, at the end of December, 1845, it had made most rapid progress; new houses, and even new streets, had risen, as if by magic. Some noble government buildings were nearly completed, to be used as barracks for the soldiers; excellent and substantial houses were erected, or in the course of erection, for the merchants;

and a large Chinese town had been built to the westward, for the principal part of the Chinese population. A beautiful road, called the Queen's Road, has been formed along the shore for several miles; and this was lined with excellent houses and many very good shops. Many of the Chinese shops are little inferior to those in Canton, and certainly equal to what used to be in Macao. In fact, a very large proportion of the Macao shopkeepers have removed their establishments to Hongkong; the former place being now useless for the purpose of trade since the English left it. The bazaar or market is also a most excellent one. Here we find all the natural productions of China, which are brought regularly from the main land; such as the fruits and vegetables indigenous to the country; fowls, ducks, teal, quails, and pheasants; meat of all kinds; and in fact every luxury which the natives or foreigners can possibly require. Besides these, English potatoes, green peas, and several other kinds of foreign vegetables, are plentiful at almost all seasons of the year.

The only other Chinese towns on the island of any note besides the new one just noticed are on the south side, and used to be called Little Hong-kong and Chuckchew: their names have been changed lately by the governor, Sir J. Davis, into *Stanley* and *Aberdeen*. They are merely fishing-towns; but the government always keep up a military station at the latter, which renders it of some importance.

Hong-kong is one of the largest islands near the mouth of the Canton river. It is about eight miles from east to west, and the widest part of it is not more than six miles; but it is very irregular, some parts being only three miles in breadth, and the land jutting out here and there, forming a succession of headlands and bays. Imagine, then, an island considerably longer than it is broad, perfectly mountainous, and sloping in a rugged manner to the water's edge, having here and there deep ravines almost at equal distances along the coast, which extend from the tops of the mountains down to the sea, deepening and widening in their course. There are immense blocks of granite in these ravines, which have either been bared by the rapid currents of water in its descent during the rains, or which have tumbled into them from the sides of the mountains at some former period of time. The water in these ravines is abundant and excellent; and hence the poetical name which the Chinese have given our island—*Hong-kong*, or more properly *Heang-keang*, the "*Island of fragrant streams.*" During the wet season—for it rains in torrents then—these little streams swell with the augmentation of fresh water, and rush down from the mountains with a velocity which sweeps everything before them. In May, 1845, one of these storms of thunder and rain visited Victoria; and the effects produced by it were perfectly astonishing; houses were undermined, roads made at a great expense only a few months before were swept away; drains were burst open; and many of the bridges and other public works rendered perfectly useless. 'The Hong-kong Register' thus notices the storm to which I allude:—"The damage was very great, both to the recently-formed roads and to many buildings in the course of erection;

and had the violence of the rain continued an hour or two longer, many houses must have been undermined and destroyed. As it was, much individual inconvenience has been sustained. About 5 o'clock the whole of Queen's Road, from the entrance to the large bazaar to the market-place, was completely flooded, to the depth of from two to four feet. All the streets leading upwards to the hill served as feeders to this lake. In Peel Street particularly the torrent rushed along, bearing everything before it, and the street still resembles a dried-up watercourse, covered with stones and wrecks of buildings. The passages from the Queen's Road to the sea were all full; the one leading through Chunam's Hong for hours presented the appearance of a rapid river, and many of the houses on each side were only saved from the flood by mud-walls hastily raised. About 6 o'clock the rain moderated, but for some time after the road was quite impassable. A Coolie, attempting to ford the stream rushing down D'Aguilar Street, was borne off his feet, but saved himself by catching hold of the frame of a mat-shed. The drain lately formed could not carry off the water, which committed great devastation, flooding a new house in its vicinity to the depth of nearly three feet, and destroying some new walls. All the open drains in the upper streets have suffered, many are entirely destroyed, leaving scarcely a trace of the street. A stream from a distant watercourse flowed along the road above the bungalow, occupied by the attorney-general, and, descending with great fury upon the roof of one of his out-offices, carried away a great part of it. In many places the Queen's Road has been covered with soil, sand, &c., to the depth of more than two feet, and nearly all the cross drains are choked up. The bridge at the Commissariat has been carried away, and that in the Wang-nai-chung has also disappeared. Several lives were lost by the fall of a house in which some Chinese resided; and it is said the stream at Pokfowlum burst upon a mat hut in which were a number of Coolies employed upon the new road; three saved themselves in a tree, but many more are missing, and are supposed to have been carried out to sea."

There is very little flat ground on the island capable of being brought under cultivation; indeed the only tract of any extent is the "Wang-nai-chung," or, as the English call it, the "Happy Valley," about two miles east from the town; and even that is not more than twenty or thirty acres in extent. There are several other small plots of ground near the bottom of the hills, and some few terraced patches amongst them, but the whole is of very trifling extent. In former times the Chinese used to cultivate crops of rice and vegetables in the Wang-nai-chung Valley, but the place proved to be very unhealthy; and the Government, supposing that the malaria might proceed from the water necessary to bring the crops to maturity, prohibited the natives from cultivating them, and set about draining the land. From this description it will be seen that our settlement on this island is entirely dependent on the dominions of his Celestial Majesty for supplies, which he, of course, can cut off when he pleases. Shortly after the Governor, Sir John Francis Davis, took the helm of affairs in China, he, with the advice of the Legislative Council of Hong-kong, passed a law for registering all the inhabitants of the island, English and Chinese, the latter of course being under the rule of Her Britannic Majesty's representative. The Chinese population, ever jealous of foreigners, fancied there was more in this than met the eye, and that it was done for the purpose of *squeezing* them, and they actually rebelled against the decree. A meeting of all the Compradores and other great men took place, and one of the results was, that the "supplies" were stopped. For several days everything stood still, the Coolies would not work, the boats would not bring provisions, in fact, the Chinese were in a fair way of starving the "Legislative Council of Hong-kong" into making better laws; and they succeeded at last in making them alter the celebrated Registration Act into one more agreeable to their feelings.

From the tops of the mountains the view is grand and imposing in the extreme; mountain is seen rising above mountain, rugged, barren, and wild—the elevation of the highest being nearly two thousand feet; the sea as far as the eye can reach is studded with islands of the same character as Hong-kong; on one side our beautiful bay lies beneath us, crowded with shipping and boats, and, on the other, the far extending waters of the China sea.

The climate of Hong-kong is far from being agreeable, and has proved very unhealthy, both to Europeans and to the native Chinese. During the months of July and August—the hottest in the year—the maximum heat shown by my thermometer was 94° Fahr., and the minimum in the same time was 80°. The difference between the heat of day and night is generally about 10 degrees. In winter the thermometer sometimes sinks as low as the freezing point, but this is a rare occurrence. Even in the midst of winter, when the sun shines, it is scarcely possible to walk out without the shelter of an umbrella, and if any one has the hardihood to attempt it he invariably suffers for his folly. The air is so dry that one can scarcely breathe, and there is no shade to break the force of the almost vertical rays of the sun. At other times in winter, the wind blows cold and cutting from the north, and fires are necessary in the houses; indeed, at all seasons the climate is liable to sudden changes of temperature.

The botany of the island possesses a considerable degree of interest, at least would have done so some years ago, when the plants indigenous to it were less known than they now are. By far the most beautiful plants met with on the low ground are the different species of *Lagerstrœmia*. There are two or three varieties, having red, white, and purple flowers, and in the summer months, when they are in bloom, they are quite the hawthorns of China,—surpassing in their gorgeous flowers even that beautiful family. I have generally met with them in a wild state very near the sea-shore. A little higher up we find the beautiful *Ixora coccinea* flowering in profusion in the clefts of the rocks, and its scarlet heads of bloom under the Hong-kong sun are of the most dazzling brightness. The ravines are crowded with ferns and creeping shrubs of different kinds, not however of much interest to the lover of ornamental flowering plants. Here, however, under the ever-dripping rocks, we find the beautiful *Chirita sinensis*, a plant with elegant foxglove lilac flowers, which I sent to the Horticultural Society soon after I arrived in China, and which is now to be found in many of the gardens of England.

The trees on the island are few, and generally in a stunted condition. The fir (*Pinus sinensis*) is common here, as it is all along the coast of China; *Cunninghamia sinensis* is rare on Hong-kong, although frequently met with on the main land; the tallow-tree is also indigenous, but no use is made of its fruit. Many kinds of the fig tribe are common, and one, the *Ficus nitida*, a kind of banyan, sometimes forms a very ornamental tree. Several species of bamboo seem to grow very well, and in the situations where they are found are strikingly ornamental.

The only trees to the cultivation of which the Chinese pay any attention are the fruit-bearing kinds; and in some places there are very fair orchards containing the Mango, Leechee, Longan, Wangpee, Orange, Citrons, and Pumelows.

Although there are many more species of shrubs and trees indigenous to Hong-kong, yet after all the island has a barren and desolate appearance. The nature of the soil will always be a great barrier in the way of any improvement in this state of things; but even this, to a certain extent at least, may be overcome by the liberality of the Government, or even by the energy and taste of private individuals, and Hong-kong or Victoria may become in a few years very different from what it now is. We have only to look at what has been done as an earnest of what may follow. Trees lately planted are already growing beautifully in the grounds of Messrs. Dents, the Honourable Major Caine, Messrs. Jardine, and Messrs. Matheson, and at Mr. Stewart's a considerable way up the hill.

The island is not rich in indigenous animals. I have frequently seen wild goats feeding in the most inaccessible parts of the rocky crags; there are also deer and foxes, but these are extremely rare. The only animals of the feathered tribe one meets with are, two or three species of kingfishers, some small singing birds and a few wood-pigeons where there are any trees or bushes to shelter them. The main land is much better stocked with birds. From thence the natives bring to the market large quantities of pheasants, partridges, quail, ducks, teal, and sometimes woodcocks and snipes. These birds are seldom seen wild amongst the mountain of Hong-kong, and, when they are, they have only accidentally strayed from the main land. Luckily for the poor Chinese, their waters are much more productive than the land, and an inconceivable variety of fish is daily brought to the markets, and forms, with rice, the staple article of their food.

There are numerous fine quarries of granite along the coast, from which the stone has been obtained for the new town of Victoria. Much of the granite in different parts of the island is in a state of decay, and some ingenious persons have fancied that to this may be ascribed the prevalence of that malignant disease called the

"Hong-kong fever," which has baffled medical skill, and carried hundreds to the tomb.

The autumnal months, August, September, and October, are most unhealthy. In 1843, when I first visited the island, it was in a lamentable condition. A place called the "West Point," where some barracks stood, and which was to all appearance as healthy as any other, proved fatal to the greater part of a detachment of our troops quartered there. The mortality was such that Lord Saltoun, then commander-in-chief, was obliged to remove the wretched remnant, and ordered the barracks to be pulled down. The "Wang-nai-chung," that "*happy* Valley" already noticed, was another most unhealthy spot. One of my fellow-passengers, Mr. Dyer, and his partner, who came out with high hopes of succeeding in business under the new regulations, went to live in this place, where, in a few days, they were seized with fever, and in a few more they had both gone to "that undiscovered country from whose bourne no traveller returns." In other parts of the island, which were at that time considered more healthy, fever prevailed to a great extent. Among those who were carried off, and whose death caused the greatest regret, were Major Pottinger, and the Honourable J. R. Morrison, Chinese interpreter, son of the celebrated Dr. Morrison. The former had been only out for a few days, and was on the point of returning home with despatches for the Government. Many other instances might be mentioned; but these are sufficient to show the deplorable condition of our new settlement at this time; and so malignant and fatal was this disease, that few who were seized ever recovered. The only advice the doctors gave was at once to leave the island and fly to Macao.

The south side of Hong-kong was at this time considered much more healthy than the north, where the new town of Victoria was being built. The prevailing opinion amongst the inhabitants then was that the town ought to have been placed on the south side, which had the advantage of being exposed to the refreshing breeze of the south-west monsoon, from which the north was in a great measure shut out by the range of mountains. This theory, however, was soon disproved, for latterly the troops stationed at Aberdeen, on the south side, have suffered more than those in Victoria.

The native population in Victoria consist of shopkeepers, tradesmen, servants, boat-people, and Coolies, and altogether form a most motley group. Unfortunately there is no inducement for the respectable Chinese merchant to take up his quarters there, and until that takes place we shall always have the worst set of people in the country. The town swarms with thieves and robbers, who are only kept under by the strong armed police lately established. Previous to this, scarcely a dark night passed without some one having his house broken into by an armed band, and all that was valuable being carried off or destroyed. These audacious rascals did not except the Governor even, for one night Government House was robbed; and another time they actually stole the arms of the sentries. These armed bands, sometimes a hundred strong, disappeared, as they came, in a most marvellous manner, and no one seemed to know whence they came or whither they went. Such attacks are fortunately now of rare occurrence. In all my wanderings on the island, and also on the main land hereabouts, I found the inhabitants harmless and civil. I have visited their glens and their mountains, their villages and small towns, and from all the intercourse I have had with them I am bound to give them this character. But perhaps the secret of all was, that I had nothing for them to take, for I was always most careful not to have anything valuable about me, and my clothes, after scrambling amongst the rocks and brushwood, were not very tempting even to a Chinaman.

Since the island of Hong-kong has been ceded to England, the foreign population in it has been much changed. In former days there were only a few mercantile establishments, all known to each other, and generally most upright and honourable men. Now people from all countries, from England to Sydney, flock to the Celestial country, and form a very motley group.

Viewed as a place of trade, I fear Hong-kong will be a failure. The great export and import trade of Southern China must necessarily be carried on at Canton, as heretofore, there being, at present at least, no inducement to bring that trade to Hong-kong. It will, nevertheless, be a place of great importance to many of the merchants, more particularly to those engaged in the opium trade; and will, in fact, be the head-quarters of all houses who have business on the coast, from the facilities of gaining early information regarding the state of the English and Indian markets, now that steam communication has been established between this country and the south of China. Moreover, with all its faults, its importance may yet be acknowledged in the event of another war. Our countrymen cannot have so entirely forgotten the kind of protection which used to be afforded them by the Portuguese at Macao as to make them wish to be put in the same circumstances again; and it is of no little importance to know that their lives and property are safe under the British flag, which has

> . . . . "braved a thousand years
> The battle and the breeze."

CHAPTER II.

Leave Hong-kong for Amoy — Opium Station at Namoa — Liberty the English enjoy there — Chinese Population, and their Modes of living — A new Admiral makes new Laws — Cherry Brandy alters his Views — The Account which, as in Duty bound, he sends to Peking — Amoy — Remarks on its Trade — Travels in the Country amongst the People — The want of a Tail — The Hills — Island of Koo-Lung-Soo — Effects of War — Strange Rocks — Unhealthy Nature of the Island — Botany and Birds — Visit to one of the chief Mandarins — His House and Grounds.

I LEFT the pleasant bay of Hong-kong on the 23rd of August, and sailed for Amoy. As we came out of the harbour by the western entrance, and rounded the south side of the island, I had an excellent view of the little town of Chuckchew, and the military station established there. The town, or village, for it is but a small place, is pleasantly situated on the shores of a deep bay, and fully exposed to the refreshing breezes of the south-west monsoon, and is generally considered much more healthy than the town of Victoria, on the opposite side of the island.

It was now my lot to be seized with that dreadful fever which I have already noticed as so prevalent in our new settlement at this time. I lay in a very precarious state for several days, without the means of procuring medical aid; but the sea air probably did more for me than anything else, and, under Providence, was the means of saving my life. After encountering a strong gale of wind, which we rode out in a deep bay for three days, we at last reached the opium station at Namoa.

Namoa is the name of a small island about half way between Hong-kong and Amoy, and is well known as one of the stations where the contraband trade in opium is carried on between foreign vessels and the Chinese smugglers. At this time I was fresh from England, and full of all the notions which we form there of the sacredness of the Chinese empire. I then thought that, although I might perhaps get a view of the Celestial country, no barbarian feet would be allowed to pollute the sacred soil. Great was my surprise and pleasure when I found the captains of vessels wandering about all over the island unmolested. They had made roads to a considerable extent, and had built a cottage as a sort of smoking-lodge when they landed in the evenings for recreation. They had also erected stables, and had small Chinese ponies for riding all over the island; in fact, they seemed quite the lords of the soil, and were not subjected to the least annoyance from the natives.

Hundreds of Chinamen gather round this spot, where they have erected huts and a bazaar, or market, for supplying the shipping, and, what appears not a little strange to European eyes, whenever the ships move to any other anchorage in the vicinity, the whole of the inhabitants, houses, market, and all, move along with them, so easily do these individuals change about from one place to another. One of the captains informed me that it was in contemplation to leave that particular spot shortly, and that, if I happened to visit it a day or two after this event, all the motley groups would be gone, and the place entirely deserted. Nor was this statement at all exaggerated, for, on my return a few months afterwards, the change of station had taken place, and not a vestige of the little village remained: men, women, and children, with their huts, boats, and all that belonged to them, had followed the ships, and had again squatted opposite to them on the beach.

The different modes which these people have of obtaining a livelihood are really astonishing: with one of these I was particularly struck. There are boats of all kinds engaged in bringing off stock, such as ducks, fowls, and other things, to the ships, but one kind consisted only of five or six thick pieces of bamboo fastened together in the form of a raft, and with this the poor fellows paddled along with two oars, the water washing all over the raft, and frequently also over its contents. The fowls which some of these people brought off were in a most pitiable plight, and certainly could not exist long in such a state.

A few months after this time a complaint was made to Sir Henry Pottinger, then governor of Hong-kong, by the Chinese authorities regarding this state of affairs at Namoa. It set forth that the subjects of her Britannic Majesty had built houses, made roads, and in fact were making another Hong-kong at the island of Namoa, which, according to the treaty, they had no right to do. The old Chinese admiral, who had shut his eyes to all these irregular proceedings, had been removed, and another, remarkable for his *prowess and bravery* in the suppression of piracy on that coast! had been appointed to this station, and it was the latter with whom the complaint originated. Sir Henry Pottinger acknowledged the irregularity of the proceeding, but blamed the Chinese authorities for allowing it for such a length of time, and claimed a period of six months to give time for the sale or removal of any articles the English might have on shore. This was agreed to on the part of the Chinese.

And now comes the part of the business which so nicely illustrates the peculiar character of the Chinese. When I visited Namoa, in October, 1845, I made inquiry regarding the state of affairs on shore, and found that a little civility, and a few bottles of cherry brandy, had wonderfully softened the good old admiral, and that a communication had been received stating that some little show of compliance was actually necessary: they must pull down the house, for example, but the stables and horses might remain as before, and the captains might go on taking their accustomed exercise and recreation on the island, as they had been in the habit of doing. It was even hinted that no objection would be made to their putting up another cottage, if they chose to do so. In the mean time, a fine account had doubtless gone to Peking, showing how the barbarians had been driven from the island which they had dared to set foot upon; perhaps a battle had been fought, and a few of our ships and their crews taken and destroyed, which would give a certain amount of éclat to the affair. This is the way things are managed in China! Matters being in this state, I had no difficulty in prosecuting my botanical researches amongst the hills. These hills are of the same barren nature as those formerly noticed, and the natural productions, both in the animal and vegetable kingdoms, resemble those of Hong-kong.

The island of Namoa is about fifteen miles long, and of irregular breadth; in some places about five miles. The principal town is situated on the northern side, having a very fine bay, swarming with fishing-boats; indeed the whole of the coasts of this celebrated country are studded with small sailing-boats belonging to fishermen, who seem to be a most industrious and hard-working race of men; many of them in this island go perfectly naked, a practice which I have not observed so common in any other part of China.

Leaving Namoa, and sailing up the coast towards Amoy, the stranger is continually struck with the barren rocky nature of the coast, and in some parts has a view of hills of sand, the particles of which, when a hurricane blows, mix with the wind, and whiten the ropes of vessels and render it most unpleasant to be in the vicinity. Here and there he has a view of what appear to be rather fertile plains amongst the hills, cultivated with sweet potatoes, rice, and the other staple productions of the country. On the top of the highest hills along the coast, and as far as the eye can reach inland, pagodas are seen towering, which serve as excellent marks to the mariner as he sails along the shores. As we approached nearer to Amoy we passed Chapel Island, remarkable for having a large natural tunnel right through its centre, which has a most striking and curious appearance when vessels come in a line with it. In the afternoon we anchored in the harbour of Amoy between that island and Koo-lung-soo.

Amoy is a city of the third class, seven or eight miles in circumference, and contains about 300,000 inhabitants. It is one of the filthiest towns which I have ever seen, either in China or elsewhere; worse even than Shanghae, and that is bad enough. When I was there in the hot autumnal months, the streets, which are only a few feet wide, were thatched over with mats to protect the inhabitants from the sun. At every corner the itinerant cooks and bakers were pursuing their avocations, and disposing of their delicacies; and the odours which met me at every point were of the most disagreeable and suffocating nature. The suburbs are rather cleaner than the city; but as it is not customary to use carriages of any kind in this part of China, the roads are narrow.

It is from this place and the adjacent coast that the best and most enterprising Chinese sailors come. Many, or rather most of those who emigrate to Manila, Singapore, and other parts of the straits, are natives of Amoy and the coast of Fokien, and hence this place has generally been the head-quarters of the foreign junk-trade. During the war it was remarked by our officers that the merchants here showed more knowledge of English customs than those at other places did, and all were acquainted with our settlement at Singapore, and spoke highly of it.

Since this port has been thrown open several foreign merchants have established themselves, and the trade, although small when compared with that of the more northern port of Shanghae, is still considerable. Indian cotton, cotton twist, long-cloths of English and American manufacture, and opium, seem to be the principal articles of import, if we except the straits produce, which is chiefly brought in their own junks. Since the arrival of the British Consul the opium-ships have been removed from the harbour, and now lie just outside its limits, where the Chinese smugglers are allowed to visit them with impunity.

Unfortunately for the trade at Amoy, the exports of which we are most in need—I mean teas and silk—are not so easily brought to it as to the northern port of Shanghae. This, of course, will be much against Amoy; but nevertheless it may do a considerable portion of business in other ways. All sorts of coins are current here: dollars, rupees, English shillings and sixpences, Dutch coins, &c. &c., are all met with, and pass current by weight. Native gold, in bars, is sometimes brought in considerable quantities, to pay for the cotton and opium, and is, I believe, considered of a very pure quality.

During my stay here I was continually travelling in the interior, going sometimes a considerable distance up the rivers, and then landing, and prosecuting my botanical researches in the adjacent country. Frequently in these excursions I came unexpectedly upon small towns and villages, and generally walked into them without the least obstruction on the part of the natives; indeed, they seemed in most cases highly delighted to see me. When the day was hot, I would sit down under the shade of a large banyan-tree, generally found growing near the houses, and then the whole village—men, women, and children—would gather around, gazing at me with curiosity not unmixed with fear, as if I were a being from another world. Then one would begin to examine my clothes, another would peep into my pockets, while several others were examining my specimens. The general opinion seemed to be that I was a medical man, and in a very short time I was surrounded with invalids of all classes and ages, begging assistance and advice. The number of persons who are diseased in a Chinese village is really astonishing. Many of them are nearly blind, and a much greater number, in this part of the country at least, were affected with cutaneous diseases of the most loathsome description, originating probably in their peculiar diet and dirty habits.

I was one day travelling amongst the hills in the interior of the island in places where I suppose no Englishman had ever been before. The day was fine, and the whole of the agricultural labourers were at work in the fields. When they first saw me they seemed much excited, and from their gestures and language I was almost inclined to think them hostile. From every hill and valley they cried "Wyloe-Fokei," or "Wyloe-san-pan-Fokei," that is, "Be off to your boat, friend;" but on former occasions I had always found that the best plan was to put a bold face on the matter and walk in amongst them, and then try to get them into good humour. In this instance the plan succeeded admirably: we were in a few minutes excellent friends; the boys were running in all directions gathering plants for my specimen-box, and the old men were offering me their bamboo-pipes to smoke. As I got a little nearer to the village, however, their suspicions seemed to return, and they evidently would have been better pleased, had I either remained where I was, or gone back again. This procedure did not suit my plans, and, although they tried very hard to induce me to "wyloe" to my "sanpan," it was of no use. They then pointed to the heavens, which were very black at the time, and told me that it would soon be a thunder-storm, but even this did not succeed. As a last resource, when they found that I was not to be turned out of my way, some of the little ones were sent on before to apprize the villagers of my approach, and, when I reached the village, every living thing, down even to the dogs and pigs, were out to have a peep at the "Fokei." I soon put them all, the dogs excepted,* in the best possible humour, and at last they seemed in no hurry to get rid of me. One of the most respectable amongst them, seemingly the head man of the village, brought me some cakes and tea, which he politely offered me. I thanked him and began to eat. The hundreds who now surrounded me were perfectly delighted. "He eats and drinks like ourselves," said one; "Look," said two or three behind me, who had been examining the back part of my head rather attentively, "look here, the stranger has no tail;" and then the whole crowd, women and children included, had to come round me, to see if it was really a fact that I had no tail. One of them, rather a dandy in his way, with a noble tail of his own, plaited with silk, now came forward, and, taking off a kind of cloth, which the natives here wear as a turban, and allowing his tail to fall gracefully over his shoulders, said to me

* The Chinese house-dog has a great antipathy to foreigners, and will scarcely make friends with them.

in the most triumphant manner, "*Look at that.*" I acknowledged it was very fine, and promised, if he would allow me to cut it off, I would wear it for his sake. He seemed very much disgusted at the idea of such a loss, and the others had a good laugh at him.

The hills in this part of the country are more barren than any I ever recollect to have seen either before or since; consisting entirely of bare rocks and gravelly sand, as hard and as solid as stone, with scarcely a vestige of vegetation. In height they vary from five hundred to two thousand feet above the level of the sea. Further inland the ground is more level: it is also much more fertile, and yields good crops of rice, sweet potatoes, and earthnut, besides a considerable quantity of ginger and sugar.

The island of Koo-lung-soo is situated opposite to the town of Amoy, and commands it. At the time of the war this island was taken by the English troops, and occupied until the spring of 1845, when the Chinese paid a part of the ransom money, and it was again placed in their hands. It is scarcely two miles long, and of irregular breadth, and seems to have been, before the war, the residence of some of the principal inhabitants in this part of the country. Most of the houses on the island are in ruins, but their remains show what they were, and prove the wealth of their former residents. I could not look upon the ruined walls, the pretty fish-ponds, all overgrown with weeds and filled up with rubbish, the remains of gardens ruinous as the houses, without wishing most sincerely that war, and all its attending calamities, might long be kept from my own peaceful, happy home, and soon be unnecessary in every part of the world. According to all accounts, the less respectable part of the natives had done more to make the houses of this island have a ruinous appearance than our troops during the war, by pulling down everything that they could possibly carry away and dispose of.

Some immense blocks of stone (granite) are here supported naturally on the tops of the hills in the strangest manner, and are objects of great interest to the traveller. One, in particular, appears as if some giant arm had raised it to its present position, and left it there solely to astonish the beholder in after-ages, and leave him to wonder not only how it came there, but how it could remain in its present position; and, most assuredly, a very small quantity of gunpowder exploded below it would hurl it from the hill to the plain beneath. Another huge rock stands near the entrance of the harbour; this, however, seems to have been on the point of giving way, for it is now supported by a mass of stone-work on one side. The natives have a tradition concerning this rock, and say that as long as it stands the town of Amoy will never fall before a foreign enemy. Unfortunately for the prophecy, Amoy, like the rest of the places attacked by the English, was taken, although the rock still stands as before.

The island, particularly on the north-eastern and eastern sides, is very unhealthy; fever and cholera prevail to a great extent during the south-west moonsoon, and are most fatal. Our troops suffered far more from the climate, when they had possession of the place, than from the guns of the Chinese at the taking of Amoy. In the autumn of 1843 the sickness amongst the officers and men of the 18th Royal Irish was almost unprecedented: dismay was painted in every countenance, for every one had lost his comrade or his friend. It was dismal indeed. I have known many who were healthy and well one day, and on the morrow at sunset their remains were carried to their last resting-place. The little English burial-place was already nearly full, and the earth was red and fresh with recent interments, scarcely a day passing without two or three being added to the number of the dead. And yet, what was rather strange, a detachment of the 41st M. N. I., commanded by Captain Hall, were, officers and men, all perfectly healthy; they were, however, on a different part of the island.

I fear that the more we know of China the more will be dispelled the notions of its being a healthy country, which we had formed from the experience of those who lived in their shaded airy houses at Macao and Canton. During my rambles on Koo-lung-soo I stumbled on the tombstones of some Englishmen, who, according to the inscriptions on them, had been interred upwards of one hundred and fifty years: their graves had been preserved during that long period by the Chinese, who seem to pay great respect to the tombs of the dead. Lately the stones had been replaced and the tombs repaired by one of our captains on the coast, who for this respectful and praiseworthy act had acquired amongst his comrades the name of *Old Mortality*.

In the midst of such rocky mountains and barren

scenery, it will not be expected that I could have much success in my botanical researches. In the gardens there were several pretty shrubs, but the greater part of them were well known, such, for example, as the *Jasminum Sambac, Olea fragrans, China rose, Chrysanthemums*, and various other common species. There are, however, some very pretty roses on the island, producing small double flowers of great neatness and beauty, although destitute of perfume. These I sent home to the garden of the Horticultural Society at Chiswick.

Birds are very rare, and the species most meagre in number: indeed this may be expected, as there is no shelter for them. A small mina with white wings is met with in large flocks; white-necked crows are common, as well as paddy-birds, Indian kites, and two or three varieties of kingfishers. During my stay here I was much assisted by Captain Hall of the 41st N. I., who was fond of botany, and well acquainted with the localities of all the plants in the neighbourhood.

One day I went in company with this gentleman and the Rev. Mr. Abele, an American missionary, to pay our respects to one of the principal mandarins, and to see his houses and gardens. His residence is in the suburbs of the town, on the side of a rocky hill, close to the beach. When we entered the outer court we were received by a number of officers of inferior rank, and conducted to a kind of office, where, after politely desiring us to sit down, they offered us their pipes to smoke, and snuff-boxes, or rather phials of glass and stone, containing something which was like Scotch snuff, and rather agreeable. There were two couches or beds in the room, on one of which I observed a small lamp burning and an opium-pipe lying by its side, by which I conjectured we had disturbed an opium-smoker in the midst of his enjoyment. Tea was immediately set before us, as is the custom in this country; but it was very indifferent, and, as Mr. Abele informed us that we should get much better when we were introduced to the principal mandarin, we only tasted it in compliment to our good friends.

In a few minutes the mandarin himself came to conduct us into a more splendid apartment. It was a large airy room, one side fitted up with finely carved cases, in the centre of which stood a timepiece and some beautiful jars filled with flowers. I here had an opportunity of seeing the great veneration with which the Chinese regard anything that is old. One of these pieces of porcelain, he informed us, had been in his family for five hundred years, and had the peculiar property of preserving flowers or fruits from decay for a lengthened period. He seemed to prize it much on account of its age, and handled it with great veneration. The other side of the room was elevated a little, and fitted up for the "sing-song," or theatricals, of which the Chinese, from the highest to the lowest, are passionately fond. Tea was soon brought in, in a teapot, in the European fashion, and not in the manner usual amongst the Chinese; for the custom with them is first to put the tea into the cup, and then to pour the water over it, the visitor drinking the beverage and leaving the leaves in the bottom of the cup—an admirable mode for such persons as the Aberdeen gentleman who, some years since, when coffee was not so common as it is now, complained that "his landlady did not give him the thick as well as the thin." Sugar is never used by the Chinese with their tea.

The mandarin, after making various inquiries about us—what our names were? what our occupations? how long we had been from home? and more particularly how old we were?—and after minutely inspecting our clothes, the coloured waistcoats apparently gratifying him very much, asked us to walk out and see the grounds around the mansion. The house stands near the base of the hill, and the garden lies behind it: the whole is really pretty; the large banyan-trees overhanging the walks, and the huge and rugged rocks forming caves and shades from the sun. A very fine spring issues from the hill-side, from beneath a rock. This water the proprietor praised very much, and we all drank heartily of it to please him: really such a spring, in a place like this, is invaluable. A telescope was brought to us, which he evidently considered a great curiosity. He placed it upon a large stone table, carefully adjusting it to the desired view, and then asked us to look through it; but we were not accustomed to use the instrument in that way, and took it up in our hands in the usual manner. He seemed surprised that we could see through it this way. After showing us all the curiosities in the garden, he took us back into the house, where tea was again set before us, with the addition of six or seven kinds of cake, which, however good they may be considered by the Chinese, I must confess I did not like. I have since tasted excellent buns and short cakes in Chusan and Shanghae. After some further conversation we withdrew, the mandarin inviting us to renew our visit as often as we pleased. It was now dark, and we were lighted to the river with torches, followed, as usual, by some hundreds of the Chinese, who were all respectful and civil. Indeed, we were always honoured with a body-guard of this description wherever we went.

CHAPTER III.

Leave Amoy — Gale in the Formosa Channel — Driven back to Chimoo — Chimoo Bay — Chinese Mode of paying Taxes — Character of the Natives — Journey to the Hills — Chimoo Pagoda — Interesting Scenery — Attacked and Robbed — My Servant's Opinion of the State of Matters — Get back in Safety to the Shore —Novel Mode of crossing the wet Sands—The Bay of Chinchew.

HAVING travelled all over the country adjacent to Amoy, and completed my researches, at the end of September I sailed again towards the Formosa Channel, on my way to our most northern stations of Chusan, Ning-po, and Shanghae. The monsoon, however, had now changed from south-west to north-east, and we experienced very stormy weather, with strong northerly currents, which, of course were directly against us. The vessel was at last obliged to put into the Bay of Chinchew from stress of weather, and, having sprung her bowsprit in the gale, it was impossible for her to proceed. At one time the sea was running so high, and the vessel plunging so much, that the whole of her decks were frequently under water. Some idea may be formed of the storm when I mention that a large fish weighing at least thirty pounds was thrown out of the sea upon the skylight on the poop, the frame of which was dashed to pieces, and the fish fell through, and landed upon the cabin table.

In a day or two our cargo was got out and put into another vessel, in which I also embarked, and we again proceeded on our voyage. This attempt was even more disastrous than the last, for, after being out for several days, and having got nearly through the Formosa Channel, we met one of those deadful gales so well known to the navigators of these seas. Our newest and strongest sails were split to pieces, the bulwarks washed away, and in spite of the best seamanship, and every exertion, we were driven back far below the bay from which we started about a week before. I shall long remember one of these fearful nights. The poor Lascar crew were huddled together under the long-boat, to shelter themselves from the wind: the sea was running very high, and washing our decks fore and aft, as if we had been a narrow plank tossing on the waves. I had gone below, and the Captain had come down for a second to look at the barometer, when we felt a sea strike the vessel with terrible force, and heard a crash which sounded as if her sides had been driven in; at the same moment the glass of the skylight came down about our ears, and the sea forced its way into the cabin. I certainly thought the little schooner had gone to pieces; but Captain Landers rushed on deck to ascertain the damage which had been done, and to try to repair it. The night was very dark; but he soon found that our weather bulwarks had been stove in, and the long-boat carried over to leeward from its place in midships, where it was fixed. Luckily the lee bulwarks held it fast, otherwise the boat and the whole of our crew would have been swept together into the angry foaming ocean, where no mortal arm could have rendered them any assistance. Two glazed plant-cases filled with plants from Amoy, which were on the deck, were dashed to pieces, and their contents, of course, completely destroyed. In the long voyage from England to China, even in rounding the celebrated "Cape of Storms," I never experienced such weather as I met with on the east coast of China, at the commencement of the north-east monsoon. After being three days in the storm, having only as much sail on the vessel as to steady her, the gale moderated a little, and we were able to hoist more sail, and make for the land, which proved to be a place called Chimoo, which was far below the point which we started from a week before.

Chimoo Bay is about fifty miles north of Amoy. It has been an opium station for foreign ships for some years; and here, even during the war, that trade was carried on in spite of the mandarins. The natives of the different towns on the shores of this bay are an independent and lawless race. An anecdote was related to me by one of the captains, which gives a fair idea how things are managed in this part of the country.

Some of the opium merchants came on board one of the ships in the bay, and requested the loan of some guns, for each of which they offered to deposit a large piece of Sycee silver, which was, of course, much more than its value; and promised to return the guns in a day or two. When asked what they intended to do with them, they replied, that the mandarins and officers of government were expected shortly to levy the taxes, and that the people were determined not to pay. They said they only wanted four or five guns for the purpose: these were granted them; and in a day or two, when they returned them, inquiry was made if they had been successful. "O yes," they said: "we have driven the mandarins over the hills." It certainly had been no very difficult matter to effect this object.

The inhabitants in the towns and villages around the bay are frequently at war with each other; in this they resemble the borderers of our own country in ancient feudal times, when "might was right." As in those days, too, a sort of black mail is levied, and treaties of peace are concluded, one of the parties paying a stipulated sum to the other. This, however, I am sorry to say, is not the worst trait in their character: they are the greatest thieves and robbers in existence; as I myself found to my cost.

One day I had sent my Chinese servant on shore with orders to gather all the plants he could find in a certain direction, which I pointed out to him before he left the ship; but he returned to me the next morning with only a few useless things, which he had evidently gathered very near the landing-place on the shore. I felt much annoyed at this, and scolded him pretty sharply for his conduct; but he excused himself by saying that he durst not go in the direction to which I had pointed, as he would have been beaten and robbed by the Chin-chew men. This I did not believe at the time, and imagined that it was laziness on his part, for, like most of the Chinese, who receive a specified sum per month for their services, he was rather remarkable for this propensity; I therefore determined to set out myself on the day following, and give him the treat of a long walk for his misconduct. The following morning was fine, and I jumped into a China boat which I had hired for the purpose, and reached the shore, after being completely drenched by the breakers, which roll high along the shores of this bay, and render the landing, particularly in small boats, rather dangerous. When I got on shore, and proceeded to walk in the direction I intended, the boatmen and others came round me, and attempted to dissuade me from going, by intimating that I was sure to be attacked by the Chinchew men, and robbed or murdered. I also saw signs of warfare, in the shape of matchlocks and long bamboo poles, in the hands of the Chinamen, who, as my servant informed me, were obliged to carry them in self-defence. I began to wish, then, that I had brought off from the ship a few of the crew for protection—indeed Captain Woodrow kindly offered to send some with me when I set out: however, it was now too late; and I determined to put a bold face on the matter and proceed. I set out towards the hills, on one of which stands the Chimoo pagoda, which I was anxious to visit on my route, as I expected to get a good view of the country from its summit.

Many acres of ground here, all along the shore, are used for evaporating sea-water and forming salt, which is a great article of trade in China. As the traveller proceeds inland, the ground, capable of cultivation, is covered with crops of sweet potato and earth-nut, which form the staple productions of this part of the country in the autumnal months. Between the different fields one often stumbles upon the graves of the natives, sometimes finely ornamented with those half-circular erections so common in the south of China, and at other times without any ornament whatever; this of course depending upon the wealth of the relatives. The hills are like those near Amoy, rocky and barren, having here and there a few wild plants growing on the sides of the ravines; some of which, however, are very beautiful. The pagoda, already mentioned, stands on the top of the highest hill, and affords an excellent landmark to the vessels on the coast.

On my way towards the hills I was frequently surrounded by hundreds of the Chinese, and was evidently considered a great *natural curiosity*. The country, although barren, teems with inhabitants; indeed, I almost thought the very stones were changing into Chinamen, so rapidly did the crowd accumulate at times. The sight was droll enough:—here were I and my servant on one side of some ravine, with our specimen boxes and other implements, gathering samples of everything we could find; there, on the top of the other, stood three or four hundred of the Chinese, of both sexes and all ages, looking down upon us with wonder painted in every countenance. And then, their features, their manners and costume, were all so striking to a stranger, that I believe our surprise and curiosity were mutual. They were generally civil, but I ran a risk at last of getting into trouble, on account of a silk neckcloth which I had on, and to which some of them took a great fancy, telling me that it would look so well round their heads—for in this part of China they wear a handkerchief like a turban. I was much amused with the various plans they employed to get it from me: one brought a handful of chillies, which he held out in one hand, and with the other pointed to the neckcloth, intimating that he would close the bargain in that way; another did the same with a few earth-nuts, and some brought me a few weeds; all, however, taking care to offer nothing of value. I began blundering Chinese to them as well as I could, upon which two of the men ran off to the village as fast as they could, desiring me to wait until they returned. I could not divine the reason of this; but in order to please them, I complied with their wishes. They soon returned, bringing with them a bottle of sam-shoo, or Chinese spirits; which they supposed I had asked for, and which they now tendered for the neckcloth, evidently considering that this offer must be irresistible. The crowd, however, was now becoming rather too great, and I walked on towards the hills, and began to ascend them—a plan which I always adopted when I wanted to get away from the Chinese, as they are generally too lazy to follow far where much exertion is required. The manœuvre answered my purpose, for I was soon left to my own meditations. When I reached the highest hill, on which the pagoda stands, and looked down on the level plain over which I had passed, I was at no loss to comprehend from whence the numbers came by whom I had been surrounded, as large villages or towns now met my eye in all directions which had not been visible when I was on the plain.

On reaching the pagoda I was astonished to find it in a most dilapidated condition, almost ruinous, although the main part of it, which had been strongly built, was nearly entire. A few stone josses or gods—a dome, with a double wall, containing a winding staircase leading to the different balconies, through which the wind howled in a most dismal manner—are all that I can particularise about the pagoda. I went over the whole of it, and obtained an excellent view of the surrounding country for many miles on all sides. As far as the eye can reach it has the same barren and rocky character. No one noticed or molested me in any way.

After enjoying the view of the country from the top of the hills, I descended to the low ground by a different way from that by which I had come; but no sooner did I reach the plain than I was again surrounded by the natives. It was getting late in the afternoon, and my servant, I believe, felt rather tired, as I had intended he should when we started in the morning. He now began to scheme a little to save himself from walking any farther than he could possibly help; and as I sometimes traversed rather wide circular routes in search of plants, he generally took the nearest way in the direction in which he knew we had ultimately to go. A few of the natives now began to follow me rather closely, and from their manner I suspected that their intentions were not good; but as they pretended to take me to some place where I should see some good plants and flowers, I allowed them to accompany me, and tried to keep them all in good humour. We arrived at last in sight of a large mansion, standing in a retired part of the country, and I was proceeding with perfect confidence towards it, when the Chinamen began to press more closely round me; and upon feeling a hand in my pocket I turned quickly round, and saw the thief running off with a letter which he had abstracted. As soon as he saw he was discovered, he threw it on the ground and made off; but when I put my hand into my pocket I found that I had lost several things of more value. This incident stopped my progress, and made me look about for my servant, whom I saw at some distance attacked by about eight or ten of the fellows. They had surrounded him, presenting their knives, and threatening to stab him if he offered the least resistance, at the same time endeavouring to rob and strip him of everything of the slightest value, and my poor plants collected with so much care were flying about in all directions. I felt that we were in a dangerous situation, and, instantly leaving my pickpockets, set off to his assistance as fast as I could. When the Chinamen saw me coming, they all took to their heels and left him, making off towards their companions, who were looking on from a distance. My servant was pale with fright when I reached him, and very much excited; nor did he fail to remind me of all he had said the day before. I felt there was no denying we were in dangerous company, and that the only thing to be done was to get out of it as soon as we could. Accordingly I made straight for the village where we had left the boat, and my servant took good care to follow close to my heels. As we approached the landing-place the boatman came to meet us in high spirits, saying he had expected us long ago, and was fearful that the Chinchew men had either robbed or murdered us. It was now ebb tide, and there was about half a mile of bare sand to cross, with the surf breaking furiously beyond it. The boatman at first said it was impossible to go to the ship before morning, and the people of the village promised me good chow-chow (food) and quarters for the night. I thanked them for all their kind offers, but told them that I should be much better pleased to go on board of the *Ka pan* with three masts, as I was to sail to Chusan early next day. Upon this, a sign was made to some other boatmen hard by, and immediately all were in motion. A boat was carried by a number of men across the sands to the water. I jumped upon the back of a stout Chinaman, who scampered like a race-horse across the wet sands, and deposited me in the boat; and they rowed us through the rolling surf in a masterly manner. I reached the ship all safe and sound, although completely drenched with wet, but with my opinion of the Chinese considerably lowered by the adventures of the day.

The bay which bears the name of *Chinchew* has also a station for merchants' vessels, a few miles further north than that of Chimoo. I mention this place to show the great change which has taken place in the Chinese since the late war. The captains of the ships here, as at Namoa, have now horses to take exercise in the morning and evening.

A little incident occurred about this time, which speaks for itself. It was necessary, from some cause or other, to remove the officers' stable, and build it on another part of the shore. The men employed for this purpose, when taking away the stones from the one place to the other, were stopped by some natives of the lower order, who took the stones and appropriated them to their own use. In going past the site of the old stable a few days afterwards, our people were surprised to see the stones all brought back; doubtless through the interference of some superior officer amongst the Chinese. This incident shows, I think, that the mandarins are anxious to preserve peace with the English, although some people, who pretend to secret sources of information, assert that in the interior they are preparing for another war.

The country, both with regard to vegetation and general features, is the same as at Chimoo: I was, however, much struck with the formation of one part of the mainland near the entrance to the bay. Part of the hill was rocky, but other parts were formed by immense banks of sea-sand, which appear to have been driven up from the bottom of the ocean by some terrific storm or convulsion of nature. Sea-shells, stony shingle, large fragments of rock, as well as sand, contribute their share in swelling the mighty mass, and all formed a great contrast with the appearance of everything around it.

The natives bear the same character as those all along the coast in this province—that of thieves and pirates; but they are the best and most enterprising sailors in China, and you meet them in every port you go to. Their trade will be much injured by the admission of English vessels into the northern ports.

I must here notice the great kindness and assistance which I have always received from the captains of vessels at these opium stations, who were always ready to lend me a helping hand, and forward my views by every means in their power.

CHAPTER IV.

Land at Chusan — Description of the Island — Town of Tinghae — Agriculture — Staple Productions — Hemp Plants — Palm of which Ropes are made — Trefoil cultivated for Manure — Oil Plant — Flora — Hills covered with Azaleas, &c.— The Tallow Tree — Green Tea Shrub — Bamboos and other Trees — Fruits — Yang Mai and Kum-Quat — Inhabitants and Shops in Tinghae — English Names on Shop Doors — A new Language — Mode of classing Foreigners — Diseases of the Eye common — Salt-making — Method of preparing the Vegetable Tallow — Mode of hatching Eggs by artificial Heat.

OUR little vessel being sufficiently repaired, we were able to proceed on our voyage. This time we were more fortunate, and reached the Chusan group of islands in ten days from Chimoo. When we neared the islands I was delighted with the change in the aspect of the country; and as we anchored off Keto Point, waiting for the tide, Captain Landers kindly allowed me to have the ship's boat and crew to go on shore. The first glance at the vegetation convinced me that this must be the field of my future operations, and I had then no doubt that my mission would end most successfully. Here the hills were no longer barren, but either cultivated, or clothed with beautiful green grass, trees, and brushwood. I returned to the vessel in high spirits, and in a few hours afterwards we were at anchor in the fine bay of Chusan.

Chusan is a large and beautiful island, twenty miles

in length, and ten or twelve in breadth at the broadest part. In approaching it the view of the numerous other islands which stud the sea in all directions is striking and picturesque; noble mountains towering above the other land, and fertile valleys sloping gradually to the ocean. The island itself is a succession of hills, valleys, and glens, presenting an appearance not unlike the scenery in the Highlands of Scotland. At the head of every valley there are mountain passes, over which the inhabitants cross when they wish to visit the interior of the island. The valleys are rich and beautiful, surrounded by mountains which in many parts are covered with trees, and in others under cultivation: these, in their turn, again open and expose other valleys no less fertile, rich in vegetation, and watered by the clear streams from the mountains. Thus the traveller can visit the whole of the island, his way winding through valleys and over mountain passes, until his prospect is at last arrested by the sea, of which he has had frequent glimpses during the journey. Did our island of Hongkong possess the natural advantages and beauties of Chusan, what a splendid place it might have been made by our enterprising English merchants in a very few years!

The principal town is Tinghae, well known as the place twice taken by the English troops during the last war. It is but small, compared with any of the other five ports where foreigners are now trading: the walls are not more than three miles in circumference, and the suburbs not very extensive; it contains about 26,000 inhabitants. When I was there the island was in the hands of the English, being retained by them until 1846, under the treaty of Nanking, and Tinghae was of course the head-quarters of the troops: we had also military stations at Sing-kong and Singkie-mun, the western and eastern parts of the island. Major-General Sir James Schoedde, the officer in command, to whom I had letters from Lord Stanley, very kindly procured me quarters in a house within the walls, and I immediately commenced operations. I was fortunate in becoming acquainted with Dr. Maxwell, of the 2nd Madras native infantry, who was stationed there. This gentleman, an ardent lover of botanical pursuits, had been most indefatigable in his researches, and was consequently able to give me much valuable information.

The soil of the hills is a rich gravelly loam; in the valleys it is more stiff, from having less vegetable matter mixed with it, and from being almost continually under water. The rocks of granite, however, of the same kind as those noticed on the barren southern hills, exist here also; and, although they are generally covered with soil and vegetation, they have doubtless been at some former times as bleak and barren as their southern neighbours.

All the valleys and hill-sides are under cultivation; paddy is the principal crop on the low grounds, and sweet potatoes on the hills. In the spring and early summer months, crops of wheat, barley, beans, peas, and maize are grown on the hilly and rising grounds, the low paddy-land being too wet for such crops. Cotton is also grown on the island, but the quantity is inconsiderable; it is only for the home use of the small farmers on whose land it grows. There is a plant called *Urtica nivea*, both wild and cultivated, which grows about three or four feet in height, and produces a strong fibre in the bark, which is prepared by the natives, and sold for the purpose of making ropes and cables. The same species is said to yield a very fine fibre, which is used in the manufacture of grass-cloth. Another strong fibre is obtained from the bracts of a palm-tree cultivated on the hill-sides of Chusan, as well as in similar situations all over the province of Chekiang. These articles answer the purposes to which they are applied extremely well; but the rope made from the Manila hemp is of much greater strength and durability. From the bracts of this same palm the natives of the north make what they call a *So-e*, or garment of leaves, and a hat of the same material, which they put on during rainy weather; and, although they look comical enough in the dress, still it is an excellent protection from wind and rain. In the south of China the *So-e* is made from the leaves of the bamboo and other broad-leaved grasses.

After the last crop of rice has been gathered in, the ground is immediately ploughed up and prepared to receive certain hardy green crops, such as clover, the oil-plant, and other varieties of the cabbage tribe. The trefoil, or clover, is sown on ridges, to keep it above the level of the water, which often covers the valleys during the winter months. When I first went to Chusan, and saw this plant cultivated so extensively in the fields, I was at a loss to know the use to which it was applied, for the Chinese have few cattle to feed, and these are easily supplied from the road-sides and uncultivated parts of the hills. On inquiry I was informed that this crop was cultivated almost exclusively for manure. The large fresh leaves of the trefoil are also picked and used as a vegetable by the natives.

The oil-plant, *Brassica chinensis*, is in seed and ready to be taken from the ground in the beginning of May. This plant is extensively grown in this part of China, both in the province of Chekiang and also in Kiangsoo, and there is a great demand for the oil which is pressed from its seeds. For the information of readers not acquainted with botany, I may state that this plant is a species of cabbage, producing flower-stems three or four feet high, with yellow flowers, and long pods of seed like all the cabbage tribe. In April, when the fields are in bloom, the whole country seems tinged with gold, and the fragrance which fills the air, particularly after an April shower, is delightful.

The small ox-plough, and the celebrated water-wheel, which is here worked by hand, are the two principal implements in husbandry; the plough seems a rude thing, but it answers the purpose remarkably well, and is probably better for the Chinese in their present state, with their oxen and buffaloes, than our more improved implement. An immense quantity of water is raised with great ease by the water-wheel, and is made to flow into the different rice-flats with great rapidity. I have often stood for a considerable time looking on and admiring the simplicity and utility of this contrivance.

The flora of Chusan, and all over the main land in this part of the province of Chekiang, is very different from that of the south. Almost all the species of a tropical character have entirely disappeared, and in their places we find others related to those found in temperate climates in other parts of the world. I here met, for the first time, the beautiful *Glycine sinensis* wild on the hills, where it climbs among the hedges and on trees, and its flowering branches hang in graceful festoons by the sides of the narrow roads which lead over the mountains. The *Ficus nitida*, so common around all the houses and temples in the south, is here unknown; and many of those beautiful flowering genera which are only found on the tops of the mountains in the south have here chosen less exalted situations. I allude more particularly to the *Azaleas*, which abound on the hill-sides of this island. Most people have seen and admired the beautiful azaleas which are brought to the Chiswick fêtes, and which, as individual specimens, surpass in most instances those which grow and bloom on their native hills: but few can form any idea of the gorgeous and striking beauty of these azalea-clad mountains, where on every side, as far as our vision extends, the eye rests on masses of flowers of dazzling brightness and surpassing beauty. Nor is it the azalea alone which claims our admiration; clematises, wild roses, honeysuckles, the Glycine noticed above, and a hundred others, mingle their flowers with them, and make us confess that China is indeed the "central flowery land."

The tallow-tree (*Stillingia sebifera*) is abundant in the valleys of Chusan, and large quantities of tallow and oil are yearly extracted from its seeds: tallow-mills are erected in several parts of the island for this purpose. The *Laurus camphora*, or camphor-tree, is also abundant, but no camphor is extracted or exported from the island. The green-tea shrub (*Thea viridis*) is cultivated everywhere; but, if we except a small quantity which is annually sent over to the main land—to Ning-po and the adjacent towns—the whole of the produce is used by the inhabitants themselves. Every small farmer and cottager has a few plants on his premises, which he rears with considerable care, but seems to have no wish to enter on its cultivation on a larger scale. Indeed, it is questionable if it would answer, as the soil is scarcely rich enough; and, although the shrub grows pretty well, it is far from being so luxuriant as it is in the larger tea districts on the main land. The forests of different varieties of bamboo are very striking, and give a kind of tropical character to the Chusan scenery. I do not know anything more beautiful than the yellow bamboo, with its clean and straight stem, and graceful top and branches waving in the breeze: it always reminded me of our young larch forests at home. The fir-tree, found in the south, is also common in this part of China: it seems to be an exception to a general rule, being met with all over the country, and in every degree of latitude. Here the *Cunninghamia sinensis*, another of the pine tribe, is also found in abundance: it is more rare in the south. Besides these, there are several species of cypress and juniper, which are always found growing around the tombs of the wealthy, which are scattered over the valley and hill-sides.

In fruits Chusan is meagre indeed. All the peaches, grapes, pears, plums, oranges, &c., which are brought to the markets of Tinghae in the summer season, are from the main land. There are, however, two fruits cultivated on the island which are of considerable excellence; the one is called *Yang-mai:* it is a scarlet fruit, not unlike an arbutus or strawberry, but having a stone like a plum in the centre; the other is the *Kum-quat*, a small species of Citrus, about the size of an oval gooseberry, with a sweet rind and sharp acid pulp. This fruit is well known in a preserved state by those who have any intercourse with Canton, and a small quantity is generally sent home as presents every year. Preserved in sugar, according to the Chinese method, it is excellent. Groves of the kum-quat are common on all the hill-sides of Chusan. The bush grows from three to six feet high; and, when covered with its orange-coloured fruit, is a very pretty object.

The natives of Chusan are a quiet and inoffensive race, and were always civil and obliging to me. Like the vegetation of their hills, they are very different from their countrymen of the south, and the change, I am happy to say, is for the better and not for the worse. Doubtless there are thieves and bad characters amongst them; but these are comparatively few, and are kept in better check by the government, the result of which is, that unprotected property is in a great measure safe, and cases of theft are almost unknown. The people may be divided into three classes—the countrymen or agricultural farmers and labourers, the shopkeepers in the towns, and the mandarins or officers of government. The trade of Tinghae and the other towns seems to consist chiefly in articles of food and clothing, and, owing to the number of British soldiers who were there from the time of our taking possession of the island until it was again handed over to the Chinese, this trade was of course in a flourishing condition. Fruits and vegetables were brought in great quantities from the main land ; fish were plentiful ; good sheep were sold at about three dollars each ; and the Chinese even got so far over their religious prejudices as to keep the market well supplied with bullocks, which were sold at prices varying from eight to twelve dollars. It was astonishing how quickly they got accustomed to our habits, and were able to supply all our wants. Bread baked in the English mode was soon exposed for sale in the shops,* and even ready-made clothes were to be had in any quantity. The tailors flocked from all quarters : a large proportion of the shops near the beach were occupied by them, and they doubtless reaped a rich harvest, although they made and sold every article of dress on the most reasonable terms. Then there were curiosity shops without number, containing josses or gods carved in bamboo or stone, incense-burners, old bronzes, animals of strange forms which only exist in the brains of the Chinese, and countless specimens of porcelain and pictures. Silk-shops, too, were not wanting, and here were to be had beautiful

* A mode of baking and cooking in use here is ingenious. A large rice-pan is filled with water, with a fire below it : upon this is placed a kind of sieve, made of bamboo, and filled with bread or other articles to be cooked ; several of these sieves, one above another, have all their contents cooked at the same time, the steam rising through the lower to the upper ones. The sides of course fit nicely, and prevent the steam from escaping, and there is a close cover which fits on to the uppermost one. Our common brick oven is also in use here.

pieces of manufactured silk, much cheaper and better than could be purchased in Canton. The embroidery in these shops was of the most elaborate and beautiful description, which must be seen before it can be appreciated; this the Chinese were making into articles such as scarfs and aprons for English ladies.

The shopkeepers in Tinghae supposed an English name indispensable to the respectability of their shops and the success of their trade, and it was quite amusing to walk up the streets and read the different names which they had adopted under the advice and instruction of the soldiers and sailors to whom they had applied on the subject. There were "Stultz, tailor, from London;" "Buckmaster, tailor to the army and navy;" "Dominie Dobbs, the grocer;" "Squire Sam, porcelain merchant;" and the number of tradesmen "to Her Majesty" was very great, among whom one was "Tailor to Her Most Gracious Majesty Queen Victoria and His Royal Highness Prince Albert, by appointment," and below the name was a single word, which I could not make out for some few seconds,—*Uniformsofalldescriptions.* Certificates from their customers were also in great request, and many of these were most laughable performances. The poor Chinese were never quite at their ease about these certificates, as they were so often hoaxed by the donors, and consequently were continually showing them to other customers and asking "*what thing that paper talkie; can do, eh?*" The answer was probably in this strain—"Oh, yes, *Fokei*, this can do, only a little alteration, more better." Poor Fokei runs and brings a pen, the little alteration is made, and it is needless to add that the thing is ten times more ridiculous than it was before.

Almost all the natives who came in contact with the English understood a little of their language; and as they had also a smattering of Portuguese, Malay, and Bengalese, they soon mixed them up all together, and drew out of the whole a new tongue, which the most accomplished linguist would have very great difficulty in analysing. And what is most amusing, they fancied all the time that this was capital English.

The way in which the Chinese classed the foreigners on the island was somewhat droll. There were three degrees of rank which they generally bestowed upon them,—Mandarins, or, as they pronounced it, *Mandalees*, *Sien-sangs*, and *A-says*. In the first class they included all persons of rank holding government situations, as well as the officers of the army and navy; the higher being styled "Bulla Bulla Mandalees," and the lower "Chotta Chotta Mandalees," corruptions of Hindostan words, signifying very large and very small. The merchants were honoured with the title of *Sien-sang;* and the common soldiers, sailors, and the rest of the lower orders, were all classed under the head of *A-says.* The word Mandarin is not Chinese, but has always been used by the Portuguese at Macao, as well as by the English, to denote a Chinese government officer; Sien-sang is a Chinese term, and signifies master or teacher, being generally used by the people as a title of respect, in the same way as we commonly use our word Sir: but *A-say* is quite a new appellation. "I say," or "Ay say," is a very common expression amongst our soldiers and sailors; and when the northern towns were taken by us during the war, the Chinese continually heard our men shouting it out to each other, and naturally concluded that this was the name of the class to which the lower orders belonged. It was quite common to hear them asking each other whether such a one was a Mandarin, a Sien-sang, or an A-say.

Cutaneous diseases are less common amongst the natives here than amongst those in the south of China, probably owing to the more healthy nature of the climate. They are, however, dreadfully affected with diseases of the eye and ultimate blindness. This is, doubtless, caused in a great measure by the operations of the native barber, who, whenever he shaves the heads of his customers, also tickles their eyes and probes their ears, and the result is that they become both blind and deaf. The lashes of the eye, probably also from this cause, frequently grow inwards, and the hairs rubbing on the eyeball soon cause inflammation. Many of the poor natives were cured by my friend Dr. Maxwell, who, in the kindest and most philanthropic manner, set apart a portion of every day for the purpose. They flocked to him from all parts of the island, submitting cheerfully and without a murmur to operations of a most painful nature. Many most remarkable cures resulted from his skill, and his fame spread not only all over the island, but also to the main land—to Chinhae and Ning-po—from whence numbers came and begged to be admitted on his list of patients. One day, when I was out with the Doctor on a botanising expedition, as we were passing a small cottage at the foot of the hills, a man and his wife rushed out, and begged us to enter their humble dwelling. We did so, chairs were set for us, tea was brought, and the worthy pair thanked the doctor in the most feeling and grateful manner for his former kindness to them. The man had been nearly blind and unable to work for his family, when, hearing of the wonderful English doctor, he came over to Chusan, and soon received his sight.

Many of the inhabitants of Chusan and the neighbouring islands gain their living by making salt on the shores. Large heaps of clay are scraped together in winter on the flats close by the sea; and when the weather becomes warm in summer, these heaps are spread out, and regularly watered with sea-water several times a day, which quickly evaporates, and leaves a highly saline mixture. When by this means the soil is completely saturated, the next operation is to make a filter. This the natives do by forming a round basin of clay and mud; in the bottom of this they put a quantity of straw or grass, and some charcoal or ashes on the top; they then surround the whole with another layer of mud, and place a quantity of the saline earth in the centre. Water is then regularly poured over this earth, and the particles of salt are carried down through the filter in a liquid state. A pipe made of bamboo, which had been placed below, leads the liquid into a well dug at the side, into which it comes clear, pure, and highly saline. This mixture is now carried off to pans, where it is boiled until the whole of the water is evaporated. I cannot say whether the Chinese have any means of purifying the salt. In Chimoo Bay the natives evaporate sea-water with the aid of the sun alone, and do not saturate the soil as they do in Chusan; but there the sea-water is perfectly clear. Amongst the Chusan group of islands the water is yellow and muddy, being rendered so by the large rivers which are pouring in their waters from the main land, and more particularly by the Yang-tse-kiang.

For the following account of the Chinese method of extracting the tallow from the seeds of the *Stillingia sebifera* I am indebted to Dr. Rawes, of the Madras army, who was some time resident in the island of Chusan:—

"The seeds are picked at the commencement of the cold weather, in November and December, when all the leaves have fallen from the trees,—this I saw at Sing-kong when out shooting in the Sah-hoo valley, close by our quarters through the village. The seeds are in the first place taken to the building where the process of making the tallow is carried on, and picked and separated from the stalks. They are then put into a wooden cylinder, open at the top, but with a perforated bottom. This is placed over an iron vessel (about the same diameter, or rather larger than the wooden cylinder, and about six or eight inches deep) containing water, by which means the seeds are well steamed, for the purpose of softening the tallow and causing it more readily to separate. The furnace I saw had four or five iron vessels in a row, was about three feet high, four or five feet broad, and eight or ten feet long. The fire was placed at one end and fed with the husk of the rice, dry grass, and such-like cheap materials, which make a great flame, and the flue was of course carried directly under the whole of the iron vessels.

"When the seeds have steamed ten minutes or a quarter of an hour, they are thrown into a large stone mortar, and are gently beaten by two men with stone mallets for the purpose of detaching the tallow from the other parts of the seed. They are then thrown upon a sieve, heated over the fire, and sifted, by which process the tallow is separated, or nearly so, although they generally undergo the process of steaming, &c., a second time that nothing may be lost. The other part of the seed is ground and pressed for oil.

"The tallow now resembles coarse linseed-meal, but with more white spots in it, and derives its brown colour from the thin covering over the seed (between it and the tallow), which is separated by the pounding and sifting. In this state it is put between circles of twisted straw, five or six of which are laid upon each other, and thus forming a hollow cylinder for its reception. When this straw cylinder (we may call it so) has been filled, it is carried away and placed in the press, which is a very rude and simple contrivance, but which, like everything Chinese, answers the purpose remarkably well. The press consists of longitudinal beams of considerable thickness, placed about a foot and a half, or two feet, asunder, with a thick plank at the bottom, forming a kind of trough, and the whole is bound together with iron. The tallow is pressed out by means of wedges driven in very tightly with stone mallets, and passes through a hole in the bottom of the press into a tub, which is sunk there to receive it. It is now freed from all impurities, and is a semifluid of a beautiful white colour, but soon gets solid, and in cold weather is very brittle. The inside of the tubs which collect the tallow are sprinkled or dusted over with a fine red earth, well dried, which prevents the tallow from adhering to their sides. It is thus easily removed in a solid state from the tubs, and in this condition the cakes are exposed for sale in the market. As the candles made from this vegetable tallow have a tendency to get soft and to melt in hot weather, they are commonly dipped in wax of various colours, as red, green, and yellow. Those which are intended for religious purposes are generally very large, and finely ornamented with golden characters.

"The cake, or refuse, which remains after the tallow has been pressed out of it, is used for fuel, or to manure the land, and so is the refuse from the other part of the seeds, from which oil is extracted."

One of the greatest lions in Chusan is an old Chinaman, who every spring hatches thousands of ducks' eggs by artificial heat. His establishment is situated in the valley on the north side of the city of Tinghae, and was much resorted to by the officers of the troops and strangers who visited the island. The first question put to a sight-seer who came here was, whether he had seen the hatching process, and, if he had not, he was always recommended to pay a visit to the old Chinaman and his ducks.

When I set out upon this excursion for the first time, it was a beautiful morning in the end of May, just such a morning as we have in the same month in England, but perhaps a little warmer. The mist and vapour were rolling lazily along the sides of the hills which surround the plain on which the city of Tinghae is built; the Chinese, who are generally early risers, were already proceeding to their daily labours; and although the greater part of the labouring population are very poor, yet they seem contented and happy. Walking through the city, and out at the north gate, I passed through some rice-fields, the first crop of which had been just planted, and a five minutes' walk brought me to the poor man's cottage. He received me with Chinese politeness; asked me to sit down, and offered me tea and his pipe, two things always at hand in a Chinese house, and perfectly indispensable. Having civilly declined his offer, I asked permission to examine his hatching-house, to which he immediately led the way.

The Chinese cottages generally are wretched buildings of mud and stone, with damp earthen floors, scarcely fit for cattle to sleep in, and remind one of what Scottish cottages were a few years ago, but which now, happily, are among the things that were. My new friend's cottage was no exception to the general rule; bad-fitting, loose, creaking doors, paper windows, dirty and torn; ducks, geese, fowls, dogs, and pigs in the house and at the doors, and apparently having equal rights with their masters. Then there were children, grandchildren, and, for aught that I know, great-grandchildren, all together, forming a most motley group, which, with their shaved heads, long tails, and strange costume, would have made a capital subject for the pencil of Cruikshank.

The hatching-house was built at the side of the cottage, and was a kind of long shed, with mud walls, and thickly thatched with straw. Along the ends and down one side of the building are a number of round straw baskets, well plastered with mud, to prevent them from taking fire. In the bottom of each basket there is a tile placed, or rather the tile forms the bottom of the basket; upon this the fire acts,—a small fireplace being below each basket. Upon the top of the basket there is a straw cover, which fits closely, and which is kept shut whilst the process is going on. In the centre of the shed are a number of large shelves placed one above another, upon which the eggs are laid at a certain stage of the process.

When the eggs are brought, they are put into the baskets, the fire is lighted below them, and an uniform heat kept up, ranging, as nearly as I could ascertain by some observations which I made with a thermometer, from 95° to 102°, but the Chinamen regulate the heat by their own feelings, and therefore it will of course vary considerably. In four or five days after the eggs have been subject to this temperature, they are taken carefully out, one by one, to a door, in which a number of holes have been bored nearly the size of the eggs; they are then held against these holes, and the Chinamen look through them, and are able to tell whether they are good or not. If good, they are taken back, and replaced in their former quarters; if bad, they are of course excluded. In nine or ten days after this, that is, about fourteen days from the commencement, the eggs are taken from the baskets, and spread out on the shelves. Here no fire-heat is applied, but they are covered over with cotton and a kind of blanket, under which they remain about fourteen days more, when the young ducks burst their shells, and the shed teems with life. These shelves are large, and capable of holding many thousands of eggs; and when the hatching takes place, the sight is not a little curious. The natives who rear the young ducks in the surrounding country know exactly the day when they will be ready for removal, and in two days after the shell is burst the whole of the little creatures are sold, and conveyed to their new quarters.

CHAPTER V.

First Visit to Ning-po — The Bridge of Boats — City and Pagoda — Medical Missionary — Temperature — Chinese Mode of keeping themselves warm — Charcoal Stoves — My Lodgings — Chinese Gamblers — Description of Shops — Silks and Embroidery — Jade Stone — Cotton Printing — Rope-making — Curiosity Shops and Contents — "Furniture Street" and Furniture — Banking Establishment — No prospect of Foreign Trade — Temples, and Devotion of some of the People — Dwarfed Trees — Mode of dwarfing explained — Mandarins' Gardens visited and described — View from northern Hills — Agriculture — Native Flora of these Hills — Graves of the Dead — Coffins exposed.

I VISITED Ning-po for the first time in the autumn of 1843. It is a large town, situated on the main-land, nearly west from the Chusan group of islands, on the east coast of China, and contains about 380,000 inhabitants. It stands about twelve miles from the sea, at the junction of two fine streams, which by their union form a noble river capable of being navigated by the larger vessels and junks. One of these branches runs from the west, and the other from the south, meeting at Ning-po; and over the latter the Chinese have constructed a bridge of boats for the traffic with the suburbs on the opposite shore. This bridge is a most simple and ingenious contrivance, consisting of a number of large boats moored at equal distances across the river, forming the basis on which the upper woodwork rests, and enabling the whole to rise and fall to a certain extent with the tide. By this means there is sufficient room under the bridge to allow fishing and passage boats to pass through at all times of the tide, providing it is not running too strong. At spring tides the water rushes through these spaces between the boats with great velocity, and sometimes it is next to impossible to get through.

The city itself is strongly fortified with high walls and ramparts about five miles round, and the space inside the walls is almost entirely filled with houses, in most parts densely crowded together. There are two or three very fine streets—finer, indeed, and wider than those of any other Chinese town which I have visited. A good view of the city and the surrounding country, as far as the eye can reach, is obtained from the top of a pagoda about one hundred and thirty feet high, having a staircase inside by which the top can be reached. (See following page.) This pagoda is named "*Tien-foong-tah*," or the "Temple of the Heavenly Winds;" it is evidently very old, and, like many others of the same kind, is in a state of decay. Whenever I visited this place, the priests (Budhists) were always in attendance with their offerings of cake and tea, for which a small gratuity was expected.

When I first landed at Ning-po, the British consul Mr. Thom, had not arrived, and I was quite at a loss where to go, or to whom to apply for quarters. Leaving my boat and servant on the river, I strolled away into the city to reconnoitre, thinking that something might turn up which I could use for my advantage. I was soon surrounded by crowds of the natives, and amongst them some blackguard boys, who had been corrupted to a great extent by the troops during the war, but who luckily understood a little of the English language, and

Temple of the Heavenly Winds.

were able to be of essential service to me. They informed me that there was one "*Hong-mou-jin*"—(red-haired man)—a term which they apply to all western nations—already in the city, and immediately led the way to his quarters. When we arrived at the house I was surprised to find a former acquaintance. He was an American

Medical Missionary, and was dressed *à la Chinoise*, tail and all complete, but truth compels me to state that his dress was rather a ludicrous one. I recollect one evening after dark going out into one of the main streets, accompanied by the doctor, to see an offering which was there presented to the gods, and I soon found that he in his Chinese dress was a greater object of attention than I was in my English one. I had obtained a room in the same house with my friend, who was visited daily by great numbers of the Chinese, and who, although not a very good Chinaman, was most zealous in the cause of medical missions.

As the winter approached the weather became extremely cold, and in December and January the ice on the ponds and canals was of considerable thickness. The most attractive shops in the city now were the different clothing establishments, where all articles of wearing apparel were lined with skins of various kinds, many of them of the most costly description. The very poorest Chinese has always a warm jacket or cloak lined with sheepskin, or padded with cotton, for the winter; and they cannot imagine how the Europeans can exist with the thin clothing they generally go about in. When the weather was cold I used always to wear a stout warm great-coat above my other dress, and yet the Chinese were continually feeling the thickness of my clothes, and telling me that surely I must feel cold. Their mode of keeping themselves comfortable in winter differs entirely from ours; they rarely or never think of using fires in their rooms for this purpose, but, as the cold increases, they just put on another jacket or two, until they feel that the warmth of their bodies is not carried off faster than it is generated. As the raw damp cold of morning gives way to the genial rays of noon, the upper coats are one by one thrown off, until evening, when they are again put on. In the spring months the upper garments are cast off by degrees, and when the summer arrives the Chinese are found clad in thin dresses of cotton, or in the grass-cloth manufactured in the country. In the northern towns the ladies sometimes use a small brass stove, like a little oval basket, having the lid grated to allow the charcoal to burn and the heat to escape; this they place upon their tables or on the floor, for the purpose of warming their hands and feet. Nurses also carry these little stoves in their hands under the feet of the children. Such, however, is the thickness and warmth of their dresses, that it is only in the coldest weather they require them. Little children in winter are so covered up, that they look like bundles of clothes, nearly as broad as they are long, and, when the padding is removed in warm weather, it is difficult to imagine that you see before you the same individuals.

I never felt so cold in England as I did during this winter in the north of China, and yet the thermometer did not indicate a very low degree. The house in which I lived was so open, that the wind rushed in at every crevice; the windows were large, not glazed, as with us, but papered, and in many places perfectly open. During the day I got on very well, as I was always out and moving about from morning until dark. But the long evenings, with the wind whistling through the windows, and blowing upon my candle, were dreary and cold enough.

To vary the monotony of the scene, as well as to warm myself, I used frequently to take a stroll down the main street. The Chinese, as a nation, are great gamblers; even the poorest of them cannot resist the temptation, and in this street after nightfall there used to be numerous stalls of oranges, sweetmeats, and trifling curiosities, at each of which there were dice of some kind, and a "wheel of fortune," surrounded by the Chinese in great numbers, trying their luck with a few copper cash, and evincing by their looks and language the most intense interest in the stopping of the wheel or the throwing of the dice.

Besides the shops already noticed for the sale of clothes and skins, there are many others worthy of our attention. There are a number of excellent silk-shops and warehouses a little off the main street, which, like our old-established houses at home, have but little external show to attract notice. Here, too, are large quantities of that beautiful northern embroidery which is so much admired by all who have had an opportunity of seeing it. It is entirely different from that commonly procured at Canton, and much more elaborate and expensive. A considerable demand for articles of dress which would be fashionable in England has induced the Chinese to get them made, and they are now exposed for sale in all the towns in the north frequented by the English. Ladies' aprons, scarfs, shawls, work-bags, and many other articles made up in the English style, and beautifully embroidered, are the things most in demand.

The Chinese estimate their celebrated jade-stone very highly, and here there are numerous shops, both for cutting it, and exposing it for sale, carved into all those curious and fantastic forms for which this people are so well known. The process of cotton-printing in its most simple and original form may be seen in most of the streets here, as well as in other towns in China. Rope-making is carried on extensively in the suburbs near the river, and some strong cables and ropes for junks are made from the bracts of the palm, formerly noticed, and from the bark of the urticaceous plant, commonly called hemp by the English, in the north of China. There are, of course, the usual quantity of curiosity shops, containing bamboo ornaments carved into all possible forms; specimens of ancient porcelain, which are said to "preserve flowers and fruit from decay for an unusual time;" lacquered ware, and other ornaments brought by the junks from Japan; many beautifully carved rhinoceros-horns, bronzes, and other articles to which the Chinese attach great importance, purchasing them at exorbitant rates, apparently far beyond their value. But what struck me as being most unique was a peculiar kind of furniture, made and sold in a street generally called "Furniture Street" by foreigners who visit Ning-po. There were beds, chairs, tables, washing-stands, cabinets, and presses, all peculiarly Chinese in their form, and beautifully inlaid with different kinds of wood and ivory, representing the people and customs of the country, and presenting, in fact, a series of pictures of China and the Chinese. Every one who saw these things admired them, and, what was rather strange, they seem peculiar to Ning-po, and were not met with at any other of the five ports, not even in Shanghae. As all this beautiful work is expensive, it is, of course, only used in the houses of the wealthy.

There are some large banking establishments in Ning-po, having connection with all the other towns in the north, and it is here, therefore, that the value of money is regulated, the "stocks" rising and falling exactly as they do in England. There can be little doubt that it is a place of great wealth. There are a large number of retired merchants in the city and suburbs, who have made their fortunes in early life, and who now seek to enjoy themselves amid the luxuries and retirement of Ning-po. But these circumstances, unfortunately, do not fit it for a place of active foreign trade; and hence, although it is large, rich, and populous, our merchants find the northern port of Shanghae of far greater importance as regards the sale of European and American manufactures, and the purchase of tea and silk,—the staple productions of the country. And yet, judging from appearances, one would think that a considerable foreign trade might be carried on at Ning-po, as it is in itself a large town, is in the midst of a populous country, and has excellent water-communication with all parts of the empire.

Many of the temples in this town have been much admired by foreigners, but I must confess that, to me, the very best of them had a childish and tinselly appearance, which I could not admire. The one called the Fokien Temple is best and most showy. The Confucian Temple was formerly a large and celebrated place, but it was nearly destroyed during the war, and up to the time when I left China no attempt had been made to rebuild it, or put it in a state of repair: the Chinese seemed to consider that the touch of the *barbarian* had polluted the sacred edifice. The Budhists' temples are crowded with painted wooden images of their gods. The "three precious Budhas," the "past, present, and future," are generally enormously large, being often thirty or forty feet in height. To these, and to the numerous small images, the poor deluded natives bow the knee, burn incense, and engage in other exercises of devotion. The traveller meets with these temples, or jos-houses, as they are commonly called, in all the streets, at the gates of the city, and even on the ramparts, and cannot but admire the devotional spirit of the inhabitants, although he may wish that it was directed to a higher and purer object. I have often looked on when these simple people,—the women more particularly,—seemed actually, like Jacob of old, "wrestling with God in prayer," and using various means to ascertain whether the mind of the Deity had softened towards them, and granted their requests. Two small pieces of wood, flat on one side and rounded on the other, are generally used to accomplish this end: these were thrown up in the air, and, if they fell on the desired side, it was well; if not, some more incense was burned, and again and again they prostrated themselves before the altar, and seemed engaged in earnest prayer. Many of their religious ceremonies have a great resemblance to those of the Roman Catholic church, and I remember being much struck on a Sunday afternoon, when passing out at one of the city gates, by hearing the sounds of prayer and praise, not unlike those of the Christian churches of other lands.

I immediately walked into the place from whence the sounds came, and found, to my disappointment, that it was one of the numerous temples with which the city abounds, and that the sounds of praise which fell upon my ears were only addressed to the gods of the heathen. But many of these temples are in a most ruinous state, and are evidently not so well supported now as they have been at some former time. In fact, the town of Ning-po itself, with all its riches and all its advantages, has been in a decaying state for years, and is one example, amongst many others, of the truth of what I formerly stated concerning the general state of this country.

My first business, when I reached Ning-po, was to make inquiries regarding the gardens of the mandarins, which I had heard something of from the officers who were there when the city was taken by the English troops during the war. I had the same difficulties to encounter as I had at Amoy, owing to the jealousy of the Chinese. Ultimately, however, these too were overcome, and I obtained access to several mandarins' gardens and nurseries, out of which several new plants were procured, which proved very valuable additions to my collections. Here, as at other places, I made many inquiries after the supposed yellow camellia, and offered ten dollars to any Chinaman who would bring me one. Anything can be had in China for dollars! and it was not long before two plants were brought to me, one of which was said to be light yellow, and the other as deep a colour as the double yellow rose. Both had flower-buds upon them, but neither were in bloom. I felt quite certain that the Chinaman was deceiving me, and it seemed foolish to pay such a sum for plants which I should in all probability have to throw away afterwards; and yet I could not make up my mind to lose the chance, slight as it was, of possessing the *yellow camellia*. And the rogue did his business so well! He had a written label stuck in each pot, and *apparently* the writing and labels had been there for some years. I fancied I was as cunning as he was, and requested him to leave the plants and return on the following morning, when he should have an answer. In the mean time I asked a respectable Chinese merchant to read the writing upon the labels. All was correct; the writing agreed with what the man had told me; namely, that one of the plants produced light yellow blooms, and the other deep yellow. "Did you ever see a camellia with yellow flowers?" I inquired of my friend the merchant. "No," said he, in his broken English. "*My never have seen he, my thinkie no have got.*" On the following morning the owner of the plant presented himself, and asked me if I had made up my mind upon the subject. I told him that I would take the plants to Hong-kong, where I was going at the time; that they would soon flower there; and that, if they proved *yellow*, he should have his money. This, however, he would not consent to; and at last we compromised the matter, I agreeing to pay half the money down, and the other half when the plants flowered, providing they were "true." On these conditions I got the camellias, and took them with me to Hong-kong. It is almost needless to say that when they flowered there was nothing yellow about them but the stamens, for they were both semi-double worthless kinds.

The gardens of the mandarins in the city of Ning-po are very pretty and unique; they contain a choice selection of the ornamental trees and shrubs of China, and generally a considerable number of dwarf trees. Many of the latter are really curious, and afford another example of the patience and ingenuity of this people. Some of the specimens are only a few inches high, and yet seem hoary with age. Not only are they trained to represent old trees in miniature, but some are made to resemble the fashionable pagodas of the country, and others different kinds of animals, amongst which the deer seems to be the favourite. Junipers are generally chosen for the latter purpose, as they can be more readily bent into the desired form; the eyes and tongue are added afterwards, and the representation altogether is really good. One of the mandarins of Ning-po, anxious, I suppose, to confer some mark of especial favour upon me, presented me with one of these animals,—plants, I should say;—but as it was of no real use to me, and as my collections of other things were large, I was obliged to decline his present, which he evidently considered of great value, and no doubt wondered at my want of taste.

Another example will show the passion which exists amongst the Chinese for things of this kind. When I was travelling on the hills of Hong-kong, soon after my first arrival in China, I met with a most curious dwarf *Lycopodium*, which I dug up and carried down to Messrs. Dent's garden, where my other plants were at the time. "Hai-yah," said the old compradore, when he saw it, and was quite in raptures of delight. All the other coolies and servants gathered round the basket to admire this curious little plant. I had not seen them evince so much gratification since I showed them the "old-man Cactus" (*Cereus senilis*), which I took out from England, and presented to a Chinese nurseryman at Canton. On asking them why they prized the Lycopodium so much, they replied, in Canton English, "*Oh, he too muchia handsome; he grow only a leete and a leete every year; and suppose he be one hundred year oula, he only so high,*" holding up their hands an inch or two higher than the plant. This little plant is really very pretty, and often naturally takes the very form of a dwarf tree in miniature, which is doubtless the reason of its being such a favourite with the Chinese.

The dwarfed trees of the Chinese and Japanese have been noticed by every author who has written upon these countries, and all have attempted to give some description of the method by which the effect is produced. The process is in reality a very simple one, and is based upon one of the commonest principles of vegetable physiology. We all know that anything which retards in any way the free circulation of the sap, also prevents to a certain extent the formation of wood and leaves. This may be done by grafting, by confining the roots, withholding water, bending the branches, or in a hundred other ways which all proceed upon the same principle, This principle is perfectly understood by the Chinese, and they make nature subservient to this particular whim of theirs. We are told that the first part of the process is to select the very smallest seeds from the smallest plants, which is not at all unlikely, but I cannot speak to the fact from my own observation. I have, however, often seen Chinese gardeners selecting suckers and plants for this purpose from the other plants which were growing in their garden. Stunted varieties were generally chosen, particularly if they had the side branches opposite or regular, for much depends upon this; a one-sided dwarf tree is of no value in the eyes of the Chinese. The main stem was then in most cases twisted in a zigzag form, which process checked the flow of the sap, and at the same time encouraged the production of side branches at those parts of the stem where they were most desired. When these suckers had formed roots in the open ground, or kind of nursery where they were planted, they were looked over and the best taken up for potting. The same principles, which I have already noticed, were still kept in view, the pots used being narrow and shallow, so that they held but a small quantity of soil compared with the wants of the plants, and no more water being given than what was barely sufficient to keep them alive. Whilst the branches were forming, they were tied down and twisted in various ways; the points of the leaders and strong growing ones were generally nipped out, and every means was taken to discourage the production of young shoots which were possessed of any degree of vigour. Nature generally struggles against this treatment for a while, until her powers seem in a great measure exhausted, when she quietly yields to the power of art. The Chinese gardener, however, must be ever on the watch; for should the roots of his plants get through the pots into the ground, or happen to be liberally supplied with moisture, or should the young shoots be allowed to grow in their natural position for a short time, the vigour of the plant which has so long been lost will be restored, and the fairest specimen of Chinese dwarfing destroyed. Sometimes, as in the case of peach and plum trees, which are often dwarfed, the plants are thrown into a flowering state, and then, as they flower freely year after year, they have little inclination to make vigorous growth. The plants generally used in dwarfing are pines, junipers, cypresses, bamboos, peach and plum trees, and a species of small-leaved elm.

Amongst the mandarins' gardens in the city of Ning-po there is one in particular which is generally visited by all strangers, and is much admired. It is situated near the lake in the centre of the city. The old man to whom it belongs has long retired from trade with an independent fortune, and he now enjoys his declining years in the peaceful pursuits of gardening, and is passionately fond of flowers. Both his house and garden are unique in their way, but they are most difficult to describe, and must be seen to be appreciated. In this part of the country the building of artificial rockwork is so well understood, that the resemblance to nature is perfect, and it forms a principal feature in every garden. This old gentleman has the different parts of his house joined together by rude-looking caverns, and what at first sight appears to be a subterraneous passage, leading from room to room, through which the visitor passes to the garden which lies behind the house. The small courts, of which a glimpse is caught in passing through, are fitted up with this rockwork; dwarf trees are planted here and there in various places, and creepers hang down naturally and gracefully until their ends touch the little ponds of water which are always placed in front of the rockwork.

These small places being passed, we are again led through passages like those already noticed, when the garden, with its dwarf trees, vases, rockwork, ornamental windows, and beautiful flowering shrubs, is suddenly opened to the view.

It must be understood, however, that all which I have now described is very limited in extent, but the most is made of it by windings and glimpses through rockwork and arches in the walls, as well as by hiding the boundary with a mass of shrubs and trees.

Here old Dr. Chang—I believe that was his name—was spending the evening of his days in peaceful retirement. When I called upon him he was extremely polite, and, after making a great many very low bows, requested me to take the seat of honour by his side. The servants were then ordered to bring tea, a beverage which is offered to every stranger, and which was of the very finest description. Messengers were sent round to all the old man's particular friends, who each hurried to see the foreigner. One by one they dropped in, until the room was nearly full. The servants, who seemed to think themselves quite as good as their masters, mixed with the company, and made their remarks upon me with the greatest freedom. Everything about me was examined and criticised most minutely, particularly my watch, which they seemed to admire very much. I was frequently requested, as a great favour, to allow them to see the works, and to hold it to their ears, in order that they might hear the sound which it made. The old mandarin now led me round his house, and showed me all the curiosities which it contained, and of which he was a great collector. Old bronzes, carved woods, specimens of porcelain, and other articles of that kind, were arranged with great taste in several of the rooms. From the house we proceeded to the garden, but as it was winter, and the trees leafless, I could form but little idea of the rarity or beauty of the plants which it contained. I took my leave, after drinking some more tea, promising to visit the old man again whenever I returned to Ning-po.

I visited also at this time several other mandarins who had gardens, and from all of them I received the greatest civility. Some small articles which I brought out with me as presents were of the greatest use, not only in procuring me a civil reception, but also in enabling me to get plants or cuttings of rare species which were only found in the gardens of the rich, and which, of course, were not for sale.

The level plain on which the city of Ning-po is built is at least thirty miles across, surrounded on all sides by a circle of hills, but opening on the east to the sea, where the town of Chinhae stands, and forms, as it were, the seaport town of Ning-po. The view from the hills is very fine—the broad extensive plain forming, as it were, a vast amphitheatre, traversed by beautiful winding rivers and by canals in all directions; thus enabling the natives to convey the produce of their country and its merchandise to Ning-po, and from thence to Hang-chow-foo, and any other part of the world. Rice is the staple production of the low land in this part of the country during the summer months, and the oil-plant is cultivated extensively on the same land in winter and spring, being in seed and ready to harvest by the time for sowing the first crop of rice. Large quantities of the trefoil which I have noticed before are also grown here, and for the same purposes; indeed, the agricultural productions, both of the low lands and on the sides of the hills, are really the same as those formerly described on the island of Chusan.

The native flora of the hills to the north of Ning-po is nearly the same as that found on Chusan and the neighbouring islands, but more extensive. It is a curious fact, that I always found the main land of China more productive in species of animals and plants than the neighbouring islands, although these islands were large, and only separated from the main land by a narrow extent of sea. I met here, for the first time in a wild state, the beautiful yellow *Azalea sinensis*. These hills are somewhat more barren than most of the others in this part of the country, and there are few trees on them of any size. They are very different from those which I have yet to describe, a few miles to the south of Ning-po.

The graves of the dead are scattered all over the plain, and give the stranger a good idea of the immense population of the country. In travelling from Ning-po to the hills I could not account for the vast number of tombs which I met with on my way; but when I reached the summit of the hills, and looked down upon the wide-spreading plain, covered with towns and villages in all directions, densely peopled with human beings, it was easily accounted for. Here, as at Chusan and Shanghae, the traveller is continually coming upon coffins, placed on the surface of the ground, and in many instances decaying, and exposing the skeleton remains of the dead. I was much struck by frequently meeting with large numbers of coffins piled one above another, in heaps of from thirty to forty, chiefly those of young children. I was told that they are buried periodically, but from their appearance many of them must have remained in the same place for years, and their tenants must long ago have mouldered into dust.

CHAPTER VI.

Remarks on the Chinese Language — Ice-houses near Ning-po described — Their Simplicity and Utility — Novel Modes of Fishing — Fishing Cormorants met with — Their Actions described — Two Pair purchased — Account of their Food and Habits.

In sailing up the river towards *Ning-po* I observed a great number of thatched houses, and desired my Chinese servant to go to the boatman and inquire what they were. He went immediately to the man at the helm, and, after a conversation of at least ten minutes' duration, came back hanging his head, and slunk away without reporting the result of his inquiries. "Well," said I, "what is the use of all these houses which we now see on the shore?" With all the gravity in the world, he replied that the boatman said they were places built to keep Chinese soldiers in during the cold winter months. "Nonsense," said I, "they cannot fill all these places with soldiers." "*Well,*" said he, "*he have talkie my so fashion.*" As I could not conceive this to be true, I went to the man myself, and, with the little knowledge of the language which I then possessed, soon found out that the buildings in question were ice-houses, for which commodity, he informed me, there was a great demand during the summer months. This shows that the Chinese language differs so much in different provinces, that a native of Canton and another in the north cannot understand each other: and indeed this is so much the case, that my Macao servant was almost entirely useless to me in the north, in so far as the language was concerned. In this instance the Chinese word "*Ping*"—or I should rather say sound—means both soldier and ice, and it immediately struck my servant, who I suppose had never seen ice in his life, that the buildings in question were soldiers' houses instead of ice-houses.

I was much struck with the simplicity of the construction of these ice-houses, and my only doubt about them was whether or not the ice would keep well in them throughout the hot summer months. The results of my investigation I sent in the following letter to Professor Lindley, who published it in the 'Gardener's Chronicle' for 1845:—

"A short time before I left England you published in the 'Gardener's Chronicle' a number of letters and plans for the construction of ice-houses, but, as far as I can remember, nothing at all resembling the Chinese one which I shall now describe to you. On the right bank of the Ning-po river, above the town and fort of Chinhae, and in various other parts of the north of China, I have met with these ice-houses. When I inspected them for the first time last winter (1843), their construction and situation differed so much from what I had been accustomed to see at home—differing, too, in things which I used to consider as indispensable to an ice-house—that I had great doubts regarding their efficiency; but at the present time, which is now the end of August, 1844, many of these houses are yet full of ice, and seem to answer the end most admirably. You are probably aware, from my former descriptions of the country, that the town of Ning-po stands in the midst of a level plain from twenty to thirty miles across. These ice-houses are built on the sides of the river in the centre of the plain, completely exposed to the sun — a sun, too, very different in its effects from what we experience in England, — clear, fierce, and burning, which would try the efficiency of our best English ice-houses as well as it does the constitution of an Englishman in China.

Ice-houses near Ning-po.

"The bottom of these ice-houses is nearly on a level with the surrounding fields, and is generally about twenty yards long, by fourteen broad. The walls, which are built of mud and stone, are very thick, twelve feet in height, and are, in fact, a kind of embankment rather than walls, having a door on one side level with the floor, for the removal of the ice, and a kind of sloping terrace on the other, by which the ice can be thrown into the house. On the top of the walls or embankment a tall span roof is raised, constructed of bamboo, thickly thatched with straw, and in appearance exactly like an English haystack. And this is the simple structure which keeps ice so well during the summer months, and under the burning sun of China!

"The Chinaman, with his characteristic ingenuity, manages also to fill his ice-houses in a most simple way, and at a very trifling expense. Around the house he has a small flat level field connected with the river. This field he takes care to flood in winter before the cold weather comes on. The water then freezes and furnishes the necessary supply of ice at the very door. Again, in spring these same fields are ploughed up and planted with rice, and the water which drains from the bottom of the ice-house helps to nourish the young crop. Of course here, as in England, when the house is filled the ice is carefully covered up with a thick coating of straw. Thus the Chinaman, with little expense in building his ice-house, and an economical mode of filling it, manages to secure an abundant supply for preserving his fish during the hot summer months.

"It now, I think, becomes a question whether we could not build ice-houses at less expense and more efficient, upon the Chinese plan, than upon the old underground system common in England. The accompanying sketch will enable you to form an idea of the appearance which these ice-houses present to the traveller in going up the Ning-po river. *Ning-po, August*, 1844."

Since this letter was published I have had frequent opportunities of testing the qualities of the Chinese ice-house, both at Ning-po and also at Chusan and Shanghae, and I have found that it answers the purpose admirably. The winter of 1844-1845 was unusually mild in this part of China; little or no ice was formed on the ponds and canals, and of course the ice-houses could not be filled; but many of them contained large quantities which had been laid up the year before, and by this means the market was suppled with ice which had been in store at least a year and a half, and would probably have kept some time longer.

The ice is of great importance to the Chinese, who depend so much for their food upon the fish which is caught in their waters. They are enabled by this means to keep their fish during the hottest weather for a considerable time, and transmit them in this way to different parts of the country.

Immense quantities of fish are daily caught in the river above the town. Their mode of catching them is ingenious and amusing. One day I was going up a considerable distance in a boat, and set out a little before low water, that I might have the full benefit of the flow of the tide, and get as far up as possible before it turned. On the side of the river, a few miles above Ning-po, I observed some hundreds of small boats anchored, each containing two or three men; and, the tide turning just as I passed, the whole fleet was instantly in motion, rowing and sculling up the river with the greatest rapidity. As soon as the men reached a favourable part of the stream they cast out their nets and began to make a loud noise, splashing with their oars and sculls, with the intention, I suppose, of driving the fish into the nets. After remaining in this spot for about a quarter of an hour, all the boats set off again, farther up, for the next station, when the crew commenced again in the same noisy manner, and so on, for a long way up the river, as long as the tide was flowing; they then returned with the ebb, loaded with fishes for the next morning's market.

There is another mode of catching fish, which I have frequently seen in the northern provinces, even more curious than that which I have just noticed. Every one acquainted with Chinese history knows that fish abound in all the rivers and lakes of the north; indeed, every little pond swarms with them. I was greatly surprised when I first saw the fish-catcher following his profession in these places. He is literally amphibious. He is to be seen perfectly naked, half walking, half swimming; now he raises his arms and hands above his head, and, bringing them down, strikes a sharp blow upon the water, making a loud and splashing noise. His feet are not idle: they warn him that a fish is at hand, and they are now feeling for him amongst the mud at the bottom of the pond. The next moment the fisherman has disappeared: he is now under water, and he remains so long that you think something has happened to him. There is, however, no cause of fear; a few seconds more and he appears, rubbing his face and eyes with one hand, and in the other triumphantly holding up the poor little fish which he has just captured. It is immediately placed safely in his basket, and the work goes on as before. The surface of the water is struck and splashed, as I have just described, in order to frighten the fish, which are swimming amongst the feet of the Chinamen. Being frightened, they dive immediately to the bottom amongst the mud, where they are felt by the feet, and are soon taken by these expert divers.

But the most singular of all the methods of catching fish in China is that of training and employing a large species of cormorant for this purpose, generally called the fishing cormorant. These are certainly wonderful birds. I have frequently met with them on the canals and lakes in the interior, and, had I not seen with my own eyes their extraordinary docility, I should have had great difficulty in bringing my mind to believe what authors have said about them. The first time I saw them was on a canal a few miles from Ning-po. I was then on my way to a celebrated temple in that quarter, where I intended to remain for some time in order to make collections of objects of natural history in the neighbourhood. When the birds came in sight I immediately made my boatmen take in our sail, and we remained stationary for some time to observe their proceedings. There were two small boats, containing one man and about ten or twelve birds in each. The birds were standing perched on the sides of the little boat, and apparently had just arrived at the fishing-ground, and were about to commence operations. They were now ordered out of the boats by their masters; and so well trained were they, that they went on the water immediately, scattered themselves over the canal, and began to look for fish. They have a beautiful sea-green eye, and, quick as lightning, they see and dive upon the finny tribe, which, once caught in the sharp-notched bill of the bird, never by any possibility can escape. The cormorant now rises to the surface with the fish in his bill, and the moment he is seen by the Chinaman he is called back to the boat. As docile as a dog he swims after his master, and allows himself to be pulled into the San-pan, where he disgorges his prey, and again resumes his labours. And, what is more wonderful still, if one of the cormorants gets hold of a fish of large size, so large that he would have some difficulty in taking it to the boat, some of the others, seeing his dilemma, hasten to his assistance, and with their efforts united capture the animal and haul him off to the boat. Sometimes a bird seemed to get lazy or playful, and swam about without attending to his business; and then the Chinaman, with a long bamboo, which he also used for propelling the boat, struck the water near where the bird was, without, however, hurting him, calling out to him at the same time in an angry tone. Immediately, like the truant schoolboy who neglects his lessons and is found out, the cormorant gives up his play and resumes his labours. A small string is put round the neck of the bird, to prevent him from swallowing the fish which he catches; and great care is taken that this string is placed and fastened so that it will not slip farther down upon his neck and choke him, which otherwise it would be very apt to do.

Since I first saw these birds on the Ning-po canal I

have had opportunities of inspecting them and their operations in many other parts of China, more particularly in the country between the towns of Hang-chow-foo and Shanghae. I also saw great numbers of them on the river Min, near Foo-chow-foo. I was most anxious to get some living specimens, that I might take them home to England. Having great difficulty in inducing the Chinese to part with them, or, indeed, to speak at all on the subject, when I met them in the country, owing to our place of meeting being generally in those parts of the interior where the English are never seen, I applied to Her Majesty's Consul at Shanghae (Captain Balfour), who very kindly sent one of the Chinese connected with the consulate into the country, and procured two pairs for me. The difficulty now was to provide food for them on the voyage from Shanghae to Hong-kong. We procured a large quantity of live eels, this being a principal part of their food, and put them into a jar of mud and fresh water. These they ate in a most voracious manner, swallowing them whole, and in many instances vomiting them afterwards. If one bird was unlucky enough to vomit his eel, he was fortunate indeed if he caught it again, for another, as voracious as himself, would instantly seize it, and swallow it in a moment. Often they would fight stoutly for the fish, and then it either became the property of one, or, as often happened, their sharp bills divided the prey, and each ran off and devoured the half which fell to his share. During the passage down we encountered a heavy gale at sea, and, as the vessel was one of those small clipper schooners, she pitched and rolled very much, shipping seas from bow to stern, which set everything on her decks swimming. I put my head out of the cabin-door when the gale was at its height, and the first thing I saw was the cormorants devouring the eels, which were floating all over the decks. I then knew that the jar must have been turned over or smashed to pieces, and that of course all the eels which escaped the bills of the cormorants were now swimming in the ocean. After this I was obliged to feed them upon anything on board which I could find; but when I arrived at Hong-kong they were not in very good condition: two of them died soon after; and as there was no hope of taking the others home alive, I was obliged to kill them, and preserve their skins.

The Chinaman from whom I bought these birds has a large establishment for fishing and breeding the birds about thirty or forty miles from Shanghae, and between that town and Chapoo. They sell at a high price even amongst the Chinese themselves—I believe from six to eight dollars per pair, that is, from 30*s.* to 40*s.* As I was anxious to learn something of their food and habits, Mr. Medhurst, jun., interpreter to the British consulate at Shanghae, kindly undertook to put some questions to the man who brought them, and sent me the following notes connected with this subject:—

"The fish-catching birds eat small fish, yellow eels, and pulse-jelly. At five P.M. every day each bird will eat six taels (eight ounces) of eels or fish, and a catty of pulse-jelly. They lay eggs after three years, and in the fourth or fifth month. Hens are used to incubate the eggs. When about to lay their faces turn red, and then a good hen must be prepared. The date must be clearly written upon the shells of the eggs laid, and they will hatch in twenty-five days. When hatched take the young and put them upon cotton spread upon some warm water, and feed them with eels' blood for five days. After five days they can be fed with eels' flesh chopped fine, and great care must be taken in watching them.

"When fishing, a straw tie must be put upon their necks, to prevent them from swallowing the fish when they catch them. In the eighth or ninth month of the year they will daily descend into the water at ten o'clock in the morning, and catch fish until five in the afternoon, when they will come on shore. They will continue to go on in this way until the third month, after which time they cannot fish until the eighth month comes round again. The male is easily known from the female, in being generally a larger bird, and in having a darker and more glossy feather, but more particularly in the size of the head, the head of the male being large, and that of the female small."

Such are the habits of this extraordinary bird. As the months named in the note just quoted refer to the Chinese calendar, it follows that these birds do not fish in the summer months, but commence in autumn, about October, and end about May—periods agreeing nearly with the eighth and third months of the Chinese year.

TEA GARDENS AT SHANGHAE.

To face p. 91, vol. i.

CHAPTER VII.

Shanghae visited at the end of 1843 — My Lodgings — Prejudices and Superstitions of the Inhabitants — The City described — Shops and Merchandise — Food — An important Station for Foreign Trade — The Exports of the Country; Teas and Silk easily brought to it — The adjacent Country described — Its Canals — Agriculture — Tombs of the Dead — Trees and Shrubs — Gardens and Nurseries — Difficulty of access to them — Cunning and Deceit of the Chinese — A Chinese Dinner — Theatricals.

SHANGHAE is the most northerly of the five ports at which foreigners are now permitted to trade with the Chinese. Its population is estimated at 270,000. It is situated about a hundred miles, in a north-west direction, from the island of Chusan. The city stands on the bank of a fine river, about twelve miles from the point where it joins the celebrated Yang-tse-Kiang, or "Child of the Ocean." The Shanghae river, as it is generally called by foreigners, is as wide at Shanghae as the Thames at London Bridge. Its main channel is deep, and easily navigated when known, but the river abounds in long mud-banks, dangerous to large foreign vessels unless they happen to go up with a fair wind, and manage to get a good pilot on board at the entrance of the river.

I visited this place for the first time at the end of 1843, as soon as the port was opened by Her Majesty's Consul, Captain Balfour, and took up my quarters in a kind of bank or government shroff establishment, in company with two or three gentlemen who were here for purposes of trade. As none of us carried a cooking establishment with us, our meals were necessarily of the roughest description, neither exactly Chinese nor English, but something between the two. Our bed-rooms were miserably cold: often, in the mornings, we would find ourselves drenched in bed with the rain; and if snow fell, it was blown through the windows and formed "*wreaths*" on the floor. Nevertheless, the excitement produced on our minds by everything around us kept us in excellent health and in good spirits, and we made light of many things which in other circumstances we might have considered as hardships. Whenever we moved out of the house hundreds of people crowded the streets, and followed in our wake, as anxious to catch a glimpse of us as the crowds in London are to see the Queen. Every door and window was crammed with men, women, and children, who gazed upon us with a kind of stupid wonder, as if we had been inhabitants of the moon, and not the ordinary sons of earth. The children more particularly looked upon us with a kind of fear and dread, doubtless implanted in their young minds by their parents, who had less or more of the same feelings themselves. The name we bore—*Kwei-tsz*, or devil's child—was also calculated to produce erroneous impressions, particularly on the minds of the young, and made them regard us with superstitious horror. In these times it was quite common for us to hear such expressions as the following:—"The devil's children are coming," or "Come and see a devil's child;" and not unfrequently

"Kwei-tsz" was called out to us in derision. Several complaints were made of this conduct to the British Consul by parties who believed it to be very bad policy at the first commencement of the trade to submit to any marks of contempt, however slight; and strong remonstrances were promptly made by him to the Taoutae, or head mandarin, of Shanghae. This policy was the very best which could have been pursued with the Chinese authorities; and the consequence was, that in a very short time the offensive appellation was rarely heard in the streets of Shanghae; and if some little urchin, remembering the lesson so early taught him, came out with it unawares, he was immediately rebuked by the respectable part of the bystanders.

The following incident shows the kind of superstitious dread in which we were held by the inhabitants. A friend and myself were asked to a dinner given on board one of the vessels in the river, and, as the cabin was much more comfortable than our cheerless, fireless rooms on shore, we remained until nearly eleven o'clock. Not only are the gates of a Chinese town closed after dark, but all communication even with the streets in the suburbs is cut off by numerous gates and doors, which are fastened up about ten or eleven o'clock at night. This has doubtless been a very ancient custom, to prevent any sudden surprise by an enemy, or by the unruly populace themselves, and is still kept up in more peaceful times. When, therefore, we landed, we found all the gates in the suburbs closed and locked; and we had to pass through one at least before we could reach our quarters. Not a sound was heard; every house was closed; and all that dense multitude which thronged the street by day had sunk into repose. "How shall we get through?" said my friend. "Shake the gate," said I; "perhaps the noise will bring some one; or perchance, as it seems pretty old, it may give way." We took hold of the gate and gave it a good shake, calling out at the same time for some one to come and open it. The watchman's light was now seen coming towards us, and my friend again called out to him to make haste. At last two men with their lanterns came up, in that dreamy state which I have already noticed as a characteristic feature in the Chinese race, and muffled up with skins, as the night was very cold. They could not see distinctly who were on the other side of the door; and, as we mumbled a word or two of Chinese, they were put completely off their guard, and supposed we were benighted Chinamen. The bolts were drawn, the door opened, and behold, two of the dreaded "red-haired race" stood before them. I shall never forget their astonishment when they got their eyes upon us after the gate was opened; and whether they actually believed us to be beings of another world, or supposed we had another army at our back to take the city a second time, it is impossible to say, but quick as lightning they both turned their backs and fled, leaving us to shut the gates, or admit an army, if we chose. We walked quietly home, and neither saw nor heard anything more of the bold guardians of the night.

The city of Shanghae is surrounded with high walls and ramparts built upon the same plan as all other Chinese fortifications of this kind. The circumference of the walls is about three and a half miles, and the greater part of the inside is densely studded with houses; the suburbs, particularly all along the side of the river, are very extensive. Although the gates of the city are closed soon after dark, the people are allowed to pass through afterwards on the payment of a few "cash." When the gate is opened to one, a whole crowd are ready to rush through along with him, the first only paying the "cash." Such is the custom; so that if a poor man comes to the gate he has only to wait until one richer than himself arrives, when, the fee being paid, they pass through together. Joss-houses are met with in all directions, both in the city and suburbs; at certain parts on the ramparts, also, these temples are built and crowded with idols, where the natives come to burn incense, bow the knee, and engage in the other ceremonies of heathen idol-worship. Fortune-tellers and jugglers are also in great request, and reap a rich harvest by working upon the credulity of their countrymen. You meet these characters in all the streets and public squares in Shanghae, and, what is very strange, the *sing-song*, or theatricals, of which the Chinese are particularly fond, are frequently exhibited in the temples. This is much opposed to our ideas of religion and propriety; but, somehow or other, the customs of our Celestial friends are in many instances directly opposed to ours.

The streets are generally very narrow, and in the daytime are crowded with people actively engaged in business. The merchandise which is the most striking to a stranger walking through the streets is the silk and embroidery, such as I formerly noticed at Ning-po, cotton and cotton goods, porcelain, ready-made clothes of all kinds beautifully lined with skins and fur, bamboo pipes six feet long and nicely arranged in the shops, pictures, bronzes, and numerous curiosity-shops for the sale of carved bamboo ornaments, old pieces of porcelain, and things of that kind, to which the Chinese attach great value. But articles of food form of course the most extensive trade of all; and it is sometimes a difficult matter to get through the streets for the immense quantities of fish, pork, fruit, and vegetables which crowd the stands in front of the shops. Besides the more common kinds of vegetables, the shepherds' purse, and a kind of trefoil or clover, are extensively used amongst the natives here; and really these things, when properly cooked, more particularly the latter, are not bad. Dining-rooms, tea-houses, and bakers' shops, are met with at every step, from the poor man who carries his kitchen or bakehouse upon his back, and beats upon a piece of bamboo to apprise the neighbourhood of his presence, and whose whole establishment is not worth a dollar, to the most extensive tavern or tea-garden crowded with hundreds of customers. For a few cash (1000 or 1200 = one dollar) a Chinese can dine in a sumptuous manner upon his rice, fish, vegetables, and tea; and I fully believe that in no country in the world is there less real misery and want than in China. The very beggars seem a kind of jolly crew, and are kindly treated by the inhabitants.

Shanghae is by far the most important station for foreign trade on the coast of China, and is consequently attracting a large share of public attention. No other town with which I am acquainted possesses such advantages: it is the great gate—the principal entrance, in fact—to the Chinese empire. In going up the river towards the town a forest of masts meets the eye, and shows at once that it is a place of vast native trade. Junks come here from all parts of the coast, not only from the southern provinces, but also from Shantung and Peechelee: there are also a considerable number annually from Singapore and the Malay Islands. The convenience of inland transit is also unrivalled in any part of the world. The country, being as it were the valley of the Yang-tse-kiang, is one vast plain, intersected by many beautiful rivers, and these again joined and crossed by canals, many of them nearly natural, and others stupendous works of art. Owing to the level nature of the country, the tide ebbs and flows a great distance inland, thus assisting the natives in the transmission of their exports to Shanghae, or their imports to the most distant parts of the country. The port of Shanghae swarms with boats of all sizes, employed in this inland traffic; and the traveller continually meets them, and gets a glimpse of their sails over the land, at every step of his progress in the interior. Since the port has been opened, these boats bring down large quantities of tea and silk to supply the wants of our merchants who have established themselves here, and return loaded with the manufactures of Europe and America, which they have taken in exchange. Our plain cotton goods are most in demand amongst the Chinese, because they can dye them in their own peculiar style, and fit them for the tastes of the people. From what we know of the geographical nature of the country, there can be no doubt that all the green teas, and perhaps the greatest portion of the black, can be brought to Shanghae at less expense than they can be taken to Canton, or any of the other southern towns, except, perhaps, Ning-po; and as the tea-men incur less risk in taking their money home from the north, owing to the peaceable nature of the inhabitants, this will be another very great inducement to bring their teas to Shanghae. The large silk districts of northern China are close at hand; and there can be no doubt that a large proportion of that commodity in a raw state will be disposed of at Shanghae. Taking, therefore, all these facts into consideration—the proximity of Shanghae to the large towns of Hang-chow, Soo-chow, and the ancient capital of Nanking; the large native trade, the convenience of inland transit by means of rivers and canals; the fact that teas and silks can be brought here more readily than to Canton; and, lastly, viewing this place as an immense mart for our cotton manufactures, which we already know it to be,—there can be no doubt that in a few years it will not only rival Canton, but become a place of far greater importance. And when I add that the climate is healthy, the natives peaceable, and foreign residents respected, and allowed to walk and ride all over the country, to any distance not exceeding a day's journey, it will be acknowledged that, as a place to live at, it has many advantages over its southern rival.

I have already said that this part of China is a

complete network of rivers and canals. These were often most annoying to me in my travels over the country, when I happened to get off the Emperor's highway, a circumstance of no rare occurrence. I have often been obliged to press a boat into my service much against the will of the owners, more particularly when I visited this region for the first time, because I was then unacquainted with the localities, and the Chinese always seemed to fear I might take, or rob, their boats if I succeeded in getting into them, such were the opinions formed of foreigners at that time.

One day, in particular, I had been a considerable distance inland to the westward of Shanghae, and on my return, by some means or other, I got off the beaten track, and in pursuing my way, as I supposed in the proper direction, I was "brought up" by a large and deep canal. About two miles from where I stood I saw a bridge, and, as it was nearly dark, I made for it as fast as I could. Unluckily, however, just as I thought my difficulties were over, being within gunshot of the bridge, I was again stopped by another canal, which crossed the former one at right angles. I was now completely brought to a stand-still, but in a few minutes I perceived a boat approaching, and a man tracking it on the same side as that on which we were. As soon as it came near, we called out to the men on board to pull the boat towards us, and allow us to get across to the other side. They seemed much frightened and, after making the man who was tracking the boat come on board, they pulled her into the middle of the canal, and then sculled away with all their might. They would soon have passed far beyond our reach, and left us to feel our way in the dark, or plunge through the deep muddy canal. Necessity, they say, has no law. "Call out to them," said I to my servant, "that if they do not immediately stop I will fire into the boat," and at the same moment I fired one of my barrels a little way ahead. This was quite sufficient. They immediately came towards us, and put us quickly over to the other side. I paid them for their trouble, and desired them to be more civil to the next traveller they might meet in the same circumstances. They went off in high spirits, and we heard them laughing and joking about the adventure long after they had passed out of our sight.

As an agricultural country, the plain of Shanghae is by far the richest which I have seen in China, and is perhaps unequalled by any district of like extent in the world. It is one vast beautiful garden. The hills nearest to Shanghae are distant about thirty miles. These have an isolated appearance in the extensive plain, and are not more than two or three hundred feet high. From their summit, on a clear day, I looked round in all directions, and was only able to see some few hills, apparently having the same isolated character, far away on the horizon, to the south; these, I have since ascertained, are near the Tartar city of Chapoo. All the rest of the country was a vast level plain, without a mountain or a hill to break the monotony of the view. The soil is a rich deep loam, and produces heavy crops of wheat, barley, rice, and cotton, besides an immense quantity of green vegetable crops, such as cabbages, turnips, yams, carrots, egg-plants, cucumbers, and other articles of that kind which are grown in the vicinity of the city. The land, although level, is generally much higher than the valleys amongst the hills, or the plain round Ning-po; and, consequently, it is well adapted for the cultivation of cotton, which is, in fact, the staple production of the district. Indeed this is the great Nanking cotton country, from which large quantities of that article are generally sent in junks to the north and south of China, as well as to the neighbouring islands. Both the white kind, and that called the "yellow cotton," from which the yellow Nanking cloth is made, are produced in the district.

The soil of this district is not only remarkably fertile, but agriculture seems more advanced, and bears a greater resemblance to what it is at home, than in any part of China which I have seen. One here meets with a farmyard containing stacks regularly built up and thatched in the same form and manner as we find them in England; the land, too, is ridged and furrowed in the same way; and were it not for plantations of bamboo, and the long tails and general costume of the natives, a man might almost imagine himself on the banks of the Thames.

A very considerable portion of the land in the vicinity of the town is occupied by the tombs of the dead.* In all directions large conical-shaped mounds meet the eye, overgrown with long grass, and in some instances planted with shrubs and flowers. The traveller here, as well

* It is stated in Davis's 'Chinese,' that the dead are all buried on the sides of the barren hills.

as at Ning-po and Chusan, constantly meets with coffins placed on the surface of the ground out in the fields, carefully thatched over with straw or mats to preserve them from the weather. Sometimes, though rarely, when the relatives are less careful than they generally are, I met with coffins broken or crumbling to pieces with age, exposing the remains of the dead. I was most struck with the coffins of children, which I met with everywhere; these are raised from the ground on a few wooden posts, and carefully thatched over to protect them from the weather—reminding the stranger that some parent, with feelings as tender and acute as his own, has been bereaved of a loved one, whom he, perhaps, expected should cheer and support him in his declining years, and whose remains he now carefully watches. Those in the higher ranks of life have generally a family burial-place at a little distance from the town, planted with cypress and pine trees, with a temple and altar built to hold the josses or idols, and where the various religious ceremonies are performed. A man with his family is stationed there to protect the place, and to burn candles and incense on certain high days. Others, again, are interred in what may be called public cemeteries, several of which I met with in the vicinity of Shanghae. These are large buildings, each containing a certain number of spacious halls or rooms, and having the coffins placed in rows around the sides.

A flat and highly cultivated country, such as I have just described, cannot be expected to be rich in indigenous plants. There are, however, many beautiful clumps of the bamboo growing round all the villages and small farm-houses, which give a kind of tropical character to the scenery, but it is the *only* type of the tropics met with in this district, at least as regards trees. I have already mentioned the clumps of cypress and pine trees planted in the cemeteries of the rich, which are seen studded all over the country, and form one of its most striking features. Among these, I met for the first time with the beautiful *Cryptomeria japonica*, a species of pine not unlike the *Araucarias* of Norfolk Island and Brazil. When growing luxuriantly it is highly ornamental, rising from the ground as straight as a larch, and sending out numerous side branches almost horizontally from the main stem, which again droop towards the ground in a graceful and "*weeping*" manner. The wood of the tree has a kind of twisted grain, and possesses great strength and durability. It is highly valued by the Chinese, and from its beauty and straightness is often used by the mandarins and priests for those long poles which are generally seen in front of their houses and temples. It is also well known and highly prized by the natives of Japan.

The only tree which I met with of very large size in this district is the *Salisburia adiantifolia*, commonly called the Maiden-hair tree, from the resemblance its leaves bear to a fern of that name. This is one of the plants which the Chinese are fond of dwarfing, and it is, consequently, often seen in that state in their gardens. Its fruit is sold in the markets in all Chinese towns by the name of "*Pa-kwo*," and is not unlike dried almonds, only whiter, fuller, and more round. The natives seem very fond of it, although it is rarely eaten by Europeans. The weeping-willow, apparently the same species as we possess in England, is also common on the sides of all the rivers and canals, as well as in the gardens of the Chinese; and there is also a species of elm, but it never attains any great size, and can therefore be of little value.

Although there is a paucity in the number of plants which are really indigenous to this district, yet Shanghae is rich in species which have been brought from other parts of the empire, and are here exposed in gardens for sale: but there are here no mandarin gardens similar to those at Ning-po, this being essentially a mercantile city, and all the residents engaged in active business. The difference between the two towns, in this respect, is indeed very striking. To make up, however, for the deficiency of private collections, I found a number of nursery gardens containing excellent assortments of plants for sale, many of which were new to me, and are unknown in Europe; and, being at the same time very ornamental, were consequently of great value. At first I had great difficulty in finding out these gardens. The Chinese, from motives which it would be difficult to define—perhaps jealousy or fear—were unwilling to give me the slightest information about any of these places outside of the town. They told me there were numbers of flower-shops in the city, but denied having any knowledge of nurseries or gardens in the country.

"If you want flowers," said they, "there they are in the shops; why do you not buy them? Shanghae men do this, and you should do the same."

"But then shops do not contain the things which I want," said I.

"Then give us the names of the things you want, and we will get them for you."

"But how can I give you the names? I do not understand your language; you would, of course, send to your nurseries for them if I could only furnish you with their names."

"Yes."

"Oh, then, you have nursery gardens in the country?"

"Yes; but they are a very long way off."

Of course I knew enough of the Chinese by this time to doubt every word they told me, unless I had good reasons for believing them to be speaking the truth, which I had not in this case. I also saw at a glance, from the state of the plants, that they had not only been grown in the country, but I knew from their condition that they could have come but a very short distance, for they had been dug out of the ground with a portion of the soil adhering to the roots. For some few days, however, all my efforts were completely baffled, until a lucky circumstance enabled me to get the better of my Chinese friends. My servant and myself were returning home from the country, after an unsuccessful day's search, when, as we neared the north gate of the city, I shot a bird, which was new to me, being at that time engaged in making a collection of the skins of Chinese birds. I was of course immediately surrounded by all the boys in the neighbourhood, who were quite in raptures at my gun, as it was so different from their own clumsy matchlock. "Now," said I to the juvenile crowd around me, "who can show me the way to the nearest flower-garden, where I can purchase some flowers?" "Lyloe, lyloe,"* said half a dozen of them at once, and I found, to my surprise and pleasure, that I was almost close to the gate of a very good nursery belonging to an individual who had a flower-shop in the city, and with whom I had had the conversation related above. It was now getting too dark to see the plants well, but I marked the spot, and returned on the following day. This time, however, I was not successful; for, as I approached, a boy, who was on the watch, scampered away to the gardener's house and gave notice of my appearance; and long before I reached the gate it was closed and barricaded, and no persuasion nor entreaty could remove their fears or induce them to allow me to enter. The next day, and the next again, the very same thing took place, although I took different roads, in the hopes of finding the young sentinel off his guard. I was now obliged to have recourse to other means to gain my end. Her Majesty's consul, Captain Balfour, had from the first taken great interest in the success of my pursuits, and kindly offered me every assistance in his power, should I find any difficulties in my way. I therefore related the circumstance to him, and requested him to allow one of the Chinese officers attached to the consulate to accompany me to the garden, and explain that my object was to purchase plants, and not to take anything away against their will. From our experience of Chinese character, we were well aware that, if this were properly explained, the poor people, whose liveli-

* "Come, come."

hood depended upon the propagation and sale of plants, would be very glad to allow me to make purchases at their garden. I therefore set out again on the following day, accompanied by an officer from the consulate. When we approached the garden my young friend was at his post as usual, and ran off immediately, and forthwith the gate was closed and barricaded as before. We walked quietly up to it and knocked, but there was no answer, and the place seemed all at once to be deserted. The officer well knew that the family had hid themselves just inside the gate, and commenced talking to them, and laughing at their fears. In a few seconds we heard a movement amongst the bushes, and then the inmates, gaining courage, ventured to approach the gate to reconnoitre. At last, being apparently satisfied, the bolts were withdrawn and we were admitted within the sacred precincts of the garden, when I soon found several very valuable plants. The ice was now broken, and, with the assistance of the Chinese officer, I got the names and localities of several other gardens, which I soon found out ; and although it was the winter season, and vegetation in a state of repose, I was able in a few weeks to get together a collection of plants which, when they flowered, proved not only quite new, but highly ornamental. A few months wrought a great change upon these diffident and timid people, and at length they not only received me with pleasure, but begged me to bring my friends and acquaintances to see their flowers. I frequently did so, and, as we always treated them with kindness and consideration, a favourable impression was made upon their minds, which, I have no doubt, will long continue. When I was leaving Shanghae, in 1845, on my return to England, I went to remove a collection of plants which I had in one of these gardens: as I was doing so, the proprietor said to me, "The next time you come to Shanghae I shall have left this garden, and gone to one which I have taken in the next district, where I shall be glad to see you, and supply you with the plants you want."

"Thanks, my good friend," said I; "but as my labours in the 'central flowery land' are ended, I shall now return again to my own country, 'Ta-Eng-co,'* a land in the far distant west, and you shall never see me again; fare you well."

He then kindly wished me fair winds, smooth seas, and a happy meeting with my friends at home.

I merely mention this circumstance to show what a change took place in the feelings of these poor people in the course of two years, and which I regard as an earnest of what may be done with the northern Chinese, who differ widely from their haughty and insolent countrymen in the south.

Another example may be given to show the cunning and deceit of many of the Chinese here as elsewhere. A flower-painter in Chusan had informed me that several very valuable varieties of the *Moutan*, or Tree Pœony, were to be found in gardens near Shanghae. Those varieties of this flower which are yearly brought from the northern provinces to Canton, and which are now common in Europe, have blossoms, which are either

* Great England, or Great Britain, the name which our country is known by in the north of China.

rose-coloured or white: but it was always asserted, although not believed, that in some parts of China, purple, blue, and yellow varieties were produced, although these were never brought to Canton for sale. It was for these that I made the most particular inquiries, and this painter not only affirmed he had seen them, but also offered, for a small sum, to make me drawings from memory of all the different kinds. I employed him at once, and when he had finished the drawings I took them with me to Shanghae. A nurseryman who had a flower-shop in the town, to whom I showed these drawings, promised at once to procure living plants for me, but said they would be very expensive, as he would have to send to Soo-chow, a distance of nearly one hundred miles, for they were not to be procured in the vicinity of Shanghae, and a man would be absent at least eight days. I was, of course, glad to get them upon any terms, and gave the man the price he asked, which, after all, was not much out of the way, if they were to be brought a hundred miles. At the specified time the Moutans arrived, and proved most valuable kinds, which, in England, would have brought a very high sum. Amongst them there were *lilacs* and *purples;* some nearly *black;* and one which the Chinese called "*the yellow,*" which, however, was only white with a slight tinge of yellow near the centre of the petals. Altogether the collection was a valuable one, and I was highly satisfied with my bargain. Great was my surprise when I afterwards found that these plants were brought a distance of not more than six miles from the walls of Shanghae, and that the celebrated town of Soo-chow was, in fact, supplied with "Moutans" from the very same place.

Whilst at Shanghae, I, with some other Europeans, had an invitation to go to the house of a mandarin, to see a theatrical performance or "Sing-song," and to dine with him in Chinese style afterwards. Sedan-chairs were sent to take us to his house, where we were introduced to a number of his friends, and, as the invariable custom is, tea was immediately handed round. Shortly afterwards a servant came with a tray full of wet warm towels, not unlike those generally used in kitchens at home, and presented one to each of us. At first we could not conjecture what these were for; but on looking at our Chinese friends we observed them rubbing their faces and hands with them, and, although not very agreeable to us, we immediately did the same. I afterwards found that this was a common custom amongst the Chinese, and I have often been much refreshed by it after a warm walk. In hot countries like China this plan is much better and more conducive to health than either washing or bathing in cold water.

While this was going on in the house the players were getting everything ready in the large room where the performance was to take place. In a little while one of them entered the room where we were, carrying in his hand several fine long ivory cards, on which were written a number of the most popular plays of the day, any one of which the players were ready to perform at the command of our host and his friends. We were most politely consulted on the subject, which, as we did not know a single character of the language, and had the greatest difficulty in understanding what was said to us, was not of much use. Having at last fixed upon a particular piece for the evening's entertainment, we were all led into the theatre. The room was large and nearly square, having a platform at the upper end for the actors and band, and one of the sides being only separated from an open lane by a railing, so that the public might also have a view of the play. The centre of the room was completely filled with guests, and from the roof hung a number of lanterns in the Chinese style. As it was early in the afternoon when the play commenced, the lanterns were not lighted and the piece went on in day-light, the Chinese actors not excluding it as we do in our theatres in England.

The play began with some pantomime-like feats, such as we see in English theatres at Christmas. This was succeeded by something which appeared to be very pathetic, judging from the language and gestures of the performers. All was gone through in a kind of opera style, the actors singing their parts with false voices. The feats of tumbling which were now and then performed were extremely dexterous and clever, and attracted our notice more than anything else, probably because they were best understood.

The dresses of the actors were superb, and must have cost a large sum of money. There were no females amongst them, as it is not customary for them to act; but their places were supplied by men or boys chosen from amongst those who are most "lady-looking," and so well were their appearance and dresses arranged, that it would have required a practised eye to have detected the difference.

The voices of the actors were not musical, at least to English ears, but the whole was in unison with the noisy gong, and the wind instruments like bagpipes, which are in common use amongst the Chinese. In fact, noise seemed to be the thing which produced the greatest effect, and we certainly had enough of it.

I was struck by the various figures made by the actors on the stage, intended, no doubt, to represent something like those scenes or pictures which are so much studied in our theatres at home. A quadrant seems to be a great favourite, and was constantly made by them in the different acts. They have no scenery to assist the delusion, only a simple screen, which is sometimes used to represent a room out of which some actor is to make his appearance. Fencing is much practised, and is, perhaps, the most curious part of these exhibitions. Each individual has two swords, which he swings about his head in the wildest manner, at the same time throwing his feet and legs about in a most fantastic way, as if they had as much to do in the business as the hands and arms. The exhibition or play lasted for three hours, and then we left the theatre and retired into another room. While we were there the servants were busily employed in re-arranging the theatre, which was now to be converted into a dining-room.

When all was ready we were led in with great ceremony, and placed in the principal seats of honour. We had now an opportunity of seeing the extent to which the Chinese carry their ceremony and politeness amongst themselves when they are about to be seated at table. Our host and his friends were nearly a quarter of an hour before the whole of them were seated. Each one was pressing the most honourable seat upon his neighbour, who, in his turn, could not think of occupying such a distinguished place at the board. However, after a great deal of bowing and flattery, all was apparently arranged satisfactorily, and dinner commenced.

The tables were now covered with a profusion of small dishes, which contained all the finest fruits and vegetables of the season, besides many of the most expensive kinds of soups, such as the celebrated bird's-nest and others, many of which were excellent even to the palate of an Englishman. The servants were continually employed in removing the centre dishes and replacing them by others of a different kind, until at last every one seemed perfectly satisfied. Still, however, the ceremony of bringing in new dishes went on, and these were merely looked at and removed. Our maiden efforts with the chopsticks must have been a source of great amusement to our Chinese friends, but they were polite enough not to laugh at us, and did everything in their power to assist us. The play was resumed again as soon as the dinner commenced, and continued as briskly as ever. The "lady actors" at intervals came down from the platform and supplied the guests with different kinds of wines. During the entertainment a piece of money was handed to each of the guests, which they were desired to leave as a present for the actors at the conclusion of the piece. When this was given them, the whole of the *corps dramatique* came round, and each made a most polite bow of acknowledgment, and withdrew. Still, however, the dinner ceremonial went on; hundreds of fresh dishes were brought in, and as many in their turn removed. The Chinese guests were sometimes smoking, sometimes eating, just as it seemed good to them, and uniformly praising everything which made its appearance on the table.

We had now been three or four hours at table, and, although the whole affair had been very amusing, we had had enough of it, and were beginning to tire. "How long shall the dinner last?" said I to a linguist who was placed next me, and who had most politely explained everything which had occurred during the entertainment. "Oh," said he, "it will last for three or four hours longer, but if you want to go away you may do so now." We were very glad to find that Chinese etiquette permitted us to withdraw, and ordered our chairs, which were waiting in the court-yard to receive us. Our host and his friends lighted us out with lanterns, and we took our departure in the same style in which we came. So ended my first Chinese dinner. Since then such things have been no rarity, either in the palaces of the rich or in the cottages of the poor, and they have been even more frequent in the temples with the priests.

CHAPTER VIII.

Return to the South of China — The Canton River described — Forts at the Bocca Tigris — Productions of the Country — The "Sighing" Willow — Cultivation of the Nelumbium — Boats on the River — The Barber's Boat — Splendour of the Flower Boats — Appearance of the River at Festivals — Order which prevails in this floating City — Houses built over Water — Chinese Dexterity in swimming and diving — Fa-Tee Gardens — Chinese new Year — Attacked and robbed by the Chinese — A subsequent Attack made upon some Officers of the English Government.

As the island of Chusan was my head-quarters in the north of China, I now proceeded thither with my collections from Shanghae, preparatory to sailing for Hong-kong and the southern ports of the country. The Chusan hills were now covered with snow, and the weather was piercingly cold. Large quantities of pheasants and water-fowl were daily brought to the markets by the Chinese, who found the English good customers. A small species of deer was also brought from the main-land, and frequently alive. Four or five fine pheasants were often to be purchased for a dollar, and duck and teal were also remarkably cheap: I believe from two to four rupees were generally given for a deer.

The officers of the troops stationed at Chusan, who were fond of shooting, obtained excellent sport by engaging Chinese boats and going across to the hills on the main-land, there being little game of any kind upon the island itself.

Having got all my things packed, I took a passage in a vessel bound for the south, and, having a fair monsoon down the China Sea, we arrived at Hong-kong in a few days, without anything occurring worthy of notice. The various collections which I had made in the north were now put up in glazed cases and shipped for England.

As the south of China had been ransacked by former botanists, I could not expect to find much which was new or worthy of being sent home, and I therefore arranged to proceed north again in March or April, in order to have a whole season before me. In the mean time, as I had a few weeks to spare in the south, I determined on a visit to Canton and Macao, which are both within a short distance from Hong-kong.

The Canton river is certainly one of the most imposing and striking objects which the traveller meets with in this celebrated country. The sea, near its mouth, is studded all over with numerous islands, of which a good view is obtained in going over from Hong-kong to Macao; and in sailing from either of these places to Canton we pass a succession of them, most of which are mountainous, having huge masses of rock, and yellow gravelly clay, protruding here and there through the surface, and but thinly covered with vegetation of any kind.

Sometimes, however, in our progress, we obtained views of beautiful bays, with a few acres of level land near the shore, in the midst of which there are some pretty houses or huts, surrounded by a few trees and shrubs. In sailing amongst these islands one is apt to think that, in the retirement of such places, far removed from the vicious world and the "busy hum of men," the inhabitants must, indeed, be happy and innocent, having their few wants abundantly supplied by the rice which grows luxuriantly around their dwellings, and by the never-failing supply of excellent fish, which are easily caught in the sea. But these dreams of happiness and innocence are soon dispelled—these quiet villages abound with pirates, who frequently commit acts of the most cold-blooded cruelty, and render the passage between Hong-kong, Canton, and Macao, an alarming and dangerous affair. Lorchas, and other small vessels, with valuable cargoes on board, are frequently attacked, the crew and passengers murdered, and the vessels disabled or destroyed.

A few hours' sail, with a fair wind and tide, brought me in sight of the celebrated Bocca Tigris, the entrance to the Canton river. The forts destroyed during the war had been rebuilt on a more extensive scale; and, if manned with English soldiers, no hostile fleet in the world could pass them without being blown to pieces. I fancy, however, that the Chinese, although they have had a lesson in the art of war which will make them more difficult to conquer in future, would still, with all their forts, afford but a feeble resistance against the military and naval tactics of the English and other civilised nations of the West.

Inside the Bogue the river widens very much, and presents the appearance of an inland sea. The view now becomes beautiful and highly picturesque, the flat cultivated land near the shores forming a striking contrast to the barren hills on the outside of the forts; the mountains in the distance appear to encircle the extensive plain; and although, like the others, they are barren, yet they make a fine background to the picture. A few miles further up the river the shipping in Blenheim and Whampoa reaches comes into view, and the celebrated Whampoa pagoda, with several more of less note, besides numerous other towers and joss-houses, all remind the traveller that he is approaching the far-famed city of Canton, one of the richest and most important in the celestial empire. The noble river, with its numerous ramifications, forms many islands, on one of which the small town or village of Whampoa is built.

Large quantities of rice are grown, both on the islands formed by the river, and on the flats on the main-land. The tide is kept out by embankments, and the ground can be overflowed at will. These embankments are not allowed to lie idle, but are made to produce crops of plantains. When the land is too high to be flooded by the tide, the water-wheel is brought into play, and it is perfectly astonishing how much water can be raised by this simple contrivance in a very short space of time.

Sugar-cane is also grown rather extensively near Whampoa, and, in its raw state, is an article in great demand amongst the Chinese. It is manufactured into sugar-candy and brown sugar; many kinds of the latter being particularly fine, though not much used by the foreigners residing in the country, who generally prefer the candy reduced to powder, in which state it is very fine and white. I did not see our loaf-sugar in any part of China, and I conceive that it is not made there.

A great number of the common fruit trees of the country grow all over the plains and near the side of the river. The mango, guava, wangpee (*Cookia punctata*), leechee, longan, oranges, and pumeloes, are the principal kinds. Besides these, there are the cypress, thuja, banyan and other kinds of fig-trees, and a species of pine, called by the Chinese the water-pine, from its always growing by the sides of the rivers and canals. The bamboo, and a sort of weeping willow very much like our own, are also frequently met with. The name which the Chinese give to the latter is the "sighing" willow, coinciding rather curiously with our own term of "weeping;" and when taken in connexion with the historical fact of the Jews weeping by the streams of Babylon, and hanging their harps upon the willows, shows that this is regarded as the emblem of sorrow, as universally as the dark and sombre pine and cypress are considered in all countries fit companions to the cemetery and churchyard.

On the sides of the river, both below and above the city, large quantities of the water-lily, or lotus, are grown, which are enclosed by embankments in the same manner as the rice-fields. This plant is cultivated both as an ornament, and for the root, which is brought in large quantities to the markets, and of which the Chinese are remarkably fond. In the summer and autumn months, when in flower, the lotus-fields have a gay and striking appearance, but at other seasons the decayed leaves and flowers, and the stagnant and dirty water, are not at all ornamental to the houses which they surround.

One of the most striking sights on the Canton river is the immense number of boats which are moored all along the shore, near the foreign factory. There are thousands of all kinds and sizes, from the splendid flower-boat, as it is called, down to the small barber's boat, forming a large floating city, peopled by an immense number of human beings. In sailing up the river you may observe a very small boat, perhaps the smallest you ever saw, exposed on the water, being nothing more than a few planks fastened together. This is the barber's boat, who is going about, or rather swimming about, following his daily avocation of shaving the heads and tickling the ears and eyes of the Chinamen. By the by, this same barber has much to answer for, for his practice has a most prejudicial effect upon the eyes and ears of his countrymen. He, however, works his little boat with great dexterity, and with his scull manages to propel himself with ease and swiftness through the floating city of boats, larger and more powerful than his own. Then you see boats of various sizes, such as those at Macao and Hong-kong, covered over, divided into three compartments, and kept remarkably clean and neat. These are hired by either natives or foreigners for the purpose of going off to the large junks or other vessels moored out in the river, or for short excursions to the island of Honan, the Fa-Tee Gardens, or such places. The centre division of the boat forms a very neat little room, having windows in the sides, ornamented with pictures and flowers of various kinds. The compartment at the bow is occupied by the rowers, and that at the stern is used for preparing the food of the family to whom the boat belongs.

The boats of the Hong merchants, and the large flower-boats, are very splendid. They are arranged in compartments like the others, but are built in a more superb and costly manner. The reader must imagine a kind of wooden house raised upon the floor of the boat, having the entrance near the bows, space being left there for the boatmen to stand and row. This entrance, being the front, is carved in a most superb style, forming a prelude to what may be seen within. Numerous lanterns hang from the roof of these splendid showy cabins; looking-glasses, pictures, and poetry adorn their sides; and all the peculiarities of this singular people are exposed to our view in these their floating palaces.

Then there are the chop-boats, which are used by the merchants for conveying goods to the vessels at Whampoa; the passage-boats to Hong-kong, Macao, and various parts of the country; the mandarin-boats, with their numerous oars, which have a strange appearance as they pass up and down the river (I have seen a single boat of this kind with forty oars on each side); and, lastly, the large unwieldy sea-going junks. There are various modifications of all these kinds of boats, each adapted for the particular purpose for which it is designed. At festival times the river has a singularly gay and striking appearance, particularly at night, when the lanterns are lighted, and numberless boats gaily decorated with them move up and down in front of the factory. The effect produced upon a stranger at these times by the wild and occasionally plaintive strains of Chinese music, the noisy gong, the close and sultry air, the strange people,—full of peculiarities and conceit,—is such as he can never forget, and leaves upon his mind a mixed impression of pleasure, pity, admiration, and contempt. Throughout the whole of this immense floating city the greatest regularity prevails; the large boats are arranged in rows, forming streets, through which the smaller craft pass and repass, like coaches and other vehicles in a large town. The families who live in this manner seem to have a great partiality for flowers, which they keep in pots, either upon the high stern of their boats, or in their little parlours. The Chinese arbor vitæ, gardenias, cycas revoluta, cockscombs, and oranges, seem to be the greatest favourites with them. A joss-house—small indeed, in many cases, but yet a place of worship—is indispensable to all these floating houses. Here the joss-stick and the oil are daily burned, and form the incense which these poor people offer to their imaginary deity.

The city and suburbs of Canton are supposed to contain about a million of inhabitants. Upon the sides of the river, and the numerous canals in the suburbs of Canton, whole streets of wooden houses are built upon stakes which are driven firmly into the mud. These dwellings very much resemble the travelling shows which are often seen in the market-towns of England; except that posts supply the place of wheels, and that they are crowded together in hundreds, forming crooked and irregular streets. Thousands of the inhabitants live and enjoy health and happiness in such places, which would soon be graves for Europeans—such is the difference of constitution.

But what surprised me most was the old women and young children bathing in the river, which seemed as if it were their natural element, and they appeared quite as much at home there as the fishes themselves. The Chinese boat population are famous for their dexterity in and under the water. Since the island of Hong-kong became an English settlement, officers of the government, sent to apprehend thieves in the bay, have frequently failed to do so owing to this circumstance. The Chinamen, whenever they found that there was any danger of being taken, jumped all together overboard, diving out of sight, and swimming under water until they were out of the reach of their pursuers, or until they found shelter in some of the numerous boats belonging to their own clan which lay moored in the bay.

I lost no time in visiting the celebrated Fa-tee gardens, near Canton, "the flowery land," as the name implies, from whence a great number of those fine plants were first procured which now decorate our gardens in England. They are situated two or three miles above the city, on the opposite side of the river, and are, in fact, Chinese nursery gardens, where plants are cultivated for sale.

Here, then, I beheld a specimen of the far-famed system of Chinese gardening, about which we have read so much in European authors: I will therefore describe them somewhat fully. The plants are principally kept in large pots arranged in rows along the sides of narrow paved walks, with the houses of the gardeners at the entrance, through which the visitors pass to the gardens. There are about a dozen of these gardens, more or less extensive, according to the business or wealth of the proprietor; but they are generally smaller than the smallest of our London nurseries. They have also stock-grounds, where the different plants are planted out in the ground, and where the first process of dwarfing their celebrated trees is put in operation. These contain large collections of camellias, azaleas, oranges, roses, and various other well-known plants, which are purchased by the Chinese when in flower. The most striking plant in autumn or winter is the curious fingered citron, which the Chinese gather and place in their dwellings or on their altars. It is much admired both for its strange form, and also for its perfume. The mandarin orange is also much grown at Fa-tee, where the plants are kept in a dwarf state, and flower and fruit most profusely, producing large, flat, dark, red-skinned fruit. The Chinese have a great variety of plants belonging to the orange tribe: and of one, which they call the *cum-quat*—a small oval-fruited variety—they make a most excellent preserve.

But it is of course in spring that the Fa-tee gardens possess the greatest attractions. They are then gay with the tree pæony, azaleas, camellias, roses, and various other plants. The azaleas are splendid, and reminded me of the exhibitions in the gardens of the Horticultural Society at Chiswick, but the Fa-tee exhibitions were on a much larger scale. Every garden was one mass of bloom, and the different colours of red, white, and purple, blended together, had a most beautiful and imposing effect. The air at this season around Fa-tee is perfumed with the sweet flowers of *Olea fragrans* and the *Magnolia fuscata*, both of which are grown extensively in these gardens. Dwarfed trees, as may be supposed, occupy a principal station; they are trained into the most grotesque and curious forms. The plants which stand next to dwarf trees in importance with the Chinese are certainly chrysanthemums, which they manage extremely well, perhaps better than they do any other plant. So high do these plants stand in the favour of the Chinese gardener, that he will cultivate them extensively, even against the wishes of his employer; and, in many instances, rather leave his situation than give up the growth of his favourite flower. I was told that the late Mr. Beale used to say that he grew chrysanthemums in his garden for no other purpose than to please his gardener, not having any taste for this particular flower himself.

Tree pæonies are not natives of the south of China, but are brought down in large quantities every year, about the month of January, from the northern provinces. They flower soon after they arrive, and are rapidly bought up by the Chinese to ornament their houses; after which they are thrown away, as they do not thrive well so far south as Canton or Macao, and will not flower a second season. They are sold according to the number of flower-buds they may have upon them, many of them fetching rather high prices.

Although the botanist can find little that is new to him in these gardens, yet they are well worthy of a visit; and in the spring months, when most of the plants are in bloom, they have a singularly gorgeous and imposing appearance, and really deserve the poetical name of "Fa-tee," or flowery land, which the Chinese have given them.

At this period the Chinese were making great preparations for the celebration of New Year's Day, which then fell on the 18th of February. Flowers of all kinds were in great demand amongst the inhabitants, who employ them in the decoration of their houses and temples. In going up the river towards the Fa-tee gardens I met boats in great numbers loaded with branches of peach and plum trees in bloom, *Enkianthus quinqueflorus*, camellias, cockscombs, magnolias, and various other plants which flower at this season. The Enkianthus is brought down from the hills with the buds just expanding; and after being placed in water for a day or two the flowers come out as healthy and fresh as if the branches had not been removed from the parent tree. This plant is a great favourite amongst the Chinese. The common jonquil too comes in for a very extensive share of patronage; and in the streets of Canton one meets with thousands of bulbs growing in small pans amongst water and a few white stones. In this case the Chinese exhibit their peculiar propensity for dwarf and monstrous growth, by planting the bulbs upside down, and making the plants and flowers assume curious twisted forms, which appear to be so agreeable to the eyes of a Chinaman. Large quantities of all these flowers are exposed for sale in many of the shops and in the corners of the streets in Canton, where they seem to be eagerly bought up by the Chinese, who consider them quite indispensable at this particular season. Not only are the houses and temples decorated with them, but the boats on the river also come in for a most extensive share. Indeed, these boats are only floating houses, for a very great part of the population of Canton lives upon the river. The flower-boats, as they are commonly called, are particularly gay at new-year time with flowers of all hues, and gaudy flags streaming from each mast and stern. Crackers or fireworks, of which the Chinaman is so fond, are let off in large quantities for several days in all parts of the town, and form part of their religious ceremonies or offerings to their gods. Their shops are closed on New Year's Day, and for two or three days afterwards. The greater part of the natives wear their holiday clothes, and tramp about amongst their relations and friends to *chin-chin* them, and wish them a happy new year, as we do at home. Large parties are made at this season to go up to the gardens at Fa-tee; and on particular days you find there hundreds of these flower-boats crowded with young Chinese of the better classes, enjoying themselves as our own population do at Richmond or Hampton Court. Great numbers of well-dressed ladies also go over to Fa-tee in the flower-boats, and walk about in the gardens; and this is the only season when they are visible at Canton.

After having been several months in the north of China, and, with one or two exceptions, always experiencing the greatest civility from the natives, I was beginning to form a high opinion of the Chinese as a nation, and inclined to trust the people about Canton in the same manner as I had done in the northern provinces. I very soon, however, found out my mistake, and in a most disagreeable manner. There were some hills behind the city, a few miles distant, which I had often wished to visit for the purpose of examining their botanical productions. One morning I started off through the town, in the direction of these hills; and after walking between two and three miles I reached the suburbs on the side of the town opposite to that where the foreign factory stands. The sounds of "*Fankwei*,"* with which I was assailed in the early part of my walk, had now nearly ceased, and I began to imagine that I had got out from amongst the impertinent boys and low Chinese whom one continually meets in the back streets of Canton. I was now on a good road, amongst fields and gardens, and had an excellent view of the surrounding country and hills. How very strange, thought I, that the foreign residents in the factories never avail themselves of the opportunity of coming here, when they might enjoy the fresh air, and see the country, which would help to relieve the monotonous life they are compelled to lead!

As I was walking quietly along I met a Chinese soldier on horseback, who by gestures and words did everything in his power to induce me to retrace my steps. I knew nothing of the Canton dialect at this time, and, as I thought he only wished to prevent me from taking a walk in the country, I paid no attention to him, but passed onwards. Soon afterwards, however, I began to suspect the ill intentions of several groups of

* Literally, "foreign devil."

ill-looking fellows who seemed to be eyeing me narrowly as I proceeded. I now came to a little hill which seemed to be used as a cemetery: it was enclosed, but the door which led to it was wide open, and the place appeared to be quite public. In order to have a more extended view of the country, I walked in and began to ascend the hill. I had only proceeded about half way up, when a number of Chinamen who had followed me in began to crowd round me, asking for "*comeshaws*,"* and becoming every moment more numerous and urgent. I tried what civility would do with them for a little while, but by the time I reached the top of the hill I clearly perceived that I was in a trap, out of which it would be a difficult matter to extricate myself.

Up to this time, however, no one had attempted to lay hands upon me. Taking a cursory view of the surrounding country, I began to devise in my mind the best mode of getting rid of my troublesome companions. There seemed no other way than putting a bold face on the matter, and retracing my steps to Canton. "You more better come down this way," said a fellow to me in broken English, pointing to a ravine on the opposite side of the hill. My suspicions, however, were now roused, and I saw at once the object of my adviser, which was to get me into some place out of sight, where I should doubtless have been robbed of every article I had about my person, and probably stripped into the bargain. "No, no," said I, "I have nothing to do down there," and began to retrace my steps down the hill. The Chinese now closed upon me, and seemed deter-

* Presents.

mined to obstruct my progress. Some laid hold of my arms; one fellow seized my cap, and ran off with it; another did the same with my umbrella; several hands were in my pockets, and others were even attempting to get my coat off. I now saw that nothing short of getting everything I possessed would satisfy them, as each one wanted something, and "their name was legion." Collecting all my strength, I threw myself upon those who were below me, and sent several of them rolling down the side of the hill. This, however, was nearly fatal to me, for, owing to the force which I exerted, and the uneven nature of the ground, I stumbled and fell; but fortunately I instantly recovered myself, and renewed the unequal struggle, my object being to reach the door of the cemetery by which I had entered. The Chinese on the hill now called out to their friends below to shut the door and thus prevent me from reaching the open road. Seeing at once that if this were accomplished I should be an easy prey to them, I determined if possible to prevent it. Springing out of the grasp of those by whom I was surrounded, I made for the door, which I reached just as it was closed, but fortunately before it was fastened on the other side. The force with which I came against it burst it open, and threw the Chinamen on their backs who were busily fastening it. I was now in the open road, where some hundreds of the Chinese were congregated together; some of them apparently respectable, but the greater part evidently nothing but thieves and robbers. The respectable part would not, or probably durst not, render me any assistance. Stones were now flying about me in all directions, and a brick struck me with great force on the back, and nearly brought me to the ground. I was stunned for a few seconds, and leaned against the wall to breathe and recover myself, thinking that I was now comparatively safe as I was out on the open road. I was soon undeceived, however, for the rascals again surrounded me, and relieved me of several articles which had escaped them before. As the whole neighbourhood was evidently a bad one, it would have been madness to have taken shelter in any of the houses, and I therefore had to struggle with the robbers for nearly a mile, sometimes fighting, and sometimes running, until I got out of their territory, and near the more populous parts of the town. The plight I was now in may easily be conceived, but, taking everything into account, I came off better than might have been expected.

On my way home, having neither hat nor umbrella, I suffered greatly from exposure to the sun, which, in the south of China, is very powerful on a clear day, even in spring. I would have gladly gone into a shop and bought a Chinese hat, but the rascals had not left me even a copper cash for the purpose. Fortunately I had left my watch at home, otherwise that would have been taken amongst the first things, as Chinese thieves are very partial to watches and know their value well.

The Honourable F. C. Drummond, with whom I was staying at the time, informed me afterwards that the place where I had been attacked was one of the worst in the suburbs of Canton, and that three gentlemen of his acquaintance, a year or two before, had come off even worse than I had done, the Chinese having taken away nearly all their clothes.

About two years after this attack upon me three gentlemen holding government appointments in China, Mr. Montgomery Martin, the Rev. V. Stanton, and Mr. Jackson, having incautiously strolled into the suburbs, were also attacked; and the letter which they addressed officially to Her Majesty's consul, complaining of the treatment they had received, shows so clearly the state of things at Canton, that I give it entire:—

"About seven o'clock this morning, while walking for exercise along the north wall, on the outside of the city, we were attacked by several Chinese, who had been following us, and increasing in numbers, from the building known to foreigners as the Five-storied Pagoda. At first they commenced by throwing stones, which endangered our lives, and by some of which we were struck. This attack was aided and encouraged by a number of Chinese, who followed us along the top of the city wall, hurling large stones, which, if they had struck, would have killed those at whom they were aimed. Mr. Jackson was first attacked by men brandishing swords and daggers; his arms were pinioned, and his gold chain snatched from his neck. The Rev. Mr. Stanton and Mr. Martin, perceiving that Mr. Jackson was not following, returned to aid him, and were themselves seized. One of the assailants thrust a dagger at Mr. Martin's breast, two endeavoured to throw him on the ground, and, whilst struggling with them, his pockets were rifled. The same course was pursued with Mr. Jackson and Mr. Stanton. The latter lost his watch; the former still retained his, but everything else was taken. The assailants then left us: but the persons on the wall followed us for some time, hurling large stones and using menacing gestures and opprobrious language.

"Proceeding southward beneath the wall to reach the river side, we were again followed and attacked by another party. Mr. Jackson received a violent blow on his chest, and a roof was torn up to furnish large sticks to the assailants. In this attack Mr. Jackson was deprived of his watch; our clothes were torn; and at one time the people were disposed to strip us. No resistance was offered: it was hopeless to have attempted it, not only by reason of the numbers and weapons of the multitude, but also on account of the attack on us from the watch-tower and along the walls.

"The outrage was entirely unprovoked. Our own official character, and the presence of a minister of religion, was a guarantee for peaceful conduct; and had his presence not restrained Mr. Jackson and Mr. Martin, bloodshed might probably have ensued. Reaching a more populous part of the suburbs, we rested a moment and then proceeded home; but not unfrequently hearing opprobrious epithets, mingled with cries of 'Kill them, kill them!'

"From no nation in Europe would British subjects suffer this treatment. There can be no excuse for tolerating a continuance of such conduct towards us in China; and we think there cannot be a doubt that the Chinese government have it in their power effectually to put a stop, not only to the personal insults which the English daily experience, but also to prohibit effectually the repetition of the injuries we have experienced. By the prohibition to enter the city of Canton the lower classes of the Chinese are encouraged to regard us as inferiors, and to treat us with marked contumely. No measures, that we are aware of, have ever been taken by the authorities to prevent the constant insults to which the British community are subjected; and which, instead of diminishing by time, or being subdued by acts of kindness, seem to become more frequent and more virulent.

"Anxiously desirous to maintain peace and to promote amity, we make this representation, believing that, unless the Chinese authorities remedy the evils complained of, the most serious consequences must inevitably and ere long ensue."

CHAPTER IX.

Visit to the Ning-po Green Tea District — Mountain Travelling Chair — The Buddhist Temple of Tein-Tung — Scenery around the Temple — Traditionary History communicated by the Priest — Invitation to Dinner with the Priests — First Trial with Chopsticks — Politeness! of the Chinese — Usual Dinner Company — My Bed — Wild Boar Hunt — Narrow Escape — Mode of frightening the Animals from the Bamboo Plantations — Mountain Scenery — Buddhist Temple of Ah-Yu-Wang — Poo-To-San, or the Worshipping Island — Its Temples and Idols — Bronze Gods — Trees and Shrubs — Sale of Gods or Josses — Offerings to the Gods in Shanghae and Ning-po — Processions in Honour of the Gods — Christian Missions — Medical Missionary Society — Roman Catholics.

HAVING despatched my collections to England by three different vessels from Hong-kong, I sailed again, at the end of March, 1844, for the northern provinces. During the summer of this year, and in that of 1845, I was able to visit several parts of the country which were formerly sealed to Europeans, and which contained subjects of much interest.

About the beginning of May I set out upon an excursion, with the late Mr. Thom, the British consul, and two other gentlemen, to visit the green-tea district near Ning-po. We were informed that there was a large and celebrated temple, named *Tein-tung,* in the centre of the tea district, and above twenty miles distant, where we could lodge during our stay in this part of the country. Twelve or fourteen miles of our journey was performed by water, but, the canal ending at the foot of the hills, we were obliged to walk or take chairs for the remainder of the way. The mountain travelling-chair of China is a very simple contrivance. It consists merely of two long bamboo poles, with a board placed between them for a seat, and two other cross-pieces, one for the back and the other for the feet; a large Chinese umbrella is held over the head to afford protection from the sun and rain.

Mountain Chair.

The Chinese are quite philosophers after their own fashion. On our way to the temple, when tired with sitting so long in our boat, we several times got out and walked along the path on the sides of the canal. A great number of passage-boats going in the same direction with ourselves, and crowded with passengers, kept very near us for a considerable portion of the way, in order to satisfy their curiosity. A Chinaman never walks when he can possibly find any other mode of conveyance, and these persons were consequently much surprised to see us apparently enjoying our walk.

"Is it not strange," said one, "that these people prefer walking when they have a boat as well as ourselves?" A discussion now took place amongst them as to the reason of this apparently strange propensity, when one, more wise than his companions, settled the matter by the pithy observation, "it is *their nature* to do so;" which was apparently satisfactory to all parties.

It was nearly dark when we reached the temple, and, as the rain had fallen in torrents during the greater part of the day, we were drenched to the skin, and in rather a pitiable condition. The priests seemed much surprised at our appearance, but at once evinced the greatest hospitality and kindness, and we soon found ourselves quite at home amongst them. They brought us fire to dry our clothes, got ready our dinner, and set apart a certain number of their best rooms for us to sleep in. We were evidently subjects of great curiosity to most of them, who had never seen an Englishman before. Our clothes, features, mode of eating, and manners were all subjects of wonder to these simple people, who passed off many a good-humoured joke at our expense.

Glad to get off our clothes, which were still damp, we retired early to rest. When we arose in the morning the view which met our eyes far surpassed in beauty any scenery which I had ever witnessed before in China. The temple stands at the head of a fertile valley in the bosom of the hills. This valley is well watered by clear streams, which flow from the mountains, and produces most excellent crops of rice. The tea-shrubs, with their dark green leaves, are seen dotted on the lower sides of all the more fertile hills. The temple itself is approached by a long avenue of Chinese pine-trees. This avenue is at first straight, but near the temple it winds in a most picturesque manner round the edges of two artificial lakes, and then ends in a flight of stone steps, which lead up to the principal entrance. Behind, and on each side, the mountains rise, in irregular ridges, from one to two thousand feet above the level of the sea. These are not like the barren southern mountains, but are clothed nearly to their summits with a dense tropical-looking mass of brushwood, shrubs, and trees. Some of the finest bamboos of China are grown in the ravines, and the sombre-coloured pine attains to a large size on the sides of the hills.

After we had breakfasted, one of the head priests came and gave us a very pressing invitation to dine with him about mid-day; and in the mean time he accompanied us over the monastery, of which he gave the following history:—"Many hundred years ago a pious old man retired from the world, and came to dwell in these mountains, giving himself up entirely to the performance of religious duties. So earnest was he in his devotions that he neglected everything relating to his temporal wants, even to his daily food. Providence, however, would not suffer so good a man to starve. Some boys were sent in a miraculous manner, who daily supplied him with food. In the course of time the fame of the sage extended all over the adjacent country, and disciples flocked to him from all quarters. A small range of temples was built, and thus commenced the extensive buildings which now bear the name of 'Tein-tung,' or the 'Temple of the Heavenly Boys;' *Tein* signifying heaven, and *tung* a boy. At last the old man died, but his disciples supplied his place. The fame of the temple spread far and wide, and votaries came from the most distant parts of the empire—one of the Chinese kings being amongst the number—to worship and leave their offerings at its altars. Larger temples were built in front of the original ones, and these again in their turn gave way to those spacious buildings which form the principal part of the structure of the present day."

All the temples are crowded with idols, or images of their favourite gods, such as the "three precious Buddhas," "the Queen of Heaven"—represented as sitting on the celebrated lotus or nelumbium—"the God of War," and many other deified kings and great men of former days. Many of these images are from thirty to forty feet in height, and have a very striking appearance when seen arranged in these spacious and lofty halls. The priests themselves reside in a range of low buildings, erected at right angles with the different temples and courts which divide them. Each has a little temple in his own house—a family altar crowded with small images, where he is often engaged in private devotion.

After inspecting the various temples and the belfry,

which contains a noble bronze bell of large dimensions, our host conducted us back to his house, where the dinner was already on the table. The priests of the Buddhist religion are not allowed to eat animal food at any of their meals. Our dinner therefore consisted entirely of vegetables, served up in the usual Chinese style, in a number of small round basins, the contents of each—soups excepted—being cut up into small square bits, to be eaten with chopsticks. The Buddhist priests contrive to procure a number of vegetables of different kinds, which, by a peculiar mode of preparation, are rendered very palatable. In fact, so nearly do they resemble animal food in taste and in appearance, that at first we were deceived, imagining that the little bits we were able to get hold of with our chopsticks were really pieces of fowl or beef. Such, however, was not the case, as our good host was consistent on this day at least, and had nothing but vegetable productions at his table. Several other priests sat with us at table, and a large number of others of inferior rank, with servants, crowded around the doors and windows outside. The whole assemblage must have been surprised at the awkward way in which some of us handled our chopsticks, and, with all their politeness, I observed they could not refrain from laughing when, after repeated attempts, some little dainty morsel would still slip back again into the dish. I know few things more annoying, and yet laughable too, than attempting to eat with the Chinese chopsticks for the first time, more particularly if the operator has been wandering on the hills all the morning, and is ravenously hungry. The instruments should first of all be balanced between the thumb and fore-finger of the right hand; the points are next to be brought carefully together, just leaving as much room as will allow the coveted morsel to go in between them; the little bit is then to be neatly seized; but, alas! in the act of lifting the hand, one point of the chopstick too often slips past the other, and the object of all our hopes drops back again into the dish, or perhaps even into another dish on the table. Again and again the same operation is tried, until the poor novice loses all patience, throws down the chopsticks in despair, and seizes a porcelain spoon, with which he is more successful. In cases like these the Chinese themselves are very obliging, although scarcely in a way agreeable to an Englishman's taste. Your Chinese friend, out of kindness and politeness, when he sees the dilemma in which you are, reaches across the table and seizes, with his own chopsticks, which have just come out of his mouth, the wished-for morsel, and with them lays it on the plate before you. In common politeness you must express your gratitude and swallow the offering.

During dinner our host informed us that there were about a hundred priests connected with the monastery, but that many were always absent on missions to various parts of the country. On questioning him as to the mode by which the establishment was supported, he informed us that a considerable portion of land in the vicinity belonged to the temple, and that large sums were yearly raised from the sale of bamboos, which are here very excellent, and of the branches of trees and brushwood, which are made up in bundles for firewood. A number of tea and rice farms also belong to the priests, which they themselves cultivate. Besides the sums raised by the sale of these productions, a considerable revenue must be derived from the contributions of the devotees who resort to the temple for religious purposes, as well as from the sums collected by those of the order who are out on begging excursions at stated seasons of the year. The priests are of course of all grades, some of them being merely the servants of the others, both in the house and in the fields. They seem a harmless and simple race, but are dreadfully ignorant and superstitious. The typhoon of the previous year, or rather the rain which had accompanied it, had occasioned a large slip of earth on one of the hill-sides near the temple, and completely buried ten or twelve acres of excellent paddy-land. On our remarking this, the priests told us with great earnestness that every one said it was a bad omen for the temple; but one of them with true Chinese politeness remarked that he had no doubt any evil influence would now be counteracted, since the temple had been honoured with a visit from us.

After inspecting the tea-farms and the mode of manufacturing it, Mr. Thom, Mr. Morrison (a son of the late Dr. Morrison), and Mr. Sinclair returned to Ning-po, leaving me to prosecute my research in natural history in this part of the country. I was generally absent from the temple the whole day, returning at dark with the collections of plants and birds which I had been lucky enough to meet with in my peregrinations. The friends of the priests came from all quarters of the adjacent country to see the foreigner; and, as in the case of a wild animal, my feeding-time seemed to be the most interesting moment to them. My dinner was placed on a round table in the centre of the room, and although rather curiously concocted, being half Chinese and half English, the exercise and fresh air of the mountains gave me a keen appetite. The difficulties of the chopsticks were soon got over, and I was able to manage them nearly as well as the Chinese themselves. The priests and their friends filled the chairs, which are always placed down the sides of a Chinese hall, each man with his pipe in his mouth and his cup of tea by his side. With all deference to my host and his friends, I was obliged to request the smoking to be stopped, as it was disagreeable to me while at dinner; in other respects I believe I was "polite" enough. I shall never forget how inexpressibly lonely I felt the first night after the departure of my friends. The Chinese one by one dropped off to their homes or to bed, and at last my host himself gave several unequivocal yawns, which reminded me that it was time to retire for the night. My bed-room was upstairs, and to get to it I had to pass through a small temple, such as I have already noticed, dedicated to *Tein-how*, or the "Queen of Heaven," and crowded with other idols. Incense was burning on the altar in front of the idols; a solitary lamp shed a dim light over the objects in the room, and a kind of solemn stillness seemed to pervade the whole place. In the room below, and also in one in an adjoining house, I could hear the priests engaged in their devotional exercises, in that singing tone which is peculiar to them. Then the sounds of the gong fell upon my ears; and, at intervals, a single solemn toll of the large bronze bell in the belfry; all which showed that the priests were engaged in public as well as private devotion. Amidst scenes of this kind, in a strange country, far from friends and home, impressions are apt to be made upon the mind which remain vivid through life; and I feel convinced I shall never forget the strange mixture of feelings which filled my mind during the first night of my stay with the priests in the temple of Tein-tung. I have visited the place often since, passed through the same little temple, slept in the same bed, and heard the same solemn sounds throughout the silent watches of the night, and yet the first impressions remain in my mind distinct and single.

The priests, from the highest to the lowest, always showed me the most marked attention and kindness. As many of them as I wished cheerfully followed me in my excursions in the vicinity of the temple; one carrying my specimen-paper, another my plants, and a third my birds, and so on. The gun seemed an object of great interest to them, being so different from their own clumsy matchlocks; and percussion-caps were looked upon as most magical little objects. But they were great cowards, and always kept at a most respectful distance when I was shooting.

One evening a deputation, headed by the high-priest, came and informed me that the wild boars had come down from the mountains at night, and were destroying the young shoots of the bamboo, which were then just coming through the ground, and were in a state in which they are highly prized as a vegetable for the table.

"Well," said I, "what do you want me to do?"

"Will you be good enough to lend us the gun?"

"Yes; there it stands in the corner of the room."

"Oh, but you must load it for us."

"Very well, I will;" and I immediately loaded the gun with ball. "There; but take care and don't shoot yourselves." There was now a long pause; none had sufficient courage to take the gun, and a long consultation was held between them. At length the spokesman came forward with great gravity, and told me they were afraid to fire it off, but that, if I would go with them and shoot the boar, I should have it to eat. This was certainly no great sacrifice on the part of the Buddhist priesthood, who do not, or at least should not, eat animal food. We now sallied forth in a body to fight the wild boars; but the night was so dark that we could see nothing in the bamboo ravines, and perhaps the noise made by about thirty priests and servants warned the animals to retire to the brushwood higher up the hills. Be that as it may, we could neither see nor hear anything of them, and I confess I was rather glad than otherwise, as I thought there was a considerable chance of my shooting, by mistake, a priest instead of a wild boar.

The priests have two modes of protecting their property from the ravages of these animals. Deep pits are dug on the hill-sides, and, as there are springs in almost all these places, the pits are scarcely finished before they are half full of water. The mouth of each pit is then covered over with a quantity of sticks, rubbish, and grass to attract the animal; and no sooner does he begin to bore into it with his snout, than the whole gives way, and he is plunged, head foremost, into the pit, from which it is quite impossible for him to extricate himself, and he is either drowned or becomes an easy prey to the Chinese. These pits are most dangerous traps to persons unacquainted with the localities in which they are placed. I had several narrow escapes; and once in particular, when coming out of a dense mass of brushwood, I stepped unawares on the treacherous mouth of one of them, and felt the ground under my feet actually giving way; but, managing to throw my arms forward, I caught hold of a small twig which was growing near, and by this means supported myself until I was able to scramble on to firmer ground. On turning back to examine the place, I found that the loose rubbish had sunk in, and a deep pit, half full of water, was exposed to my view. The pit was made narrow at the mouth and widening inside like a great China vase, being constructed in this manner to prevent the boar from scrambling out when once fairly in it. Had I fallen in, it would have been next to impossible to have extricated myself without assistance; and as the pits are generally dug in the most retired and wild part of the mountains, my chance would have been a bad one.

The other method of protecting the young bamboos from the ravages of the wild boar is an ingenious one. A piece of bamboo wood, about eight or ten feet long, and rather thicker than a man's arm, is split up the middle to within a fourth of its length. This is made fast to a tree in the bamboo thicket, and at an angle of about forty-five degrees, the split part being left loose; a cord, also made of bamboo, is fastened to it by one end, and the other is led to some convenient place out of the thicket, where a man is stationed. When the boars come down in the dead of night to attack the young shoots, the man pulls the rope backwards and forwards, and clank, clank, clank goes the bamboo, producing a loud and hollow sound, which on a quiet evening may be heard at a great distance. The animals are frightened and make off to their dens on the hills. The first time I heard these things beating at night, all over the country, I imagined that some religious ceremony was going on, the hollow sounds of the bamboo being not unlike those produced by an instrument used in the Buddhist worship in all Chinese temples.

There are a large number of Buddhist temples scattered over all this part of the country. One named *Ah-yu-wang*, which I also visited, is, like *Tein-tung*, of great extent, and seemingly well supported. They both own large tracts of land in the vicinity of the monasteries, and have numerous small temples in different parts of the district, which are under their control. All the temples, both large and small, are built in the most romantic and beautiful situations amongst the hills, and the neighbouring woods are always preserved and encouraged. What would indicate the residence of a country gentleman in England, is in China the sign of a Buddhist temple, and this holds good over all the country. When the weary traveller, therefore, who has been exposed for hours to the fierce rays of an eastern sun, sees a large clean-looking house showing itself amongst trees on the distant hill-side, he may be almost certain that it is one of Buddha's temples, where the priests will treat him not only with courtesy but with kindness.

Poo-to, or the Worshipping Island, as it is commonly called by foreigners, is one of the eastern islands in the Chusan Archipelago, and seems to be the capital or stronghold of Buddhism in this part of China. This island is not more than five or six miles in circumference, and, although hilly, its sides and small ravines are pretty well wooded, particularly in the vicinity of the numerous temples. As it is only a few hours' sail from Chusan, it had been visited at different times by a number of our officers during the war, all of whom spoke highly of its natural beauties and richness of vegetation. I was also informed that the resident priests were fond of collecting plants, particularly Orchidaceæ, and that their collections were much increased by the itinerant habits of the begging priests, who visit the most distant provinces of the empire, as well as by the donations of the lay devotees, who come to Poo-to at stated seasons of the year, to worship and leave their offerings in the temples. I therefore determined to visit the place in order to judge for myself, and accordingly set out in July, 1844, accompanied by my friend Dr. Maxwell, of the Madras army.

Leaving Chusan at night, with the tide in our favour, we reached the island at sunrise on the following morning. We landed, and pursued our way over a hill, and down on the other side by a road which led us into a beautiful and romantic glen. It is here that the principal group of temples is built, and when we first caught a glimpse of them, as we wended our way down the hill, they seemed like a town of considerable size. As we approached nearer, the view became highly interesting.

In front there was a large artificial pond, filled with the broad green leaves and noble red and white flowers of the *Nelumbium speciosum*,—a plant in high favour with the Chinese. Everybody who went to Poo-to admired these beautiful water-lilies. In order to reach the monastery we crossed a very ornamental bridge built over this pond, which, when viewed in a line with an old tower close by, has a pretty and striking appearance.

The temples or halls which contain the idols are extremely spacious, and resemble those which I have already described at *Tein-tung* and *Ah-yu-wang*. These idols, many of which are thirty or forty feet in height, are generally made of wood or clay, and then richly gilt. There is one small temple, however, of a very unassuming appearance, where we met with some exquisite bronze statues, which would be considered of great value in England. These, of course, were much smaller than the others, but, viewed as works of art, they were by far the finest which I saw during my travels in China.

Having examined these temples, we pursued our way towards another assemblage of them, about two miles to the eastward and close on the sea-shore. We entered the courts through a kind of triumphal arch, which looks out upon the sea, and found that these temples were constructed upon the same plan as all the others. As we had determined to make this part of the island our home during our stay, we fixed upon the cleanest looking temple, and asked the High Priest to allow us, without farther delay, to put our beds and travelling baggage into it.

On the following day we inspected various parts of the island. Besides the large temples just noticed, there are about sixty or seventy smaller ones, built on all the hill-sides, each of which contains three or four priests, who are all under the superior, or abbot, who resides near one of the large temples. Even on the top of the highest hill, probably 1500 or 1800 feet above the level of the sea, we found a temple of considerable size and in excellent repair. There are winding stone steps from the sea-beach all the way up to this temple, and a small resting-place about half way up the hill, where the weary devotee may rest and drink of the refreshing stream which flows down the sides of the mountain; and in the little temple close at hand, which is also crowded with idols, he can supplicate Buddha for strength to enable him to reach the end of his journey. We were surprised to find a Buddhist temple in such excellent order as the one on the summit of the hill proved to be in. It is a striking fact that almost all these places are crumbling fast into ruins. There are a few exceptions, in cases where they happen to get a good name amongst the people from the supposed kindness of the gods; but the great mass are in a state of decay.

From the upper temple on Poo-to-san the view is strikingly grand. Rugged mountains are seen rising one above another, and capped with clouds. Hundreds of islands, some fertile, others rocky and barren, lay scattered over the sea. When we looked in one direction amongst the islands, the water was yellow and muddy; but, to the eastward, the deep blue ocean had resumed its usual colour, and the line between the yellow waters and the blue was distinctly and curiously marked.

The wood on the island is preserved in the same manner as it is around all the other Buddhist temples. The principal species of trees and shrubs met with are *Pinus sinensis*, *Cunninghami lanceolata*, yews, cypresses, the camphor-tree, tallow-tree, oaks, and bamboos. The *Camellia japonica* grows spontaneously in the woods, where we met with many specimens from twenty to thirty feet in height and with stems thick in proportion. The variety, however, was only the well-known single red. In other respects the flora of Poo-to is nearly the same as on the island of Chusan.

A few pet plants were cultivated by all the priests who were fortunate enough to have private residences at the little temples on the sides of the hills. We were much pleased with the interest these poor people took in their favourite flowers, but were disappointed in the number and variety of plants, which, from the reports of others, we expected to have found.

The island of Poo-to is set apart entirely as a residence for the priests of the Buddhist religion. Few other persons are allowed to live there, and these are either servants or in some way connected with the priests. No women are permitted to reside on the island, it being against the principles of the Buddhists to allow their priests to marry. The number of priests is estimated at 2000, but many of them are constantly absent on begging expeditions for the support of their religion. This establishment, like *Tein-tung*, has also a portion of land allotted to it for its support, and the remainder of the funds are made up by the subscriptions of the devotees. On certain high days, at different periods of the year, many thousands of both sexes, but particularly females, resort to these temples, clad in their best attire, to pay their vows and engage in the other exercises of heathen worship. Little stalls are then seen in the temples or at the doorways, for the sale of incense, candles, paper made up in the form of the ingots of Sycee-silver, and other holy things which are considered acceptable offerings to the gods, and are either consumed in the temples or carried home to bring a blessing upon the houses and families of those who purchase them. The profits of these sales, of course, go to the support of the establishment. When we consider that these poor deluded people sometimes travel a distance of several hundred miles to worship in the temples on Poo-to-san and other celebrated places, we cannot but admire their spirit of devotion. I was once staying in the temple of *Tein-tung* when it was visited for three days by devotees from all parts of the country. As they lined the roads on their way to the temple, clad in the graceful and flowing costume of the East, the mind was naturally led back to those days of scripture history when Jerusalem was in its glory, and the Jews, the chosen people of God, came from afar to worship in its temple.

Although no Christian can look upon the priests and devotees of the Buddhist creed without an eye of pity, yet he must give them credit for their conduct, since he has every reason to believe them sincere, and I am inclined to believe that justice has not been done them in this respect. Mr. Gutzlaff, in describing his visit to

Poo-to, is of a different opinion. He says, "We were present at the vespers of the priests, which they chanted in the Pali language, not unlike the Latin service of the Romish church. They held rosaries in their hands, which rested folded upon their breasts. One of them had a small bell, by the tinkling of which their service was regulated; and they occasionally beat the drum and large bell to rouse Buddha's attention to their prayers. The same words were a hundred times repeated. *None of the officiating persons showed any interest in the ceremony*, for some were looking around laughing and joking, while others muttered their prayers. The few people who were present, not to attend the worship, but to gaze at us, did not seem, in the least degree, to feel the solemnity of the service." What Mr. Gutzlaff says is doubtless true, but after residing for months in their temples, at different times, and in different parts of the country, I have no hesitation in saying that such conduct is very far from being general. In certain instances I have seen it myself, but this levity and apparent want of attention was exhibited by the servants and lookers-on, who were taking no part in the ceremony, and not by the respectable portion of the priests. On the contrary, I have generally been struck with the solemnity with which their devotional exercises were conducted. I have often walked into Chinese temples when the priests were engaged in prayer, and, although there would have been some apology for them had their attention been diverted, they went on in the most solemn manner until the conclusion of the service, as if no foreigner were present. They then came politely up to me, examining my dress and everything about me with the most earnest curiosity. Nor does this apply to priests only; the laity, and particularly the female sex, seem equally sincere when they engage in their public devotions. Whether they are what they appear to be, or how often they are in this pious frame of mind, are questions which I cannot answer. Before judging harshly of the Chinese let the reader consider what effect would be produced upon the members of a *Christian* church by the unexpected entrance of a small-footed Chinese lady, or a mandarin, with the gold button and peacock feather mounted on his hat, and his long tail dangling over his shoulders. I am far from being an admirer of the Buddhist priesthood; they are generally an imbecile race, and shamefully ignorant of everything but the simple forms of their religion, but nevertheless there are many traits in their character not unworthy of imitation.

There are two other sects in China, namely, the followers of *Kong-foo-tze* or Confucius, and the sect of *Taou* or Reason. Although these three sects form the principal part of the population, it is well known that there are a great number of Mohammedans in every part of the empire, who are not only tolerated, but admitted to offices under government in the same manner as the members of the three established sects. Jews also are found in several districts, but more particularly at a place called Kae-foong-foo, in the province of Honan.

The various religious ceremonies which the Chinese are continually performing prove at least that they are very superstitious. In all the southern towns every house has its temple or altar both inside and outside. The altar in the inside is generally placed at the end of the principal hall or shop, as the case may be, raised a few feet from the ground, and having some kind of representation of the family deity placed upon it. This is surrounded with gaudy tinsel paper, and on the first of the Chinese month or other high days candles and incense are burned on the table which is placed in front of it. The altar on the outside of the door resembles a little furnace, in which the same ceremonies are regularly performed. In the vicinity of small villages, and sometimes in the most retired situations, the stranger meets with little joss-houses or temples, gaudily decorated with paintings and tinsel paper, and stuck round about with the remains of candles and sticks of incense. In almost all Chinese towns there are shops for the sale of idols of all kinds and sizes, varying in price from a few "cash" to a very large sum. Many of those exposed for sale are of great age, and have evidently changed hands several times. I am inclined to believe that the Chinese exchange those gods which do not please them for others of higher character, and which they suppose are more likely to grant an answer to their prayers, or bring prosperity to their homes or their villages.

The periodical offerings to the gods are very striking exhibitions to the stranger who looks upon them for the first time. When staying at Shanghae, in November, 1844, I witnessed a most curious spectacle in the house where I was residing. It was a family offering to the gods. Early in the morning the principal hall in the house was set in order, a large table was placed in the centre, and shortly afterwards covered with small dishes filled with the various articles commonly used as food by the Chinese. All these were of the very best description which could be procured. After a certain time had elapsed a number of candles were lighted, and columns of smoke and fragrant odours began to rise from the incense which was burning on the table. All the inmates of the house and their friends were clad in their best attire, and in turn came to *ko-tou*, or bow lowly and repeatedly in front of the table and the altar. The scene, although it was an idolatrous one, seemed to me to have something very impressive about it; and whilst I pitied the delusion of our host and his friends, I could not but admire their devotion. In a short time after this ceremony was completed a large quantity of tinsel paper, made up in the form and shape of the ingots of Sycee silver common in China, was heaped on the floor in front of the tables, the burning incense was then taken from the table and placed in the midst of it, and the whole consumed together. By and by, when the gods were supposed to have finished their repast, all the articles of food were removed from the tables, cut up, and consumed by people connected with the family.

On another occasion, when at Ning-po, having been out some distance in the country, it was night and dark before I reached the east gate of the city, near which I was lodged in the house of a Chinese merchant. The city gates were closed, but two or three loud knocks soon brought the warder, who instantly admitted me. I was now in the widest and finest street in the city, which seemed in a blaze of light and unusually lively for any part of a Chinese town after nightfall. The sounds of music fell upon my ear, the gong, the drum, and the more plaintive and pleasing tones of several wind instruments. I was soon near enough to observe what was going on, and saw, at a glance, that it was a public offering to the gods, but far grander and more striking than I had before witnessed. The table was spread in the open street, and everything was on a large and expensive scale. Instead of small dishes, whole animals were sacrificed on the occasion. A pig was placed on one side of the table, and a sheep on the other, the former scraped clean, in the usual way, and the latter skinned; the entrails of both were removed, and on each were placed some flowers, an onion, and a knife. The other parts of the table groaned with all the delicacies in common use amongst the respectable portion of the Chinese, such as fowls, ducks, numerous compound dishes, fruits, vegetables, and rice. Chairs were placed at one end of the table, on which the gods were supposed to sit during the meal, and chopsticks were regularly laid at the sides of the different dishes. A blaze of light illuminated the whole place, and the smoke of the fragrant incense rose up into the air in wreaths. At intervals the band struck up their favourite plaintive national airs, and altogether the whole scene was one of the strangest and most curious which it has ever been my lot to witness.

There is another ceremony of a religious character which I frequently observed in the northern cities—I allude to processions in honour of the gods. I saw one of them at Shanghae which must have been at least a mile in length. The gods, or josses, were dressed up in the finest silks, and carried about in splendid sedan-chairs, preceded and succeeded by their numerous devotees, superbly dressed for the occasion, and bearing the different badges of office. The dresses of the officials were exactly the same as of those who form the train of some of the high mandarins. Some had a broad fan, made of peacock feathers, which they wore on the sides of their hats; others were clad in glaring theatrical dresses, with low caps, and two long black feathers stuck in them, and hanging over their shoulders like two horns. Then there were the ill-looking executioners, with long, conical, black hats on their heads, and whips in their hands for the punishment of the refractory. Bands of music, placed in different parts of the procession, played at intervals as it proceeded. Anxious to see the end of this curious exhibition, I followed the procession until it arrived at a temple in the suburbs, where it halted. The gods were taken out of the sedan-chairs, and replaced, with due honours, in the temple, from which they had been taken in the morning. Here their numerous votaries bent low before them, burned incense, and left their gifts upon the altar. Numerous groups of well-dressed ladies and their children were scattered over the ground in the vicinity of the temple, all bending their knees and seemingly engaged in earnest devotion. A large quantity of paper, in the form of the Sycee ingots, was heaped up on the grass as it was brought by the different devotees, and, when the ceremonies of the day were drawing to a close, the whole was burned in honour of, or as an offering to, the gods. The sight was interesting, but it was one which no Christian could look upon without feelings of the deepest commiseration.

In the course of my travels in China I often met with Christian missionaries, both Protestant and Roman Catholic, who have been labouring amongst the Chinese for many years. Until very lately the efforts of the Protestants had been chiefly confined to Macao and Canton. Since the war, however, they have had an opportunity of extending their operations, and some are now settled at all the new ports which have been opened for foreign trade, as well as on our island of Hong-kong, which will now become their head-quarters.

The medical missionaries also act in conjunction with the others, and are of great use in curing many of the diseases which prevail in the country, while, at the same time, the truths of the Christian faith are presented to the minds of their patients. Dr. Lockhart, of the London Missionary Society, who has established himself in the town of Shanghae, had his hospital daily crowded with patients, many of whom had come from very distant parts of the country. All were attended to in the most skilful and careful manner, "without money and without price." The Rev. Mr. Medhurst, who has laboured long and zealously as a Christian missionary in the East, was also at Shanghae. This gentleman is well known as an eminent Chinese scholar, and, besides preaching to the people in their own tongue, he has a printing establishment with Chinese type continually at work, for the dissemination of the truths of the Gospel. Several other gentlemen and their families had arrived at the same port previous to my departure, and were closely engaged in the study of the language. Ning-po and Amoy were also occupied by missionaries both from England and America, and I suppose, ere this time, some have also reached Foo-chow-foo, on the river Min.

From my own experience of Chinese character, and from what I have seen of the working of the Medical Missionary Society, I am convinced that it must be a powerful auxiliary to the missionaries in the conversion of the Chinese. I regret, however, to say, that up to the present time little progress appears to have been made. One portion of the people, and a large one, is entirely indifferent to religion of any kind, and the rest are so bigoted and conceited, that it will be a most difficult task to convince them that any religion is better or purer than their own.

The Roman Catholic missionaries conduct their operations in a manner somewhat different from the Protestants. They do not restrict themselves to the out-ports of the empire, where foreigners are permitted to trade, but penetrate into the interior, and distribute themselves over all the country. One of their bishops, an Italian nobleman, resides in the province of Keang-soo, a few miles from Shanghae, where I have frequently met him. He dresses in the costume of the country, and speaks the language with the most perfect fluency. In the place where he lives he is surrounded by his converts; in fact it is a little Christian village, where he is perfectly safe, and I believe is seldom if ever annoyed in any way by the Chinese authorities. When new Roman Catholic missionaries arrive, they are met by some of their brethren or their converts at the port nearest their destination, and secretly conveyed into the interior; the Chinese dress is substituted for the European; their heads are shaved, and in this state they are conducted to the scene of their future labours, where they commence the study of the language, if they have not learned it before, and in about two years are able to speak it sufficiently well to enable them to instruct the people. These poor men submit to many privations and dangers for the cause they have espoused, and, although I do not approve of the doctrines which they teach, I must give them the highest praise for enthusiasm and devotion to their faith. European customs, habits, and luxuries are all abandoned from the moment they put their feet on the shores of China; parents, friends, and home, in many instances, are heard of no more; before them lies a heathen land of strangers, cold and unconcerned about the religion for which they themselves are sacrificing everything, and they know that their graves will be far away from the land of their birth and the home of their early years. They seem to have much of the spirit and enthusiasm of the first preachers of the Christian religion, when they were sent out into the world by their Divine Master to "preach the Gospel to every creature," and "to obey God rather than man."

According to the accounts of these missionaries, the number of converts to their faith is very considerable; but I fear they, as well as the Protestants, are often led away by false appearances and assertions. Many of the Chinese are unprincipled and deceitful enough to become Christians, or in fact anything else, in name, to accomplish the object they may have in view, and they would become Buddhists the very next day should any inducement be offered them to do so. Judging from appearances, the day must yet be very distant when the Chinese, as a nation, will be converted to the Christian faith. Could those individuals in our time, who predict the near approach of the Millennium, see the length and breadth of this vast country, with its three hundred millions of souls, they would surely pause and reflect before they published their absurd and foolish predictions.

CHAPTER X.

Chusan Archipelago — Storm in a small Boat — Nearly upset — Kin-Tang, or Silver Island — Its Inhabitants — Their Surprise on seeing a Foreigner — Yang-Tse-Kiang River — Its numerous Sand Banks — Our Schooner aground — Novel Method of getting Assistance from the Chinese — Village of Woo-Sung — Opium Station — Remarks on the Opium Trade — Its Effects upon the Chinese.

IN the summer of 1844 I was frequently engaged in exploring the islands of the Chusan Archipelago, more particularly that portion which lies between Chusan and the opposite shores of the main-land. It was of course necessary for this purpose to employ Chinese boats, which are not very trustworthy. The distance from Chusan to the town of Chinhae, at the mouth of the Ning-po river, is about thirty miles. A sail across a sea such as this is generally pleasant enough, because the water, which is hemmed in on all sides, is frequently as smooth as a mill-pond. Sometimes, however, the wind comes down in gusts from the openings amongst the hills, and then the little China boats are all laid nearly upon their beam-ends before the sail can be taken in. Once, in particular, I had a narrow escape from a watery grave amongst these islands. I had engaged a boat to take me across from the city of Ning-po to Chusan; and as I was in a hurry at the time, I was anxious to reach my destination as soon as possible. The wind blew rather fresh as we were going down the Ning-po river, and when we reached the town of Chinhae, at its mouth, evening had set in, and the sky had a threatening and stormy appearance. The boatmen pointed this out to me, and were anxious to remain where we were until daylight. As I was afraid of being too late for a passage in an English vessel which was then at anchor in the bay of Chusan, I would not consent to this prudent proposal, but insisted that they should proceed across without further delay. After exhausting all their arguments, they at length unwillingly got up the anchor, and we proceeded on our voyage. The land and hills on our way from Ning-po to the mouth of the river had sheltered us, and prevented me from feeling the full force of the wind; but no sooner had we passed the forts, and reached the open sea, than I found I had done a very foolish thing in urging the boatmen to take me across in such a night, and I would gladly have gone back had it been prudent or indeed possible to have done so. It was now, however, too late, for with a strong spring tide and a heavy head sea it was impossible to get back again to Chinhae, and we therefore kept on in the direction of Chusan. "Are you not carrying too much sail in such a wind as this, and with such a heavy rolling sea?" said I to the captain of the boat, an old weather-beaten man from the province of Fokien. "No fear, no fear," he replied in his broken Chusan English, "my can manage he." "But I think there is fear, Fokei," I replied; and the words were scarcely said when a tremendous gust came down upon us, and at the same moment a heavy sea struck the side of our boat, and laid her fairly on her beam-ends. In an instant the boat filled in all her divisions from bow to stern. "Lower the sail, lower the sail, quick, quick!" cried the helmsman, "or we shall all go to the bottom." Several of the crew flew to the sail, which fortunately came down readily, and our little craft righted once more, but rolled and plunged very heavily in consequence of the great quantity of water in her hold, and seemed as if she would go down at every plunge, and leave us exposed to the fury of the waves. We again got a few feet of sail hoisted, and kept her away before the wind. It was now dark, not a star was to be seen in the heavens, the mountains, although not distinctly visible, yet loomed through the gloom, and the only objects clearly distinguished were some lights flickering on the distant shore. The crew now surrounded the helmsman, and besought him to try and get back to Chinhae, but I was sailor enough to know that, if we attempted to put the helm down and bring the boat round, in all probability we should ship another sea, and had we done so we must have gone down. I immediately went and stood by the helmsman, and kept the crew from interfering, telling him to keep on our course and try to get under the lee of some island as soon as possible. The men now began to throw off their clothes as a last resource, and so completely lost all their self-possession that no remonstrances could induce them to attend to the boat and get some of the water out of her. The captain or helmsman, however, did his duty well, and to his firmness and knowledge we doubtless owed our lives.

Providentially the wind lulled for a short time, which enabled us to hoist more sail; and soon afterwards we got to leeward of one of the numerous small islands which are scattered over this part of the coast. As soon as we had anchored all hands began baling the water out of the boat. We were in a most pitiful condition, all our clothes and beds being completely soaked with sea-water; some plants, but luckily only duplicates, which I had with me, were, of course, totally destroyed; but our hearts were light, and we were thankful that our lives had been saved. Before daylight the boat was all right again, and, as the weather had moderated, we were able to proceed on our course to Chusan.

Kin-tang, or Silver Island as it is called by the English, is a large island in this archipelago. Although near Chusan, it was seldom visited by any of the English there; but its hills and valleys were very interesting in a botanical point of view, and on that account I was in the habit of anchoring my little boat in some of its numerous bays, and exploring its botanical productions. The surprise of the simple inhabitants, many of whom had never left the island in their lives, was often very great when I came down unexpectedly upon their little villages. The reader will easily credit this if he will only picture to himself the surprise and astonishment with which a Chinese would be regarded were he to appear suddenly in some secluded village in the highlands of Scotland or Wales, where no such phenomenon had ever been seen before. I remember, on one occasion, that, having toiled up to the top of one of the beautiful hills on the island of Kin-tang, I observed on the other side of the hill, a few yards below me, a Chinese youth engaged in cutting the long grass and bushes for fire-wood. As he was employed he did not observe me, and I approached the place where he was at work, and, standing upon a rock a few feet above him, made some noise to attract his attention. He looked up, and never shall I forget the look he gave me. Had I been a being from another world he could not have been more astonished; indeed, I suppose he thought that I had fallen from the clouds, or come out from the bowels of the hills. For a second or two he stood in silent amazement, seemingly completely paralysed, and then, throwing his grass-knife away, fled down the hill over rocks and stones with a rapidity hardly credible; nor did he ever look behind, until he had crossed the narrow valley and reached the village on the opposite side. The news was soon communicated to the villagers, who rushed out of their houses and assembled in great numbers in front of their buildings. I walked slowly and quietly down towards them, and soon removed all their fears. My young friend the grass-cutter was very shy at first, but we parted excellent friends.

The port of Shanghae is situated about 80 or 100 miles to the north-west of Chusan, the latter being in lat. 30° north, and the former in 31° 20′. On leaving the Chusan group of islands, and sailing to the northward in the direction of Shanghae, we pass the Bay of Hangchow on the left, and enter the mouth of the noble Yang-tse-kiang, the "child of the Ocean," as its name implies. The country, which, up to this degree of latitude from the south, is very mountainous, now changes, and becomes perfectly level. The shores of the river are in many places lower than the river itself, which is kept within its bounds by large and strong embankments. The mountainous scenery disappears entirely, and even from the top of the highest mast of a ship no hill is seen to bound the distant horizon—all the view is a vast level plain. That is what is called the valley of the Yang-tse-kiang, and is the great northern Nanking cotton district. The land is a deep rich loam, and is without doubt the finest in China, if not in the world.

At the entrance of the river the navigation is rather difficult, particularly in thick weather, owing partly to the numerous sand-banks, which are all covered at high water, and partly to the difficulty of getting prominent landmarks. Since the opening of the trade in 1843 several ships have got entangled amongst these banks, and have been totally wrecked. When I first visited the Yang-tse-kiang it was quite a common occurrence for vessels to get aground at low water, but as the greater part of them were small opium clippers, commanded by men who knew the region well, they generally got easily off again when the tide flowed. One evening in April we were sailing up this river with a fair light breeze, which was sending us on at the rate of six or seven miles an hour. The man at the lead was singing out his soundings; and as it was "and a half three," and "by the mark three," the captain concluded that we were in the right channel, and went below for a minute or two. The leadsman was still singing out three fathoms, when, all at once, we felt the bottom of the vessel touch the ground, and in two seconds she was hard and fast in the mud. The tide was ebbing rapidly at the time, and, as one side of the schooner was in deeper water, we were obliged to get out all the spare planking we had to prop the vessel and prevent her from falling over. The next question was, how we were to get off when the tide rose. In the course of the afternoon we had observed a number of junks astern of us, coming up the river and bound for Shanghae. Some of these were now within a quarter of a mile, and had dropped their anchors until the commencement of the flood tide. After some consultation, the captain came to the determination of boarding one of them, and getting the people to shift their anchoring ground and come a little nearer the schooner, so that a rope might be passed from the one to the other, and our vessel hauled off when the tide was sufficiently high to float her. As I was able to speak a little Chinese, I was asked to go in the boat and explain what our object was, and likewise to tell them that they should be well paid for their trouble. The boat's crew armed themselves with cutlasses, and, in order to render the business more imposing, the captain put on an old uniform which had formerly belonged to a naval officer, and with a cocked hat on his head and a sword dangling at his side took his seat in the boat. The night was dark but fine, and we could just discern the masts of the nearest junk. In a few minutes we were alongside, and were challenged by the man who had the watch upon deck, and who at the same moment, seeing we were foreigners, ran to give the alarm, exclaiming that the *Hong-mou-jins*, or "red-haired men," were upon them. Without further parley we sprang into the junk, and when we looked round we found her decks deserted—the watch and everybody else having hid themselves below. The captain directed our men to go down the hatchways and try to get the Chinese upon deck, but he gave them strict orders to use them kindly. It was not a little amusing to see our tars going about this part of the business, which they did with right good will and glee. They soon dragged the Chinamen out of their hiding-places, and, much against their inclination, mustered them on deck. I now explained to their captain that our intentions were peaceful, but that our vessel was in very great danger, and that it was absolutely necessary they should get up their anchor immediately, and come to our assistance. At the same time, I told them that they should receive twenty dollars for their trouble. They now held a consultation amongst themselves, and at last came and informed us that they would render the required assistance on the following morning. This, however, would not answer our purpose, and besides, we knew enough of the Chinese to be perfectly aware that this "to-morrow" would never come, and was only said to get rid of us altogether, and leave us to our fate. We therefore told them that this arrangement would not suit us, and again requested them to get up their anchor. Another consultation was held, and, as it was quite evident to me that they were procrastinating, and that we might go on in this manner all night, I advised the master of our schooner to set his own men to work to heave up the Chinaman's anchor and hoist her sail. The sailors, who were getting rather impatient, gladly obeyed these orders, and when the junk's crew saw what was going on they also gave their assistance, so that in a few minutes we were under weigh. Having gone as near the schooner as we considered prudent, the anchor was dropped, and a strong rope made fast to the two vessels in order to draw ours off the mud when the tide rose high enough to float her. This was accomplished during the night, and we were safely anchored in three fathoms of water. At daylight, however, we found that our Chinese friends had made sail, and gone away without waiting to claim the promised reward.

The small village of Woosung, where one of the battles was fought during the last war, stands on the banks of another river, commonly known as the "Shanghae river" by Europeans, and at the point where it falls into the Yang-tse-kiang. This is one of the principal stations in China for the opium merchant vessels, and I believe latterly more of the drug has been sold here than at all the other stations put together.

So much has been said about this trade and opium-smoking, that a few remarks upon the subject will not be out of place here. It is well known that the greater part of the opium which is brought to the Chinese coast is grown and manufactured in our East Indian possessions. Those English or American merchants who deal largely in this production employ very fast-sailing vessels for bringing it from India to China, and also keep up what are called receiving ships in many of the bays or harbours along the coast of China. These receiving ships are regularly supplied by the fast-sailing vessels which bring their cargoes from India or Hong-kong. The Chinese smugglers come out from the adjoining bays and towns, in small boats, well manned and armed, in order to protect their property, which is generally of great value. Silver, in the form of South American dollars or Sycee, is bartered for the opium at all those stations on the coast where no other trade is carried on; at other places the foreign merchants often find it advantageous to barter the opium in exchange for raw silks and teas, which are the two chief exports of the country.

The statements which have been frequently made in England, both as regards the smuggling and the smoking of opium, are very much exaggerated. When I first went to China I expected to find those merchants who were engaged in this trade little else than armed buccaneers; indeed, if I do not mistake, they have been represented as characters of this kind on the English stage. Instead of this, the trade is conducted by men of the highest respectability, possessed of immense capital, and who are known and esteemed as merchants of the first class in every part of the civilised world. The trade in opium, although contraband, is so unlike what is generally called smuggling, that people at a distance are deceived by the term. It may be quite true that its introduction and use are prohibited by the Chinese government, but that prohibition is merely an empty sound, which, in fact, means nothing. The whole, or at least the greater part, of the mandarins use it, and it is not at all unlikely that his Celestial Majesty himself makes one of the number of its devotees. It is necessary, however, to publish every now and then strong threatening edicts against it, which are only consigned to oblivion in the pages of the Peking Gazette, and have no effect whatever in restraining the Emperor's loyal subjects. It is now the opinion of all intelligent foreigners, and also many of the more enlightened amongst the Chinese themselves, that the importation of opium ought to be legalised, and that it should be admitted at a small duty, as, by this means, much of the demoralising effects of smuggling would be got rid of, and a considerable revenue would flow into the coffers of the Chinese treasury.

Many instances of the feeble kind of opposition which the Chinese government employ to stop the opium-trade occurred during my residence in the country. Sometimes an admiral, renowned for his valour, was sent with a number of war junks to a particular station, where the opium-ships were anchored, for the purpose of compelling them to leave the Chinese shores. Gongs were beat, guns were fired, at a respectful distance, however, and the junks came down with all that pomp and parade which the Chinese know so well how to assume, and which seem to form a principal part of their warlike operations. In the mean time the little opium-vessels were seen quietly at anchor, apparently paying but slight attention to all these threatening demonstrations. Presently a message was sent from the admiral, ordering them to get up their anchors and stand out to sea, and never more to dare to enter the waters of his Celestial

Majesty under the penalty of being completely annihilated.

A summons like this in former days might have had some weight, but now it had none; and the only answer the messengers carried back was, "that the foreign vessels were well armed, and that they would not leave their anchorage." This was quite sufficient to cool the courage of the admiral, who was now in a dilemma; he durst not fight the "barbarians," and if he did not manage to get them out of the way, his character for courage would suffer when the affair was represented at head quarters. He therefore altered his tone, and *requested* the captains, as a great favour, to leave the anchorage and move outside for a day or two only, after which time they might return to their old quarters. This was agreed to on the part of the captains of the opium-vessels, and on the following morning they got under weigh and went out to sea. The Chinese, who were on the look-out at the time, made a great noise by beating gongs and firing guns, and followed the opium-ships until they were fairly outside. The admiral now sent up a report to his government to the effect that he had fought a great battle with the "barbarians," and had driven them away from the shores; or very probably he said that he had blown some of their vessels to pieces, and sunk the rest in the depths of the sea. In the mean time, even before the report was half-way to Peking, the opium-vessels had quietly taken up their old anchorage, and things were going on in the usual way! Such is a specimen of the way in which affairs are managed in China.

The opium from Bengal, which consists of two kinds —namely, *Patna* and *Benares*—is always of a good quality and pure; but the Bombay *Malwa* is now so much mixed up with other ingredients, that the Chinese smuggler will not buy it until he has had an opportunity of testing its quality. This is done is the following manner:—having selected the chest or number of chests which he wishes to purchase, they are opened, and he takes out three or four of the worst-looking cakes, cuts a small piece from each, and dissolves them in a copper ladle over a charcoal fire. When the opium is melted, it is poured out into a coarse paper filter. If it is not of the worst description, it readily passes through the paper into a small basin, which is placed under it. When it will not pass through the filter, the Chinese call it *Man-ling*, by which name they designate opium which is so bad, or so mixed with extraneous ingredients, that it will not dissolve in water or pass through the paper filter. This description of the drug is, of course, only bought at a very reduced price.

When the mixture passes through the filter, the paper is carefully examined, and if any sediment remains, such as sand or rubbish, with which the opium is frequently adulterated, it detracts considerably from its value. This filtered mixture is now put again into a clear copper pan, and boiled slowly over the charcoal fire, until the whole of the water is evaporated, and nothing remains but pure opium. The drug is then poured out into a small porcelain cup, and stirred round and examined with great care. At this stage of the process colour forms the principal test of its quality, and as the smuggler stirs it round, and holds it up to the light, he pronounces it be be "*tung-kow*," if it is thick like jelly; "*pak-chat*," if it has a whitish colour; "*hong-chat*," if it is red; and "*kong-see-pak*," if it is opium of the first quality, or like that sent round by the East India Company.

Opium is prepared for smoking much in the same manner as I have just described, and is kept in small cups, which are made for the purpose. The smoker lays his head upon a pillow, has a lamp by his side, and with a kind of needle he lifts a small portion of the opium to the candle; and having ignited it, he puts it into the small aperture of the bowl of the pipe. The candle is applied to the bowl during the process of inhaling, and the smoke is drawn into the lungs in the same manner as an Indian or Chinese swallows tobacco. A whiff or two is all that can be drawn from a single pipe, and, therefore, those who are accustomed to the use of the drug have frequently to renew the dose.

No one who has seen anything of the habits of the Chinese will deny that the use of opium, particularly when taken to excess, has a most pernicious effect both upon the constitution and morals of its victims. From my own experience, however, I have no hesitation in saying that the number of persons who use it to excess has been very much exaggerated; it is quite true that a very large quantity of the drug is yearly imported from India, but then we must take into consideration the vast extent of the Chinese empire, and its population of 300,000,000 of people.*

* The population of China has been estimated lately at 367,000,000.

Opium Pipe.

Lord Jocelyn, in his 'Campaign in China,' gives the following account of its effects, which he witnessed upon the Chinese at Singapore. "A few days of this fearful luxury, when taken to excess, will give a pallid and haggard look to the face, and a few months, or even weeks, will change the strong and healthy man into little better than an idiot skeleton. The pain they suffer when deprived of the drug after long habit no language can explain; and it is only when to a certain degree under its influence that their faculties are alive. In the houses devoted to their ruin, these infatuated people may be seen at nine o'clock in the evening in all the different stages; some entering half distracted to feed the craving appetite they had been obliged to subdue during the day; others laughing and talking wildly under the effects of a first pipe; whilst the couches around are filled with their different occupants, who lie languid with an idiot smile upon their countenance, too much under the influence of the drug to care for passing events, and fast merging to the wished-for consummation. The last scene in this tragic play is generally a room in the rear of the building, a species of dead-house, where lie stretched those who have passed into the state of bliss the opium-smoker madly seeks—an emblem of the long sleep to which he is blindly hurrying."

CHAPTER XI.

Shanghae in 1844 — Its Gardens and Plants — Start for the Hills in the Interior — Canals and Bridges — Adventure with my Pony — The "Tein-ching," or blue Dye, found — Hills and their Vegetation described — The Surprise of the Natives on seeing a Foreigner — Their Curiosity and Honesty! — Plants sent to England — Another Journey into the Interior — Some large Northern Cities noticed — A Midnight Visit from Thieves — The far-famed City of Soo-chow-foo visited — A Description of it — New Plants found — Central Position of Soo-chow as a Place of Trade — Baths for the Million — Return to Shanghae.

I AGAIN visited Shanghae, on the 18th of April, 1844, and spent two or three weeks there at different times. My principal object was to see all the plants in the different northern districts as they came into flower, and it was therefore necessary that I should stay as short a time as possible in each place. I have mentioned that I purchased a collection of *Tree Pœonies* during my first visit to Shanghae in the winter of 1843, which were said to be very splendid things, and entirely different in colour from any plants of the kind which were known in England. I had of course at that time no opportunity of seeing their flowers, and was now, therefore, particularly anxious to get some which were in bloom, and had intended to send my old friend back again to Soo-chow for another collection, stipulating, however, that the plants should this time have blooms upon them. One morning, however, as I was going out into the country, a short distance from Shanghae, I was surprised at meeting a garden labourer with a load of Moutans all in full flower, which he was taking towards the city for sale. The flowers were very large and fine, and the colours were *dark purples, lilacs,* and *deep reds,* kinds of which the very existence had been always doubted in England, and which are never seen even at Canton. Two English gentlemen, who were excellent Chinese scholars, being with me at the time, we soon found out the name of the Moutan district; and from the state of the roots in the man's basket I was quite certain that the plants had not been more than an hour or two out of the ground, and that consequently the place where they were grown could not be more than six or eight miles from Shanghae; a surmise which I afterwards found to be perfectly correct. This was doubtless the place where my nursery friend had procured his plants in the previous autumn, and where he would have gone again had I not been lucky enough to find that I could easily go there myself. Indeed, I afterwards discovered that there was no Moutan country in the vicinity of Soo-chow, having met a man from that place in the Shanghae district, where he had come for the express purpose of buying Tree Pæonies. I now went into the Moutan district daily during the time the different plants were coming into bloom, and secured some most striking and beautiful kinds for the Horticultural Society.

Being now well acquainted with the country in the immediate vicinity of Shanghae, I was anxious to extend my researches into the interior, particularly as far as some hills which were said to be about thirty miles distant in a westerly direction. It was extremely difficult to gain any information on this subject from the Chinese, who were particularly jealous of foreigners going any distance inland. Their suspicious feelings had also been much increased at this time by the indiscretion of some of our own countrymen, who had hired a boat and gone a considerable distance up one of the rivers, taking soundings with bamboo poles, in the manner of the Chinese. The authorities suspected that they had some particular object in view in ascertaining the depth of the river, and immediately complained to Captain Balfour, the English consul, who was consequently obliged to notice the circumstance.

Being determined, however, to make an effort to accomplish the object I had in view, I procured a pony and a pocket compass, and started off one morning early on a voyage of discovery. The hills were said to lie westerly, and in that direction I rode for eight or ten miles without seeing anything higher than a mound of earth. The compass was my only guide both in going and also in finding my way back again; the roads were generally not more than four or six feet wide; but still the country had its highways and byways, and for a length of time I was fortunate enough to keep on the former; as long as I did so, I got easily over the numerous canals which intersect the country in all directions, because, wherever these are crossed by the main road, good substantial stone bridges are erected. At last I got a glimpse of the hills in the distance, and in my anxiety to take the shortest road I lost sight of the highway, and got entangled amongst byways and canals. I was soon in a somewhat critical position; the bridges which I was constantly crossing were old, narrow, and rotten, and the feet of my pony were every now and then getting entangled between the planks. At length we came to one much worse than the others, and although I got off and did everything to persuade the pony to follow me over it, with great reluctance he attempted to do so, but, when about the centre of the bridge, his feet got fast in the rotten planking, and in the struggle to free himself the centre gave way; I had just time to spring to the bank, when the bridge and pony both fell into the canal. Luckily for me the poor animal swam to the side I was on, and allowed me to catch him when he got out of the water: he was completely covered with mud, and my saddle and bridle were of course in a sad condition. By the assistance of some labourers who were at work within a short distance, I was soon enabled to get out of this network of canals, and regain the main road; but this was a lesson to me, and as long as I was in China I never afterwards went off the main road when I was on horseback.

I reached a small town in the vicinity of the hills about two o'clock in the afternoon; the pony, having had nothing to eat since we left Shanghae, was much exhausted, and I was therefore anxious to procure a feed of corn for him at some of the shops. The news of the presence of a foreigner in the town spread like lightning, and I was soon surrounded and followed by some thousands of people of both sexes, young and old, who were all anxious to get a glimpse of my features and dress. Their behaviour on the whole, however, was civil and respectful, and the only inconvenience I had to complain of was the pressure of the crowd. For a few of the copper coin of the country, a boy had promised to take me to a shop where I could purchase something for the pony, and we wended our way through the crowd, which was every moment becoming more dense, towards, as I supposed, a corn or hay shop. At last, to my surprise, he came to a halt in front of an eating-house, and my guide came and asked me for money to go in and buy some boiled rice. "But I want a feed for the pony," said I. "Very well, give me the money, and I will fetch you a basin of boiled rice for him." "You had better bring him a pair of chopsticks also," said I, as I put the money into his hand. The idea of a pony eating with chopsticks delighted the crowd, and put them into high good humour: during my travels in the interior I often found the benefit of having a joke with the natives.

My pony seemed to enjoy the meal which was set before him, and I too had some rice from the same pot. I then proceeded on foot to examine the nearest hill, and soon came to the conclusion that it would be advantageous for me to be some days in the vicinity of this place. As I could not trust the natives with the pony, which belonged to the head mandarin in Shanghae, I determined to take him home again myself, and hire a boat, with which I could return by any of the numerous canals which branch all over the country, and stay as long as I pleased. I reached Shanghae late on the same evening, weary enough, having ridden at least sixty miles during the day.

A few days after this, having engaged a boat, I started early one morning, and taking advantage of the tide, which ebbs and flows over all this part of the country, I reached the hills on the same evening. The country through which I passed was rich and fertile, cotton forming the staple production of the fields in the neighbourhood of Shanghae. After passing the cotton district, I came into a tract of country in which a cruciferous plant seemed to be principally cultivated. From this plant a kind of indigo or blue dye is prepared; it is called *Tein-ching* by the Chinese. Very large quantities of this substance are brought to Shanghae, and all the other towns in the north of China, where it is used in dyeing the blue cotton cloth which forms the principal article of dress of the poorer classes. I brought home living specimens of the plant which produces this dye, and as these are now in flower in the gardens of the Horticultural Society, the proper scientific name of the plant will soon be ascertained.*

As I approached the hills the level of the country became lower, and at that time of the year (June) it was completely flooded, and rice was extensively cultivated. In general, the higher land of this vast plain is used in the cultivation of cotton and the cruciferous plant mentioned above; while the lower lands, those which are easily flooded, are converted into rice-fields. Here and there on my way I met with large trees of the *Salisburia*

* It has proved to be a new species, and has been named Isatis indigotica.

adiantifolia, which are the largest and most striking trees in this part of the country. Small patches of bamboo were seen around all the villages, and groups of cypress and pine generally marked the last resting-places of the Chinese, which are scattered over all the country.

The hills were very different from any which I had seen in the more southern parts of China : they are not more than 400 feet in height, and have none of that bold and rugged character which I have formerly noticed. Here and there crumbling rocks show themselves above the surface, but these are not so numerous as to affect the general pastoral-looking appearance of these hills. The country is also more richly wooded than any other part near Shanghae, and, of course, contains a greater number of species of plants. One curious fact, however, came under my notice : no Azaleas were met with in this part of the country, although the hills about sixty or eighty miles to the south abound in such plants ; and, although the other plants which accompany Azaleas on the Chusan and Ning-po hills were here growing in all their native luxuriance, these their more lovely companions were not to be found. I can scarcely believe that the hills between Ning-po and Shanghae are the most northern limit for this class of plants ; yet such from my own observations would appear to be the case.

The natives in this part of the country were vastly surprised when they saw me for the first time ; at the different villages and towns, men, women, and children of all ranks lined the banks of the canals as my boat passed along, and often requested me to come out in order that they might have a better opportunity of seeing me. When I left my boat for the purpose of ascending the hills, my boatmen used to make a good deal of money by allowing the people to go in and inspect my little cabin. A copy of the 'Pictorial Times,' which I happened to have with me, was greatly admired, and I was obliged to leave it amongst them. It is a remarkable fact, however, that nothing, as far as I know, was ever stolen from me at this time, although several hundred persons visited my boat in my absence. The boatmen must either have been very sharp, or the people must have had a superstitious dread of the property of a foreigner: to put it down to their honour is, I am afraid, out of the question!

Having finished my researches amongst the hills, I left this part of the country and returned to Shanghae. The "Helen Stuart," one of the first vessels which left Shanghae for England direct, was at this time ready for sea, and I availed myself of this opportunity to send some cases of plants to the Horticultural Society, which, I regret to say, arrived in very bad condition. When I had despatched these cases, I determined on another journey into the interior.

Every one who has been in China, or who is at all acquainted with Chinese history, has heard of the city of *Soo-chow-foo.* If a stranger enters a shop in Hong-kong, in Canton, or in any of the other towns in the south, he is sure to be told, when he inquires the price of any curiosity out of the common way, that it has been brought from this celebrated place; let him order anything superb, and it must be sent for from

Soo-chow—fine pictures, fine carved work, fine silks, and fine ladies, all come from Soo-chow.—It is the Chinaman's earthly paradise, and it would be hard indeed to convince him that it had its equal in any town on earth. In addition to its other attractions, I was informed by the Chinese nursery gardeners at Shanghae that it contained a great number of excellent flower-gardens and nurseries, from which they obtained all or nearly all the plants which they had for sale, and I was therefore strongly tempted to infringe the absurd laws of the Celestial Empire, and try to reach this far-famed place. My greatest difficulty was to meet with boatmen who would travel with me, as they were all frightened for the mandarins, who had issued very stringent orders to them after the circumstance happened which I have already noticed. They were told that they might take foreigners down the river towards the sea, and up as far as a pagoda a mile or two above Shanghae, but on no account were they to go up the western branch of the river. This was a direct infringement on the right which had been secured to us by the treaty of Nanking, and her Majesty's consul at this port soon found it necessary and prudent to interfere in the matter. Some time after this period, when what are called the boundaries were fixed, the foreign residents were allowed to go a day's journey into the interior, that is, as far as they could go and come back again in twenty-four hours.

Having at length procured a boat, we set off on our journey, the boatmen neither knowing where I intended to go to, or how long I was to be absent from Shanghae. I simply told them we were going into the country in search of plants, and that they must take a supply of rice for several days. My Chinese servant, who always accompanied me, also informed them that it was a common thing for me to wander about the country in search of plants, but that I was *perfectly harmless*, and would take care that they should not get into any trouble on my account. This gave them some confidence, and as the wind and tide were both in our favour we were soon a considerable distance away from Shanghae. As I knew pretty well in what direction Soo-chow lay, I took my course by a pocket compass which I always carried with me. After getting twenty or thirty miles from Shanghae I judged it prudent to break the subject of my wishes to my companions. First of all, I took my servant aside; he was a most active fellow, and capable of persuading the others to do anything he liked. "Now," said I to him, "I want to visit Soo-chow, and if you will persuade the boatmen to go on there I will make you a present of five dollars when we return: besides, you may tell the men that I shall double the amount of the hire which I have already promised them." Upon this a long conference ensued, the result of which was that they determined to accept my offer.

I was, of course, travelling in the Chinese costume; my head was shaved, I had a splendid wig and tail, of which some Chinaman in former days had doubtless been extremely vain; and upon the whole I believe I made a pretty fair Chinaman. Although the Chinese countenance and eye differ considerably from those of a native of Europe, yet a traveller in the north has far greater chance of escaping detection than in the south of China, the features of the northern natives approaching more nearly to those of Europeans than they do in the south, and the difference amongst themselves also being greater.

In China the canal is the traveller's highway, and the boat is his carriage, and hence the absence of good roads and carriages in this country. Such a mode of conveyance is not without its advantages, however little we may think of it in England; for as the tide ebbs and flows through the interior for many miles, the boats proceed with considerable rapidity; the traveller too can sleep comfortably in his little cabin, which is, in fact, his house for the time being.

The canal, after leaving Shanghae, leads in a northerly direction, inclining sometimes a little to the west; branches leading off in all directions over the country. Some very large towns and walled cities were passed on our route, at one of which, named *Cading*, we halted for the night just under the ramparts. I spread out my bed in my little cabin, and went to sleep rather early, intending to start by times with the tide next morning, and get as far as possible during the ensuing day. But, as my countryman says,—

> 'The best laid schemes of mice and men gang aft agee;"

and I awoke during the night by the cool air blowing in upon my head through one of the windows of the boat, which I had shut before I went to rest. I jumped up immediately and looked out, and through the darkness I could discern that we were drifting down the canal with the tide, now coming in contact with some other boat, which had been fastened up like ourselves for the night, and now rubbing against the branches of trees which hung over the sides of the canal. I lost no time in awaking my servant and the boatmen, who rubbed their eyes with astonishment, and exclaimed that some robber must have boarded us. This had never struck me before, but when I called for a light I found that all my clothes, English and Chinese, were gone. Our visitor, whoever he had been, after taking possession of all the cabin contained, cut the rope by which we were fastened, and shoved us off into the centre of the canal, along which we had drifted a considerable way before I awoke. Fortunately for me, the few dollars I had with me were in my Chinese purse beneath my pillow.

"What shall we do?" said my servant when we had made the boat fast again to some others on the side of the canal: "your clothes are all gone."

"Do?" said I, laughing; "I think the best thing we can do is to go to bed again until daylight." This being agreed to, we were soon all once more sound asleep. When morning dawned, I sent my servant into the town of Cading with a few dollars, which procured me another dress, and we proceeded on our journey.

The city of Cading is large and fortified, although the walls and ramparts are in a state of decay. It is evidently a very ancient place. Here a large quantity of the celebrated carving is done, for which the Chinese in the north are so well known. After leaving this town, the canal, which was narrow, continued in a northerly direction for a few miles, and then, all at once, our little boat shot out of it into a broad and beautiful canal, resembling a lake or broad river, running nearly east and west, and probably connecting itself with the Yang-tse-kiang river, somewhere between Woosung and Nanking. The scenery here is extremely striking; the broad and smooth canal bears on its waters hundreds of Chinese boats of all sizes, under sail, and each hurrying to its place of destination; pagodas here and there are seen rearing their heads above the woods and Buddhist temples, which are scattered over this wide and extensive plain. One of these temples crowns a solitary little hill, named *Quin-san*, which at certain seasons of the year is visited by crowds of people from Soo-chow and the neighbouring towns: the whole country, as far as the eye can reach, is one vast rice-field; and everywhere the pleasing clatter of the water-wheels falls upon the ear, and hundreds of happy and contented Chinese peasants are seen engaged in the cultivation of the soil. After continuing its westerly course for some distance, the canal divided, and the branch we took soon led us to another town named *Ta-tsong-tseu*. It is a place of great size, walled and fortified like Cading and Shanghae, and is probably larger than the latter, although perhaps not so populous. A great number of large old junks are moored on the canal round the walls, apparently used as dwelling-houses, being now unfit for any other service. This town, too, like Cading, is evidently in a decaying state, judging from the dilapidated condition of the houses and fortifications, but teems with an immense population of men, women, and particularly children.

On approaching Soo-chow some hills were seen, bounding the level plain, which I afterwards found were some few miles west from the town itself. The whole country here, as well as near Cading, is one vast rice-field. Many females are employed in driving the water-wheels, generally three or four to each wheel: these ladies have large feet, or rather their feet are of the natural size; indeed, if they were cramped in the usual way it would be impossible for them to work on the water-wheel. Small feet, however, are general amongst the lower classes who work in the fields, for of the hundreds whom I observed hoeing the cotton, or engaged in other agricultural operations, but a small proportion had feet of the natural size.

A few miles on the east of Soo-chow there is a large and beautiful lake, twelve or fifteen miles across, through which the boats from Sung-kiang-foo and other places in that direction approach the city. After passing this lake, the canal, which had widened considerably, now began to contract; bridges here and there were passed, villages and small towns lined the banks, and everything denoted the approach to a city of some size and importance. It was a delightful summer's evening on the 23rd of June when I approached this far-famed town. The moon was up, and with a fair light breeze my little boat scudded swiftly, its masts and sails reflected in the clear water of the canal; the boats thickened as we went along, the houses became more crowded and larger, lanterns were moving in great numbers on the bridges and sides of the canal, and in a few minutes more we were safely moored, among some hundreds of other boats, under the walls of this celebrated city. Having taken all the precautions in our power against another nightly visitor, my servant, the boatmen, and myself, were soon fast asleep.

With the first dawn of morning I was up, and dressed with very great care by my Chinese servant, whom I then despatched to find out the nursery gardens in the city, in order to procure the plants which I wanted. When he had obtained this information he returned, and we proceeded together into the city, in order to make my selections.

When I left the boat I confess I felt rather nervous as to the trial I was about to make. Although I had passed very well as a Chinaman in the country districts, I knew that the inhabitants of large towns, and particularly those in a town like this, were more difficult to deceive. My old friends, or I should rather say my enemies, the dogs, who are as acute as any Chinaman, evidently did not disown me as a countryman, and this at once gave me confidence. These animals manifest very great hatred to foreigners, barking at them wherever they see them, and hanging on their skirts until they are fairly out of sight of the house or village where their masters reside.

As I was crossing the bridge which is built over the moat or canal on the outside of the city walls, numbers of the Chinese were loitering on it, leaning over its sides, and looking down upon the boats which were plying to and fro. I stopped too, and looked down upon the gay and happy throng, with a feeling of secret triumph when I remembered that I was now in the most fashionable city of the Celestial Empire, where no Englishman, as far as I knew, had ever been before. None of the loiterers on the bridge appeared to pay the slightest attention to me, by which I concluded that I must be very much like one of themselves. How surprised they would have been had it been whispered to them that an Englishman was standing amongst them!

The city of Soo-chow-foo, in its general features, is much the same as the other cities in the north, but is evidently the seat of luxury and wealth, and has none of those signs of dilapidation and decay which one sees in such towns as Ning-po. A noble canal, as wide as the river Thames at Richmond, runs parallel with the city walls, and acts as a moat as well as for commercial purposes. Here, as at Cading and Ta-tsong-tseu, a large number of invalided junks are moored, and doubtless make excellent Chinese dwelling-houses, particularly to a people so fond of living on the water. This same canal is carried through arches into the city, where it ramifies in all directions, sometimes narrow and dirty, and at other places expanding into lakes of considerable beauty; thus enabling the inhabitants to convey their merchandise to their houses from the most distant parts of the country. Junks and boats of all sizes are plying on this wide and beautiful canal, and the whole place has a cheerful and flourishing aspect, which one does not often see in the other towns in China, if we except Canton and Shanghae. The walls and ramparts are high and in excellent repair, having considerable resemblance to those of Ning-po, but in much better order. The east wall, along the side of which I went all the way, is not more than a mile in length, but the north and south are much longer, thus making the city a parallelogram. That part of the city near the east gate, by which I entered, is anything but splendid; the streets are narrow and dirty, and the population seems of the lowest order; but towards the west the buildings and streets are much finer, the shops are large, and everything denotes this to be the rich and aristocratic part of the town. The city gates seem to be well guarded with Chinese soldiers, and all the streets and lanes inside are intersected at intervals with gates, which are closed at nine or ten o'clock at night. The Governor-General of the province resides here, and keeps those under his control in excellent order.

The number of nursery gardens in this city had been exaggerated by my Chinese friends at Shanghae, but nevertheless there were several of considerable extent, out of which I was able to procure some new and valuable plants. Among these I may notice in passing a white *Glycine*, a fine new double yellow rose, and a *Gardenia* with large white blossoms, like a Camellia. These plants are now in England, and will soon be met with in every garden in the country. The Soo-chow nurseries abounded in dwarf trees, many of which were very curious and old, two properties to which the Chinese attach far greater importance than we do in England.

The ladies here are considered by the Chinese to be

the most beautiful in the country, and, judging from the specimens which I had an opportunity of seeing, they certainly deserve their high character. Their dresses are of the richest material, made in a style at once graceful and elegant; and the only faults I could find with them were their small deformed feet, and the mode they have of painting or whitening their faces with a kind of powder made for this purpose. But what seemed faults in my eyes are beauties in those of a Chinaman, and hence the prevalence of these customs.

Soo-chow-foo seems to be the great emporium of the central provinces of China, for which it is peculiarly well fitted by its situation. The trade of Ning-po, Hang-chow, Shanghae, and many other towns on the south, Ching-kiang-foo, Nanking, and even Peking itself on the north, all centres here, and all these places are connected either by the Grand Canal, or by the hundreds of canals of lesser note which ramify over all this part of the empire. Shanghae, from its favourable position as regards Soo-chow, will doubtless become one day a place of vast importance, in a commercial point of view, both as regards Europe and America.

I remained for several days in this city and its neighbourhood, when, having done all that was possible under the circumstances, I set out on my way back to Shanghae. When I arrived I was obliged to go on shore in my Chinese dress, as the English one had been stolen by my midnight visitor. The disguise, however, was so complete, that I was not recognised by a single individual, although I walked up the street where I was well known, and even my friend Mr. Mackenzie, with whom I was staying, did not know me for the first few minutes after I sat down in his room.

In the town of Shanghae, as well as in many other large Chinese towns, there are a number of public hot-water bathing-establishments, which must be of great importance as regards the health and comfort of the natives. I will describe one which I passed daily during my residence in Shanghae. There are two outer rooms used for undressing and dressing; the first, and largest, is for the poorer classes; the second, for those who consider themselves more respectable, and who wish to be more private. As you enter the largest of these rooms, a placard which is hung near the door informs you what the charges are, and a man stands there to receive the money on entrance. Arranged in rows down the middle and round the sides of both rooms are a number of small boxes or lockers, furnished with lock and key, into which the visitors put their clothes, and where they can make sure of finding them when they return from the bathing-room, which is entered by a small door at the farther end of the building, and is about 30 feet long and 20 feet wide; the water occupying the whole space, except a narrow path round the sides. The water is from 1 foot to 18 inches deep, and the sides of the bath are lined with marble slabs, from which the bathers step into the water, and on which they sit and wash themselves: the furnace is placed on the outside, and the flues are carried below the centre of the bath.

In the afternoon and evening this establishment is crowded with visitors, and on entering the bath-room the first impression is almost insupportable; the hot steam or vapour meets you at the door, filling the eyes and ears, and causing perspiration to run from every pore of the body; it almost darkens the place, and the Chinamen seen in this imperfect light, with their brown skins and long tails, sporting amongst the water, render the scene a most ludicrous one to an Englishman.

Those visitors who use the common room pay only six copper cash; the others pay eighteen, but they have in addition a cup of tea and a pipe of tobacco from the proprietors. I may mention that one hundred copper cash amount to about 4½*d.* of our money; so that the first class enjoy a hot-water bath for about one farthing! and the other a bath, a private room, a cup of tea, and a pipe of tobacco, for something less than one penny!

CHAPTER XII.

Chinese Cotton Cultivation — Yellow Cotton — District where it grows — Cotton Country described — Soil — Manure, and mode of Application — Preceding Crops — Time of Sowing — Method — Rains — Summer Cultivation — Early Rain advantageous — Time of Reaping and Gathering — Cotton Farmers and their Families — Drying and Cleaning Process described — Marketing — Independence of the Seller — Crowded Streets in Shanghae during the Cotton Season — Warehouses and Packing — Home Consumption — Stalks used for Fuel.

THE Chinese or Nanking cotton-plant is the *Gossypium herbaceum* of botanists, and the "*Mie wha*" of the northern Chinese. It is a branching annual, growing from one to three or four feet in height, according to the richness of the soil, and flowering from August to October. The flowers are of a dingy yellow colour, and, like the Hibiscus or Malva, which belong to the same tribe, remain expanded only for a few hours, in which time they perform the part allotted to them by nature, and then shrivel up and soon decay. At this stage the seed-pod begins to swell rapidly, and, when ripe, the outer coating bursts and exposes the pure white cotton in which the seeds lie imbedded.

The yellow cotton, from which the beautiful Nanking cloth is manufactured, is called "*Tze mie wha*" by the

Chinese, and differs but slightly in its structure and general appearance from the kind just noticed. I have often compared them in the cotton-fields where they were growing, and, although the yellow variety has a more stunted habit than the other, it has no characters which constitute a distinct species. It is merely an accidental variety, and, although its seeds may generally produce the same kind, they doubtless frequently yield the white variety, and *vice versâ*. Hence specimens of the yellow cotton are frequently found growing amongst the white in the immediate vicinity of Shanghae; and again a few miles northward, in fields near the city of *Poushan* on the banks of the Yang-tse-kiang, where the yellow cotton abounds, I have often gathered specimens of the white variety.

The Nanking cotton is chiefly cultivated in the level ground around Shanghae, where it forms the staple summer production of the country. This district, which is part of the great plain of the Yang-tse-kiang, although flat, is yet several feet above the level of the water in the rivers and canals, and is consequently much better fitted for cotton cultivation than those flat rice-districts in various parts of the country,—such, for example, as the plain of Ning-po,—where the ground is either wet and marshy, or liable at times to be completely overflowed. Some fields in this district are, of course, low and marshy, and these are cultivated with rice instead of cotton, and regularly flooded by the water-wheel during the period of growth. Although the cotton-land is generally flat, so much so, indeed, that no hills can be seen from the tops of the houses in the city of Shanghae, it has nevertheless a pleasing and undulating appearance, and, taken as a whole, it is perhaps the most fertile agricultural district in the world. The soil is a strong rich loam, capable of yielding immense crops year after year, although it receives but a small portion of manure.

The manure applied to the cotton-lands of the Chinese is doubtless peculiarly well fitted for this kind of crop. It is obtained from the canals, ponds, and ditches which intersect the country in every direction, and consists of mud which has been formed partly by the decay of long grass, reeds, and succulent water-plants, and partly by the surface soil which has been washed down from the higher ground by the heavy rains. Every agricultural operation in China seems to be done with the greatest regularity, at certain stated times which experience has proved the best; and in nothing is this more apparent than in the manuring of the cotton-lands. Early in April the agricultural labourers, all over the country, are seen busily employed in cleaning these ponds and ditches. The water is first of all partly drawn off, and then the mud is thrown up on the adjoining land to dry, where it remains for a few days until all the superfluous water is drained out of it, and is then conveyed away and spread over the cotton-fields. Previous to this the land has been prepared for its reception, having been either ploughed up with the small buffalo plough in common use in the country, and then broken and pulverised by the three-pronged hoe, or, in those instances where the farms are small and cannot boast of a buffalo and plough, it is loosened and broken up entirely by manual labour. When the mud is first spread over the land, it is, of course, hard or cloggy, but the first showers soon mix it with the surface soil, and the whole becomes pulverised, and it is then ready for the reception of the cotton-seed. Road-scrapings and burnt rubbish are saved up with care, and used for the same purpose and in the same manner.

A considerable portion of the cotton-lands either lie fallow during the winter months, or are planted with those crops which are ready for gathering prior to the sowing of the cotton-seed. Frequently, however, two crops are found growing in the field at the same time. Wheat, for example, which is a winter crop, is reaped in the Shanghae district generally about the end of May, while the proper time for putting in the cotton-seed is the beginning of that month or the end of April. In order, therefore, to have cotton on the wheat-lands, the Chinese sow its seeds at the usual time amongst the wheat, and, when the latter is reaped, the former is several inches above ground, and ready to grow with vigour when it is more fully exposed to the influence of sun and air. The Shanghae season—that is, from the late spring frosts to those in autumn—is barely long enough for the production and ripening of the cotton, as it is easily injured by frost; and the Chinese farmer is thus obliged, in order to gain time and obtain two crops from his ground in one year, to sow its seeds before the winter crop is ready to be removed from the ground. When it is possible to have the first crop entirely removed before the cotton is sown, it is much preferred, as the land can then be well worked and properly manured, neither of which can otherwise be done. The method of sowing one crop before the preceding one is ripe and removed from the land is very common in this part of the country; and even in autumn, before the cotton-stalks are taken out of the ground, other seeds are frequently seen germinating and ready to take the place of the more tender crop.

In the end of April and beginning of May—the land having been prepared in the manner just described—the cotton-seeds are carried in baskets to the fields, and the sowing commences. They are generally sown broadcast, that is, scattered regularly over the surface of the ground, and then the labourers go over the whole surface with their feet and tread them carefully in. This not only imbeds the seeds, but also acts like a roller to break and pulverise the soil. Germination soon commences, the seeds rooting first in the manure which had been scattered over the surface of the land. In some cases the seed, instead of being sown broadcast, is sown in drills or patches, but this mode is less common than the other. These patches are often manured with bruised oil-cake, which is the remains of the cotton-seed, after its oil has been extracted. The rains, which always fall copiously at the change of the monsoon, which takes place at this season of the year, warm and moisten the earth, and the seeds swell, and vegetation progresses with wonderful rapidity. Many of the operations in Chinese agriculture are regulated by the change of the monsoon. The farmer knows from experience, that when the winds, which have been blowing from the north and east for the last seven months, change to the south and west, the atmosphere will be highly charged with electric fluid, and the clouds will daily rain and refresh his crops.

The cotton-fields are carefully tended during the summer months. The plants are thinned where they have been sown too thickly, the earth is loosened amongst the roots, and the ground hoed and kept free from weeds. If the season is favourable, immense crops are obtained, owing to the fertility of the soil; but if the weather happens to be unusually dry from June to August, the crop receives a check which it never entirely recovers, even although the ground, after that period, should be moistened by frequent showers. 1845 was a season of this kind, and the crop was a very deficient one compared with that of the previous year. The spring was highly favourable, and the plants looked well up to the month of June, when the dry weather set in, and gave them a check which they never recovered. Abundance of rain fell later in the season, but it was then too late, and only caused the plants to grow tall and run to leaf, without producing those secretions which ultimately go to the formation of flowers and seed.

The cotton-plant produces its flowers in succession from August to the end of October, but sometimes, when the autumn is mild, blooms are produced even up to November, when the cold nights generally nip the buds, and prevent them from forming seed. In the autumn of 1844 this happened on the night of the 28th of October, when the thermometer sank to the freezing point, and then ice was found on the sides of the canals and ponds.

As the pods are bursting every day, it is necessary to have them gathered with great regularity, otherwise they fall upon the ground and the cotton gets dirty, which of course reduces its value in the market. Little bands of the Chinese are now seen in the afternoon in every field, gathering the ripe cotton, and carrying it home to the houses of the farmers. As the farms are generally small, they are worked almost entirely by the farmer and his family, consisting sometimes of three or even four generations, including the old grey-haired grandfather or great-grandfather, who has seen the crops of fourscore years gathered into his barns. Every member of these family groups has a certain degree of interest in his employment; the harvest is their own, and the more productive it is, the greater number of comforts they will be able to afford. Of course there are many cotton-farms of larger size, where labourers are employed in addition to the farmer's family, but by far the greater number are small and worked in the way I have just described. It is no unusual sight to see the family goats, too, doing their share of the work. Several of these animals are kept on almost every farm, where they are, of course, great favourites with the children, and often follow them to the cotton-fields. Although the children with their little hands can gather the cotton as well as their elders, they are not strong enough to carry it about with them, and it is amusing to see their favourites the goats, with bags slung across their backs, receiving the deposits of cotton, and bearing it home to the houses, evidently aware that they too are working for the general good.

However fine the crop may be, the Chinese are never sure of it until it is actually gathered in. Much depends upon a dry autumn, for, if the weather is wet after the pods begin to burst, they drop amongst the muddy soil, and are consequently much injured, if not completely destroyed. When the cotton reaches the farmyard, it is daily spread out on hurdles raised about four feet from the ground, and fully exposed to the sun. As the object is to get rid of all the moisture, it is of course only put out in fine weather, and is always taken into the house or barn in the evening. When perfectly dry, the process of separating it from the seeds commences. This is done by the well-known wheel with two rollers, which, when turned round, draws or sucks in the cotton, and rejects the seeds. It is a simple and beautiful contrivance, and answers well the end for which it is designed. The cotton is now sent to market, and a portion of the seeds are reserved for the next year's crop.

Early in the fine autumnal mornings the roads leading into Shanghae are crowded with bands of coolies from the cotton-farms, each with his bamboo across his shoulders and a large sack of cotton swung from each end. With these they hurry into the town, for the purpose of disposing of them to the merchants, who have numerous warehouses from which they send the cotton to the other provinces of the empire. These coolies or small farmers—for many of them bring their own produce to market themselves—are very independent in their dealings. Having reached the first warehouse, the cotton is exposed to the view of the merchant, who is asked what price he intends to give for that particular quality; and should the sum offered be below the owner's expectations, he immediately shoulders his load and walks away to another merchant. At this season it is almost impossible to get along the streets near the sides of the river where the cotton warehouses are, owing to the large quantities of this commodity which are daily brought in from the country. It is bought up by the large cotton-merchants, who empty it out in their warehouses, and then repack it in a neat and compact manner before it is conveyed on board the junks.

Before the cotton is converted into thread for the purpose of weaving, it is cleaned and freed from knots by the well-known process common in our possessions in India. This is done by an elastic bow, the string of which, being passed under a portion of the cotton placed on a table, throws it in the air by the vibration which is kept up by the workman, and separates the fibre without at all breaking or injuring it. At the same time the wind caused by the sudden vibrations carries off the dust and other impurities. After this process the Chinese cotton is particularly pure and soft, and is considered by good judges not to be surpassed by any in the world. It is much superior to that imported to China from Hindostan, and always commands a higher price in the Chinese market.

Every small farmer or cottager reserves a portion of the produce of his fields for the wants of his own family.

This the female members clean, spin, and weave at home. In every cottage throughout this district the traveller meets with the spinning-wheel and the small hand-loom, which used to be common in our own country in days of yore, but which have now given way to machinery. These looms are plied by the wives and daughters, who are sometimes assisted by the old men or young boys who are unfit for the labours of the field. Where the families are numerous and industrious, a much greater quantity of cloth is woven than is required for their own wants, and in this case the surplus is taken to Shanghae and the adjacent towns for sale. A sort of market is held every morning at one of the gates of the city, where these people assemble and dispose of their little bundles of cotton cloth. Money is in this manner realised for the purchase of tea and other necessaries which are not produced by the farms in this particular district.

When the last crops are gathered from the cotton-fields, the stalks are carried home for fuel. Thus every part of the crop is turned to account: the cotton itself clothes them, and affords them the means of supplying themselves with all the necessaries of life; the surplus seeds are converted into oil; the stalks boil their frugal meals; and the ashes even—the remains of all—are strewed over their fields for the purposes of manure. But even before this takes place, the system I have already noticed—of sowing and planting fresh crops before the removal of those which occupy the land—is already in progress. Clover, beans, and other vegetables are frequently above ground in the cotton-fields before the stalks of the latter are removed. Thus, the Chinese in the northern provinces lengthen by every means in their power the period of growth; and gain as much as they possibly can from the fertility of their land. The reader must bear in mind, however, that the soil of this district is a rich deep loam, which is capable of yielding many crops in succession without the aid of a particle of manure. Nature has showered her bounties on the inhabitants of this part of the Chinese empire with no sparing hand; the soil is not only the most fertile in China, but the climate is capable of rearing and bringing to perfection many of the productions of the tropics as well as the whole of those found in all the temperate regions of the globe.

CHAPTER XIII.

Climate of China — Summer and Winter — Temperature of Hong-Kong — Of Shanghae — Monsoons — Typhoons — Signs of their Approach — Description of a Typhoon witnessed by the Author — Effect produced upon Vegetation — Rains — Wet and Dry Seasons.

IN order to understand Chinese agriculture, a knowledge of the climate of the country is of course necessary. The dominions of the Emperor of China stretch over twenty-three degrees of latitude—from 18° to 41° north, and from the 98° to the 123° of east longitude; thus including both tropical and temperate regions in its vast extent. Being placed on the east side and forming part of the large continent of Asia, it is liable to extremes of temperature—to excessive heat in summer, and extreme cold in winter—which are unknown in many other parts of the world within the same parallels of latitude. One of our best writers upon China* makes the following very sensible remarks on this subject:—"Although Peking is nearly a degree to the south of Naples—the latitude of the former place being 39° 54′, of the latter 40° 50′—the mean temperature of Peking is only 54° of Fahrenheit, while that of Naples is 63°. But

* Davis's 'Chinese.'

as the thermometer at the Chinese capital sinks much lower during the winter than at Naples, so in summer does it rise somewhat higher; the rivers are said to be frozen for three or four months together, from December to March; while during the last embassy in September, 1816, we experienced a heat of between 90° and 100° in the shade. Now it is well known that Naples, and other countries in the extreme south of Europe, are strangers to such a degree of long-continued cold, and not often visited by such heats. 'Europe,' observes Humboldt, 'may be considered altogether as the western part of a great continent, and therefore subject to all the influence which causes the western sides of continents to be warmer than the eastern; and at the same time more temperate, or less subject to *excesses* of both heat and cold, but principally the latter.'"

From my own tables, kept by Newman's best registering thermometers, I find that at Hong-kong, in the months of July and August—the two hottest months in the year—the mercury frequently stood as high as 90°, and one day at 94° Fahr. in the shade. The minimum was generally about ten degrees lower than the maximum. In the winter, from December to March, the thermometer frequently sinks nearly down to the freezing-point, and sometimes, although rarely, snow has fallen at Canton and on the adjacent hills. The influence of the sea, however, in this part of the empire, has a tendency to check the extremes of both heat and cold; but these are much greater in the northern interior. The northerly winds in the winter and spring months are severely cold in the south of China; indeed I have suffered more from cold at Hong-kong and Macao in the month of February than I have ever done in England.

At Shanghae, in the province of Keangsoo, in latitude 31° 20′ north, the extremes of heat and cold are much greater than what we experienced in the southern provinces. Through the kindness of Dr. Lockhart, who kept up my meteorological tables during my absence in different parts of the country, I have obtained a very complete set of observations for nearly two years. From these it appears that in July and August the heat is the greatest; the thermometer in the shade sometimes standing for several days at 100° of Fahrenheit. The heat during these days was almost insupportable to Europeans, who, when I was in Shanghae, were obliged to live in Chinese houses, which, from their construction, were ill calculated to exclude the heat. In the end of October the thermometer sometimes sinks as low as the freezing-point. In the evening of the 28th of that month in 1844, the remains of the cotton and other tropical plants which are cultivated in the fields during the summer were destroyed by frost. December, January, and February are the coldest months in the year, the cold then being quite as severe as it is with us in the south of England. In the winter of 1844–45 the thermometer sank as low as 26° Fahrenheit. On the night of the 18th of December, and again on January the 4th, the index was left at 24°. But that winter, according to Chinese accounts, was peculiarly mild, so much so, that the usual supply of ice could not be procured. In ordinary years the ponds and canals are frequently frozen several inches in thickness, and afford a plentiful supply of ice. I have, therefore, little doubt that in most years the thermometer may be found at least twenty degrees below the freezing-point, or at 12° of Fahrenheit, and perhaps even lower. Snow frequently falls, but the sun is too powerful to allow it to lie long on the ground.

If we except the extremes of heat and cold just noticed, the climate of Shanghae may be pronounced as fine as any in the world. Even the cold in winter is highly advantageous to the natives, and still more so to Europeans and Americans, as it strengthens their constitutions, and enables them to withstand the effects of the excessive heat. The months of April, May, and June are delightful; and although the sun is hot in the middle of the day, in the afternoon the air is soft and agreeable, and the evenings cool and pleasant. The autumnal months are generally of the same description; the wind then is cool and bracing, and the sky is much clearer than in England. The sun, for days, and sometimes for weeks together, rises in the morning, runs his course, and sets again in a clear and cloudless sky.

The prevailing winds blow from the south-west from the end of April to the middle of September; during the remaining portion of the year they are northerly and easterly: thus forming what are called the south-west and north-east monsoons. These monsoons blow with great regularity in the south of China, but are more variable towards the north. In the latitude of Chusan or Shanghae, although the monsoons prevail, the wind not unfrequently blows from other quarters. In the end of the summer season, that is, from July to October, the country is frequently visited by those dreadful gales called by foreigners typhoons. The name is a corruption of the Chinese word *Ta-fung* or "great wind." These storms commit the most fearful ravages both by land and sea. The barometer gives warning some hours before the gale commences, and, therefore, foreign ships can always send down their masts and yards, and, if possible, remove to a safe anchorage. Where that is not to be had, they have the dreadful alternative of standing out to sea. The Chinese, without the aid of the barometer, can always tell when the *Ta-fung* is coming on by the following signs. The wind, which blows from the south-west in the typhoon season, changes and blows from the north or north-east, becoming gusty and gradually increasing in strength, the sky lowers and looks wild, the sea rolls in upon the beach with a dead heavy swell, and everything portends a coming storm. When these signs appear, the fleets of fishing-boats on the coast take their nets in, crowd all sail, and make for the shore as fast as they can, where the boats are hauled up on dry land, or into some creek which is sheltered from the force of the winds and waves. The coasting junks, which are ill fitted for bad weather, lose no time in getting into some sheltered port where they can ride out the storm in safety. And, luckily, as a safeguard from the fury of these winds, nature has provided a great number of excellent well-sheltered harbours on the coast of China, all of which are well known to the pilots who are employed on board the junks.

During my residence in China I witnessed two of these terrific gales—once at sea, and once on shore.

Luckily, in the first instance, we were able to run into a deep bay, and with three anchors down rode out the gale in perfect safety. The other occurred on the 21st and 22nd of August, 1844, when I was at Ning-po. I observed the Chinese running about in great consternation, and calling to each other that the "great wind" was coming, and to make preparations for it. Mats and rattan-work, which had been placed over the doors and windows to afford shade from the sun, were hastily removed, and many of the houses, which were known to be in a weak state, were, in a rapid way, propped up and strengthened. Nor were the husbandmen less busy in the fields. The heads of the tall millet, being nearly ripe, were quickly cut, and the long stalks left to be reaped at another time. Millet is so heavy when nearly ripe, that had it been left exposed to the wind it must have been dashed to pieces, and the crop entirely lost. Crops on the sides of the rivers and canals were removed where it was possible to do so; otherwise, they would have been blown into the water, and carried away far beyond the reach of their owners. All the fruit which was nearly ripe was hastily gathered from the trees, unnecessary branches were cut away, and others tied up and supported.

The gale gradually increased in force until daylight on the morning of the 22nd, when it seemed to be at its height. In Mr. Mackenzie's house, where I was staying at the time, we passed a fearful night. The wind howled and whistled round the roof, every blast seemingly more fierce than that which preceded it, until I really thought we should have the building down upon us and be buried in the ruins. At daylight the rooms presented a dismal appearance; all the floors, chairs, and tables were covered with dust and pieces of broken tiles and mortar which had been shaken out of the roof. As the storm still raged with unabated fury, Mr. Mackenzie and myself, glad to escape from the wreck by which we were surrounded, went out to see what effect the gale was producing on the other places in the vicinity. The wind was so powerful, that it was next to impossible to keep our feet; in fact, we were frequently blown off the path, and were obliged to scramble back to it again on our hands and knees. The river, which is generally beautiful and smooth, had now risen and completely overflowed its banks, having been forced back by the strength of the wind, and was as rough as the sea itself. The whole country was one vast sheet of troubled water, for the branches of the river, and the numerous canals by which it is intersected, had all overflowed their banks, and had spread in the low paddy-fields. Most of the small boats were safe, as they were either in sheltered creeks, or drawn up beyond the reach of the water, but many of the large wood-junks which frequent this port were not so fortunate. These had been moored off the city, having, as usual, a large portion of their cargo lashed to their sides. In many instances, the combined force of the winds and waves snapped the lashings, strong as they were, and the spars of wood floated from their sides, and were either carried away by the force of the stream, or thrown on shore. Hundreds of the Chinese were now ready to seize the wood as it floated to land, and with a total disregard to the "rights of property" conveyed it at once to their own houses. No mandarin or other government officer interfered to prevent this, and the Chinese servants of the English Consul and other foreign residents actually brought a considerable quantity to the houses of their masters, and seemed surprised when reproved for their dishonesty. The English of course honourably returned the spoil to its owners, much to the surprise of the Chinese. On the opposite side of the river we observed great numbers engaged in the same lawless occupation. The city walls here run parallel with the river, and these rascals were coolly hoisting the wood over the walls and ramparts, assisted by their friends inside the city: nor was this attempted to be checked.

At about nine o'clock in the morning the wind, which commenced from the north, had veered round to the east and south, but still raged with fearful power. On retracing our steps, which we had some difficulty in doing, owing to the flooded state of the country and the force of the wind, we encountered a family group in the fields surrounding a coffin, which the wind seemed inclined to carry off in spite of all their efforts to fasten it to the ground. It is customary in this part of the country to place the remains of the dead upon the surface of the ground, sometimes supporting the coffins on short stakes, to raise them a few feet from the earth. In this instance the poor people were actually fighting with the winds, but were at last able to secure the remains of their relative, and allow him to sleep the long sleep of death in peace. At this time the barometer stood at 28° 30′, but the wind was still blowing a perfect gale until about mid-day, when it gradually became less violent. In the evening, although the sky still looked wild, it was evident the gale had passed away, and the wind was then blowing from the south-west. The river soon returned to its former limits, boats began to sail up and down, and business, which had been entirely suspended, went on again as usual. Altogether, the typhoon lasted nearly twenty-four hours.

The following morning was calm and beautiful, but the scene was one of ruin and devastation. The streets were strewed with broken tiles and mortar, many of the houses were completely unroofed, walls were blown down, and everything evinced the violence of the storm. In the fields the change was still more striking; but two days before the trees and hedges were green, the gardens were gay with flowers, and everything bore the happy smiling aspect of summer; now vegetation had changed from green to withered sickly brown, flowers had faded, trees were torn up by the roots and broken and shattered, and many of the crops were completely ruined.

The accounts which reached us from sea after this typhoon proved that the loss of life had been very great. For many days after the gale had ceased, our vessels on the coast frequently met with large portions of wreck floating about, the remains of Chinese junks, which told a fearful tale. An English vessel on her way to Chusan was obliged to cut away her masts, and was towed into the harbour a day or two afterwards by one of the government steamers. Mr. Shaw, one of her passengers, informed me that during the typhoon they had a perfect calm for some time, and that then the wind veered round to a different quarter, and blew with increased violence. This is not unfrequently the case, and during these short lulls the vessels roll and labour in a dreadful manner, owing to the heavy swell of the sea, as they are then entirely at its mercy, and have nothing to steady them.

In the preceding year this part of the country was twice visited by typhoons, viz. on the 1st of September and 1st of October. In the island of Chusan, where they were particularly violent, the most disastrous effects were produced upon the crops. The little streams in the island were swollen into large rivers, and carried away everything before them. The crops of entire fields, chiefly paddy, were in some instances swept away, and in others sanded completely up, and rendered useless. The patched-up houses of our officers, who held the island at the time, suffered severely. During the typhoon of 1844 a house built on the beach by one of the officers was actually lifting up, and would doubtless have been carried away by the force of the wind, but fortunately Brigadier Campbell, who was passing at the time, gave the alarm, and ordered out a number of men from the barracks, who held it down until it was rendered more secure.

The wet and dry seasons in the southern and tropical parts of China are more decided in their character than they are in the northern portions of the empire. At Hong-kong and in the provinces of the south the winter season, that is, from October to March, is generally dry, more particularly in November, December, and January. The most wet months in the year are those near the change of the monsoons, in May and June, and again in September, when the rains fall in torrents, probably owing to the stagnation produced in the atmosphere by the change in the direction of the winds.

In the north the rains also fall copiously at the change of the monsoons, more particularly in spring, at which time they are of the greatest utility to the crops, which are sown or planted about that time. Those parts of China, however, which are included in the temperate zone, cannot properly be said to have a wet and dry season in the same sense as these terms are generally understood in the tropics. The winter months, which are dry at Hong-kong, are far from having the same character at Shanghae, for example, where heavy and continued falls of rain and snow are of frequent occurrence. In fact, the climate of Northern China has a greater resemblance to that of the South of England or France than it has to that of the southern parts of the Chinese empire; and, although hotter, used always to remind me of the beautiful summers we have in England once in every ten or twelve years. The sky is for days and weeks together without a cloud, and in the evening a heavy dew falls and refreshes vegetation.

These remarks will assist the reader to understand more fully the theory and practice of Chinese agriculture, which form the subject of the following chapter.

CHAPTER XIV.

Chinese Agriculture — Exaggerated Statements regarding its Advancement — Soil of the Hills — Tea-Land — Soil of the Plains — Summer Crops — Rice and its Cultivation — Chinese Plough and Harrow — Number of Crops produced — Method of obtaining two Crops of Rice in Summer in the Province of Chekiang — Rice Harvest — Terrace Cultivation described — The Teinching Plant, from which the Northern Indigo is obtained — Summer Hill Crops — Cultivation of sweet Potatoes — Earth-nuts — Winter Crops — Celebrated Shan-tung Cabbage — Oil Plant — Wheat, Barley, &c. — Ripening of Winter Crops — Manures — Two Plants cultivated for this Purpose — Their Cultivation and Mode of Application — A Manure for mixing with Seeds — Its Utility — Other Manures in common Use — Manure Tanks — Night Soil and Urine — Mode of Application — Succession and Rotation of Crops.

THE *profession of agriculture in China* has been highly honoured and encouraged by the government of the country, from the earliest times down to the present day. The husbandman ranks higher here than he does in any other country in the world, and the emperor himself marks his sense of the importance of agriculture by engaging in its operations at the commencement of every season. In his character of "Son of Heaven," or mediator between the gods and his subjects, he devotes three days to solemn fasting and prayer, after which he proceeds to a field, and with his own hands holds the plough, and throws a portion of the rice-seed into the ground, thus showing the importance which government attaches to industry in the cultivation of the earth, that there may be plenty on the land to supply the wants of the teeming population.

The progress and advancement of the Chinese in agriculture as an art has been, however, greatly exaggerated by many who have adverted to this subject in their writings. The Chinese government has been always so jealous of foreigners entering the country, that those who were probably able to form a correct opinion on the subject were prevented from doing so, and were led away by the fertility of their imaginations; while, on the other hand, the Roman Catholic missionaries who travelled and resided in the interior were evidently ignorant of the art itself, as well as of the progress it had made in other countries. But it must also be borne in mind that, whilst agriculture has been advancing rapidly towards perfection amongst the nations of the western world, the Chinese in this, as with most other things, have remained stationary, and hence there must be a much greater disparity between us and them now than there was when the early writers upon China published their works. To these writers, and more particularly to those who kept on faithfully copying their works, we must attribute the erroneous opinions which have been generally held by us in everything relating to the agriculture of the Chinese. I have no doubt that, as a nation, they surpass the natives of India and other half-civilised states in this art, as they do in most other peaceful accomplishments; but it is ridiculous, now, at least, to compare them for a moment with our intelligent farmers in England or Scotland. As well might we compare their coasting junks with the navy of England, or their merchants with ours, whose ships are met with on every sea, and whose commercial operations extend to every quarter of the world. In order, however, that the reader may form an opinion for himself, I will describe in detail what passed under my own eye connected with this subject during my travels of nearly three years in the country. In that space of time I had an opportunity of seeing repeatedly the various methods of cultivation and their results, both in the north and in the south; all of which were carefully noted in my journal at the time.

I will begin with the southern provinces. These are, of course, tropical, and differ from those in the north in many respects, both with regard to soil and the nature of the plants cultivated.

The soil of the mountains in the south of China is of the poorest description. Rocks of granite are seen everywhere protruding themselves above the scanty vegetation, whilst the soil itself is composed of dry burnt clay mixed with particles of granite in a decaying or disintegrated state. This soil, naturally so poor, is kept so by the practice of periodically cutting and carrying off the long grass and stunted bushes for firewood. Sometimes the natives set fire to this upon the mountains, for the purpose of affording a scanty manure, but nevertheless the soil is miserably sterile. Almost all the hilly portions of the south of China are in a state of nature, "*stern and wild*," where the hand of man never attempts agricultural operations, and where it is almost impossible he ever can. Here and there, near the base of the hills, the far-famed terrace cultivation may be seen, where the natives grow small patches of rice and other vegetables, such as sweet potatoes and earth-nuts, but the portion of land in this part of the country used for such purposes bears but an extremely small proportion to the vast tracts in a wild state.

At Amoy, and over all that part of the province of Fokien, the mountains are even more barren than those of Quan-tung. On some of the hills on the island of Amoy the traveller may wander for miles and scarcely see even a weed. On every side there is nothing but masses of dark crumbling granite, and red burnt-looking clay. This, however, seems the northern boundary of the most barren part of China. When we reach the river Min, near Foo-chow-foo, there is a great change visible in the vegetation of the hills, caused, of course, by the richer nature of the soil. This remark applies to the northern portion of Fokien and to the whole of the province of Chekiang. I have ascended hills near the mouth of the Min at least 3000 feet above the level of the sea, which were under cultivation to the summit. The soil here was composed of a gravelly loam; and, though far from rich, it contained more vegetable matter or humus, and was also much deeper. The addition of vegetable matter rendered the soil sufficiently fertile to repay the Chinese farmer for the labour expended in bringing the crops to maturity. Some of the hills are of course much more productive than others. The tea-districts, for example, both in the province of Fokien and Chekiang, are not only more fertile, but are very different from what they are generally supposed to be. One of the most accredited accounts of China gives the following analysis of the soil of these districts:—"The tea-soil of China consists almost entirely of siliceous sand in a minute state of division—84 per cent. of sand, a quantity of carbonate of iron and alumina, *and only* 1 *per cent. of vegetable matter.*" Where or how this analysis could be obtained, I have no means of knowing—most probably from the black-tea districts near Canton; but it is certainly very far from being a correct one if meant to apply to the rich soil of the great tea districts.

But even here, and over all the most fertile mountain districts of Central China, it would be ridiculous to assert, as some have done, that the whole, or even the greater part, is under cultivation. On the contrary, by far the greater part lies in a state of nature, and has never been disturbed by the hand of man. I am anxious to state this fact in express terms, in order to set those right who have been led to believe that every inch of land in the empire, however bleak and barren, is under cultivation, having given way to Chinese industry and skill! I myself, before I visited China, was under the same impression; but the first glance at the rugged mountainous shores soon convinced me of my error. Unfortunately, our opinions of a distant unknown country are apt to go to extremes, either fancying it entirely barren, or else a paradise of fertility.

The *soil of the valleys* or plains varies quite as much

in different provinces as it does in the hills. The level of these valleys or plains is generally very low; in many instances below that of the rivers and canals. In the south the soil consists of a strong stiff clay mixed with a small portion of sand, but containing scarcely any vegetable matter or humus. This is its composition about Canton and Macao, and in fact over all the provinces of the south, unless perhaps in the vicinity of large towns, where its natural character has been altered to a certain extent by the influence of manure. Where the hills lose their barren character, four or five hundred miles to the northward from Hong-kong, a visible change takes place also in the soil of the valleys and plains. In the district of the Min, for example, instead of being almost entirely composed of strong stiff clay, it is mixed with a considerable portion of vegetable matter, and is an excellent strong loam, not unlike that which we find in some of our best wheat-lands in England and Scotland, and capable of producing excellent crops. As a general rule it may be observed that the lower the valleys are, the more the soil approaches in its nature to the stiff clay of the south, and *vice versâ*. For instance, the Shanghae district is several feet higher above the level of the rivers and canals than that of Ning-po, and the soil of the latter consists more of a stiff clay and has less vegetable matter in its composition, and is far from being so fertile as the cotton district of Shanghae.

Rice, being the chief article of food, is, of course, the staple production of the country, more particularly in the south, where two crops of it can easily be raised in the hot months, besides another crop of some more hardy vegetables in winter.

The ground is prepared in spring for the first crop of rice as soon as the winter green-crops are removed from the fields. The plough, which is commonly drawn by a buffalo or bullock, is a rude implement, but probably answers the purpose much better than ours would, which has been found to be too heavy and unmanageable for the Chinese.* As the land is always flooded with water before it is ploughed, this operation may be described as the turning up a layer of mud and water, six or eight inches deep, which lies on a solid floor of hard stiff clay. The plough never goes deeper than this mud and water, and consequently the ploughman and his bullock in wading through the field find a solid footing at this depth below the surface. The water-buffalo generally employed in the south is well adapted for this work, as he delights to wallow amongst the mud, and is often found swimming and amusing himself in the canals on the sides of the rice-fields. But it seems a most disagreeable and unhealthy operation for the poor labourer, who nevertheless goes along cheerful and happy. After the plough comes the harrow: this is chiefly used to break and pulverise the surface of the soil or to bury the manure. Hence it has not long perpendicular teeth like ours; but the labourer stands upon the top of it, and presses it down upon the muddy soil while it is drawn along. The object of both plough and harrow is not only to loosen the earth, but to mix up the whole

* Several of our ploughs have been sent out to China, and offered to the native farmers *gratis*, but they will not use them.

until it forms a puddle and its surface becomes smooth and soft. In this condition it is ready to receive the young rice-plants.

Previously to the preparation of the fields the rice-seed is sown thickly in small patches of highly-manured ground, and the young plants in these seed-beds are ready for transplanting when the fields are in a fit state to receive them. Sometimes the Chinese steep the seeds in liquid manure before they sow them; but although this practice is common in the south, it is not general throughout the empire.

The seedling-plants are carefully dug up from the bed and removed to the fields. These fields are now smooth, and overflowed with water to the depth of three inches. The plants are put in, in patches, each containing about a dozen plants, and in rows from ten to twelve inches apart each way. The operation of planting is performed with astonishing rapidity. A labourer takes a quantity of plants under his left arm, and drops them in bundles over the land about to be planted, as he knows, almost to a plant, what number will be required. These little bundles are then taken up, and the proper number of plants selected and plunged by the hand into the muddy soil. The water, when the hand is drawn up, immediately rushes into the hole, and carries with it a portion of soil to cover the roots, and the seedlings are thus planted and covered in without further trouble.

In the south the first crop is fit to cut by the end of June or the beginning of July. Before it is quite ripe another crop of seedlings is raised on the beds or corners of the fields, and is ready for transplanting as soon as the ground has been ploughed up and prepared for their reception. This second crop is ready for cutting in November.

In the latitude of Ning-po, 30° north, the summers are too short to have the land cropped in the same way in which it is done in the south. The farmers here manage to have two crops of paddy in the summer by planting the second crop two or three weeks after the first, in alternate rows. The first planting takes place about the middle of May, and the crop is reaped in the beginning of August, at which time the alternate rows are only about a foot in height, and are still quite green. After the early crop is removed the ground is stirred up and manured, and the second crop, having now plenty of light and air, advances rapidly to maturity, and is ready for the reaping-hook about the middle of November.

About one hundred miles farther north, in the Shanghae district, the summers are too short to enable the husbandman to obtain a second crop of rice, even upon the Ning-po plan, and he is therefore obliged to content himself with one. This is sown at the end of May, and reaped at the beginning of October.

A large quantity of rain always falls at the change of the north-east monsoon in May. This is of the utmost importance to the farmer, not only as regards his rice-crops, but also as to many other operations at this season of the year. We are accustomed to hear a great deal of the machine-like regularity which pervades all the operations of the Chinese; but a little investigation of the circumstances in which they are placed—at least in so far as agriculture in concerned—will convince us that their practice is regulated, not so much by caprice and those "Mede and Persian" laws, as by the laws of nature herself, upon which the success of the varied operations of agriculture mainly depends. Thus the crops of rice and cotton are sown on the low lands, and the sweet potatoes are planted on the hills, year after year, exactly at the same time. But this regularity is not the effect of prejudice, nor in obedience to the imperial orders: it is simply the result of experience, which has taught the farmer that this is the proper time for these operations, because there will then be a continuance of frequent and copious showers, which will moisten the earth and the air until such time as the young rootlets have laid hold of the soil and are capable of sending up sufficient nourishment to the stems.

During the growth of the rice, the fields are always kept flooded when water can be obtained. The terraces near the base of the hills are supplied by the mountain-streams, and the fields which are above the level of any adjoining river or canal are flooded by the celebrated water-wheel, which is in use all over the country. These machines are of three kinds. The principle in all of them is the same, the only difference being in the mode of applying the moving power; one is worked by the hand, another by the feet, and the third by an animal of some kind, generally a buffalo or bullock. The rice-lands are kept flooded in this way until the crops are nearly ripe, when the water is no longer necessary. It is also necessary, or at least advantageous, to go over

Water-wheel for Irrigation.

the ground once or twice during the summer, and stir the soil up well amongst the roots, at the same time removing any weeds which may have sprung up. If the weather is wet, the fields retain the water for a considerable time, and then it is not an uncommon sight to see the natives wading nearly up to the knees in mud and water when they are gathering in the harvest.

When ripe, the crops are cut with a small instrument not very unlike our own reaping-hook, and are generally thrashed out at once in the fields where they have grown. Sometimes, however, and more particularly in the north, the paddy is tied up in sheaves, and carried home before it is thrashed; indeed everything in the northern agriculture of the Chinese has a great resemblance to what is practised in Europe.

The *terrace cultivation* of China has been noticed by nearly all writers upon this country, and, like most other subjects, it has been either much exaggerated or undervalued. It appeared to me to be carried to the greatest perfection on the hill-sides adjacent to the river Min, near Foo-chow-foo; at least I was more struck with it there than anywhere else. On sailing up that beautiful river, these terraces look like steps on the sides of the mountains, one rising above another, until they sometimes reach six or eight hundred feet above the level of the sea. When the rice and other crops are young, these terraces are clothed in luxuriant green, and look like a collection of gardens among the rugged and barren mountains. The terrace-system is adopted by the Chinese, either for the purpose of supplying the hill-sides with water where paddy is to be grown, or to prevent the heavy rains from washing down the loose soil from the roots of other vegetables. Hence these cuttings are seen all over the sides of the hills, not exactly level like the rice-terraces, but level enough to answer the purpose of checking the rains in their descent down the mountain. For the same reason, the sweet potato and some other crops which are grown on the hills are always planted in ridges which run cross-ways, or horizontally; indeed, were the ridges made in a different direction, the heavy rains which fall in the early summer months would carry both the loose soil and crops down into the plains.

Rice is grown on the lower terrace-ground, and a stream of water is always led from some ravine and made to flow across the sides of the hills, until it reaches the highest terrace, into which it flows and floods the whole of the level space. When the water rises three or four inches in height, which is sufficiently high for the rice, it finds vent at an opening made for the purpose in the bank, through which it flows into the terrace below, which it floods in the same manner, and so on to the lowest. In this way the whole of the rice-terraces are kept continually flooded, until the stalks of the crops assume a yellow ripening hue, when, the water being no longer required, it is turned back into its natural channel, or led to a different part of the hill, for the nourishment of other crops. These mountain-streams, which abound in all parts of the hilly districts, are of the greatest importance to the farmer; and as they generally spring from a high elevation in the ravines, they can be conducted at pleasure over all the lower parts of the hills. No operation in agriculture gives him and his labourers more pleasure than leading these streams of water from one place to another and making them subservient to their purposes. In my travels in the country the inhabitants often called my attention to this branch of their operations, and I pleased them much when I expressed my admiration at the skill with which they executed it. The practice is not confined to the paddy-fields: for I remember once, when superintending the planting of some large trees and shrubs in the garden of Messrs. Dent and Co. in Hong-kong, after I had given them a large supply of water at the time they were put into the ground, I desired the gardener to repeat the dose next morning. But on the following day, when I returned to the spot, I was surprised to find a little stream divided into many branches, and meandering amongst the roots of the newly planted trees. As there was no stream there before, I went up to examine its source, and found that it had been led from a neighbouring ravine ; a work more easy than carrying a large supply of water in buckets, and at the same time more effectual.

Several other summer-crops are cultivated in the low lands. In the southern provinces, for instance, we find large quantities of the *Nelumbium speciosum* grown for its roots, which are much esteemed ; the *Trapa bicornis*, the castor-oil plant, *Scirpus tuberosus*, *Convolvulus reptans*, and several other vegetables, for which there is a great demand in all Chinese towns. The sugar-cane, also, is extensively grown both in the provinces of Quan-tung and Fokien, and probably in other parts of the empire.

In the district of Kiangsoo my attention was directed to a plant called *Tein-ching*, which is largely cultivated by the inhabitants for the sake of its blue dye. In the southern provinces a great deal of indigo (*Indigofera*) is grown and manufactured, in addition to a large quantity which is annually imported from Manila and the Straits. In the north, however, the plant which we call indigo is never met with, owing, I suppose, to the coldness of the winters; but its place is supplied by the *Tein-ching* (*Isatis indigotica*), the leaves of which are prepared in the same manner as the common indigo. The colour of the liquid at first is a kind of greenish blue, but, after being well stirred up and exposed to the air, it becomes much darker. I suppose it is thickened afterwards by evaporation ; but this part of the process did not come under my observation.

The summer productions of the hilly country are, of course, different from those of the plains. From the province of Fokien northward, to the great valley of the Yang-tse-kiang, the hills are amongst the most fertile in China. They are frequently terraced in the manner I have described, and their staple productions, if we except the rice which is grown on the lower terraces, are sweet potatoes and earth-nuts (*Arachis hypogœa*). In the southern provinces, when the winters are mild, the roots of the sweet potato frequently remain in the ground all the winter. In the north the cold is too severe, and consequently the natives are obliged to dig up and protect the roots. In April those roots which have been saved for "seed" are planted thickly in beds near the houses or in the corners of the fields. They begin to push out their young shoots immediately, and these are ready to be taken off by the beginning of May. In the mean time the ground on the hill-sides has been prepared, and horizontal ridges or drills formed about two feet apart. About the 10th or 12th of May these cuttings are taken off and planted, and seem to grow as readily as couch-grass. It is astonishing how well they succeed, considering the little care expended upon them ; but we must keep in mind that this is the commencement of the rainy season at the change of the monsoon, that the sky is generally cloudy, that scarcely a day passes without frequent showers, and that consequently the air is saturated with moisture. The earth-nuts are grown most extensively in the southern provinces, more particularly in Fokien; while the sweet potatoes are better a little farther north, where they form the chief hill crop.

The *winter crops* in the neighbourhood of Macao and Canton consist of large quantities of our European vegetables, such as potatoes, peas, onions, and cabbages, which are grown for the supply of the Europeans who reside at Hong-kong or Canton. Our potatoes are generally planted here in October, which is considered the best time to insure a good crop, but, as they always sell well in the markets, the growers manage to keep up a succession during the greater part of the year. Several varieties of the cabbage tribe, which seem indigenous to China, are grown extensively in the fields at this season both in the south and north. These never produce a solid heart like our cabbages, and are of no value when imported to England; but the celebrated "*Pak-tsae*," or white cabbage of Shan-tung and Peking, is a very different plant; it is never grown in the south of China, but is produced in the summer months in the north. Large quantities of this delicious vegetable are brought south every autumn, in the junks which sail at the commencement of the north-east monsoon in October.

In the northern provinces the principal winter productions are wheat, barley, peas, beans, the cabbage oil-plant, and various other vegetables of lesser note. These crops are grown on the hills as well as on the low lands, and on the ground which produces sweet potatoes in summer. In the Nanking district they are generally sown or planted in October upon those lands which produce rice or cotton during the summer months.

Frequently the sowing takes place before the cotton or the dry summer crops have been removed from the ground, and the young plants are seen coming up amongst these crops, and ready to take their place when they are removed. This is done in order to give a longer season for the ripening of the different crops, and is very generally practised in the northern districts. The wheat and barley ripen in Fokien in April, and in the neighbourhood of Shanghae about the middle of May. About Chinchew and Amoy the wheat-crops are so poor that the labourers pull them up by the hand, in the same manner as we do in our moorlands in England and Scotland. They are of course much better in the rich district of Shanghae, but the varieties of both wheat and barley are far inferior to ours; and as the Chinese sow them too thickly, they are generally much drawn, and the heads and corn small. The beans and peas seem to be exactly the same as our field kinds, and are certainly indigenous to the northern parts of China. Very large quantities of the cabbage tribe are cultivated for the sake of the oil which is extracted from their seeds. They are planted out in the fields in autumn, and their seeds are ripe in April and May, in time to be removed from the land before the rice-crops. It must not be supposed, however, that the whole of the land is regularly cropped in this manner, and that, as some writers inform us, it never for a moment lies idle, for such is not the case.

In the island of Chusan, and over all the rice country of Chekiang and Keangsoo, there are two plants cultivated in the winter months, almost exclusively for manure; the one is a species of *Coronilla*, the other is *Trefoil*, or clover. Large ridges, not unlike those on which gardeners grow celery, are thrown up on the wet rice-fields in the autumn, and the seeds of the plants are dropped in, in patches at five inches apart, on the surface of the ridges. In a few days germination commences, and long before the winter is past the tops of the ridges are covered with luxuriant herbage. This goes on growing until April, when it is necessary to prepare the ground for the rice. The ridges are then levelled, and the manure-plants are scattered in a fresh state over the surface of the ground. The fields are flooded, and the plough and harrow are employed to turn up and pulverise the soil. The manure thus scattered over the ground, and half-buried amongst mud and water, commences to decay immediately, and gives out a most disagreeable putrid smell. This mode of manuring is generally adopted in all the rice-lands in this part of China, and the young paddy doubtless derives strong nourishment from the ammonia given out in the decomposition of this fresh manure.

Firewood is so scarce in the country that a great portion of the straw, cotton-stalks, and grass, which would go to manure the fields, are used for firing, and therefore the plan of growing manure for the land is forced upon the farmers by necessity. The plan of using manure in a fresh state, instead of allowing it first to decay, has doubtless been found from long experience to be the best for the young paddy. The Chinese farmer is not a chemist; he knows little or nothing of vegetable physiology; but his forefathers have hit accidentally upon certain systems which are found in practice to succeed, and to these he himself adheres, and hands them down unchanged to his children.

When the first crop of rice is cut, the second, which has been planted in the alternate rows, is left to grow and ripen in the autumn; the ground is stirred up, and the stubble and part of the straw of the first crop is immediately worked up with the mud and water between the rows: this decays in the same manner as the trefoil in spring, and affords manure to the second crop. Prawns and fish of various kinds are frequently used for the same purpose and in the same way.

Burnt earth mixed with decomposed vegetable matter is another highly esteemed manure, and is common in all the agricultural districts. During the summer months all sorts of vegetable rubbish are collected in heaps by the road-sides, and mixed with straw, grass, parings of turf, &c., which are set on fire and burn slowly for several days, until all the rank vegetable matter is decomposed, and the whole reduced to a rich black earth. It is then turned over several times, when it presents the same appearance as the vegetable mould used in gardens in England. This manure is not scattered over the land, but reserved for covering the seeds, and is applied in the following manner. When the seed-time arrives, one man makes the holes, another follows and drops in the seeds, and a third puts a handful of this black earth on the top of them. Being principally vegetable matter, it keeps the seeds loose and moist during the period of germination, and afterwards affords them nourishment.

This manure is useful mechanically as well as chemically in a stiff soil, like that of the low lands of China, where the seeds are apt to be injured in the process of germination. The young crop thus planted acquires a vigour in its first growth which enables it to assimilate the matter which forms the strong stiff soil, and to strike its roots firmly into it.

What is commonly known by the name of oil-cake is broken up and used in the same manner as the vegetable earth, and is also scattered broadcast over the land. The oil-cake is the remains or refuse of the seeds of several different plants, such as the tallow-tree, various kinds of beans, and the cabbage formerly mentioned. There is a great demand for this manure in all parts of the country, and it forms a very considerable branch of trade both by sea and land. Bones, shells, old lime, soot, ashes, hair, and all kinds of rubbish, are also eagerly bought up by the farmer for the purpose of manure.

In the Fatee gardens near Canton the proprietors have a curious kind of rich mud, which they cut up into small square bits, and sell at a very high price for the growing of plants in pots. This is obtained chiefly from the ponds and lakes in the vicinity, where the *Nelumbium speciosum* grows. This soil is so much esteemed, that the price for the best kind is 1 dollar for 3 peculs,* and for the second 1 dollar for 4 peculs. The inferior sort has been frequently sent to England in plant-cases from Canton.

For crops in a vigorous growing state no kind of

* A Chinese pecul is equal to 133⅓ lbs.

manure is so eagerly sought after as night-soil; and every traveller in China has remarked the large cisterns or earthen tubs which are placed in the most conspicuous and convenient situation for the reception of this kind of manure. What would be considered an intolerable nuisance in every civilised town in Europe is here looked upon by all classes, rich and poor, with the utmost complacency; and I am convinced that nothing would astonish a Chinaman more than hearing any one complain of the stench which is continually rising from these manure-tanks. Almost every Chinese town is placed on the banks of a river or canal, and the water is generally led not only round the walls, thus forming a kind of moat, but also through many parts of the city. Long clumsy boats are placed in different departments of the town, into which the night-soil and urine are emptied and conveyed from thence into the country. The fields in the neighbourhood of cities are generally supplied with it by coolies, who go every morning to market loaded with the produce of their farms. Each brings home two buckets of this manure, slung at the ends of his bamboo pole. In England it is generally supposed that the Chinese carry the night-soil and urine to these tanks, and leave it there to undergo fermentation, before they apply it to the land. This, however, is not the case; at least, not generally. In the fertile agricultural districts in the north I have observed that the greater part of this stimulant is used in a fresh state, being of course sufficiently diluted with water before it is applied to the crops. And there can be little doubt that in this the Chinese are perfectly right, as the manure must be much more efficient in this state than when a great portion of its ammonia has passed off into the air. The Chinese, as far as I could learn, have no mode of disinfecting their manure, but they seemed to be perfectly aware that, if allowed free access to the air, a great loss must result, owing to the gases which are given out and dissipated. Without waiting, then, for fermentation or putrefaction, this manure is at once applied to the growing crops. On the afternoons, or on cloudy days, the labourers are seen carrying water from the nearest pond or canal to the manure-tank, for the purpose of diluting its contents. This being done, they fill their buckets, attaching one to each end of their bamboo in the usual way, and carry them off to their destination. When this is reached, each man takes a small wooden ladle having a long bamboo handle, and with this he scatters the liquid over the growing crop. A strong stimulant like this would probably in other circumstances have an injurious effect; but, by using it only when the crops are young and luxuriant, they assimilate its gases, and a most marked effect is produced upon their growth and productiveness. This kind of liquid manure is generally applied to wheat, barley, and all the cabbage tribe, and other garden vegetables; but not to rice, which is always flooded during its growth.

This manure is sometimes used after putrefaction and fermentation have taken place; and even in this state it is very efficient. In the gardens near Canton it is often dried and mixed with the soil taken from the bottom of the lotus-ponds, and used for growing plants in pots, or for enriching any particular tree which may be a favourite in the garden.

Although the land is sometimes allowed to lie idle for some months, yet there is no regular system of fallowing, nor is the rotation of crops much known or practised. Indeed, as regards the low lands, the soil being a kind of stiff, strong clay, capable of yielding many crops of rice in succession, without being in any way burthened or impoverished, no such mode of cultivation is necessary.

CHAPTER XV.

Return to Chusan—Its supposed Unhealthiness—Mortality amongst the Queen's Troops when first stationed there — Subsequent Salubrity — Its Advantages over Hong-kong as a British Settlement — Remarks on the Treaty with China — Ning-po — Gardens of the Mandarins — Manners of Chinese Ladies — Sail for Hong-kong — Tombs of the Chinese — Situations supposed to be the best — Soothsayers employed — Their Methods of working on the Minds of the People — Mr. Lay consulted as to the best Site for a Grave — Inscriptions on the Tombs — Periodical Visits to them by Relatives — Different Modes of Interment — Coffins exposed in the Fields — Kept in Houses — Tomb near Sung-kiang-foo — Favourite Flowers for planting on the Graves.

MY first visit to Chusan in 1843 was during the autumn and winter, but in 1844 I had an opportunity of exploring this beautiful island, at intervals, from the commencement of spring until the close of the season. At this time the first impression regarding the unhealthiness of the climate had been entirely removed, and the island was looked upon as the most healthy in the Chinese seas.

It will be recollected that, when the island was first occupied by our troops, the mortality was so great that the place was pronounced by every one to be the most unhealthy in China. Many a brave soldier fell a victim to the malignant fever which prevailed at the time. No regiment suffered more than Her Majesty's 26th, the

"Cameronians," who were encamped on a green hill which overlooked the city, and which certainly appeared to be the most healthy spot which could have been selected for the purpose. That place still bears the name of the "Cameronian Hill," and is now thickly strewed with the graves of our countrymen.

It soon became evident that this great mortality proceeded from other causes than the paddy-fields which surrounded the city of Tinghae. Invalids from Hong-kong and Amoy were sent here to recover their health; and the difference in the appearance of the troops stationed in Chusan from those in Hong-kong was most marked. Dr. Maxwell of the Madras army, who was a most excellent judge in such matters, has often expressed his opinion, that, with good medical skill and ordinary care, this beautiful island might have been rendered one of the most healthy stations for our troops in the East. Indeed, every one now seemed to regret that we had not secured Chusan as a part of the British dominions for the protection of our trade in China, instead of the barren and unhealthy island of Hong-kong; and some even went so far as to recommend that means should still be taken by our government to accomplish this desirable end. The time, however, for doing this had gone by, and I believe that every right-thinking person would have seen with regret any power exercised by a great and exalted nation like England to infringe a solemn treaty which had been entered into with a nation so utterly powerless as the Chinese; and most assuredly nothing less than this—no negotiations or promises—would have induced the Chinese to give up an island like Chusan, which commands the central and most important parts of their empire. That we committed a blunder and made a bad bargain is quite certain, but, having done so, we must abide by the consequences. Had we retained Chusan, it would not only have been a healthy place for our troops and merchants, but it would also have proved a safeguard to our trade in the north, which must ultimately become of greater importance than that at Canton. Moreover, we should have been in a central position as regards a large and important part of the world, which must sooner or later open its ports to our commerce. I allude of course to Japan and Corea, both of which are only a few days' sail from Chusan, and are still in a great measure sealed countries to Europeans. These regrets, however, are vain.*

Chusan in spring is one of the most beautiful islands in the world. It reminds the Englishman of his own

* In the event of another war taking place between England and China, it might then be a question whether or not Chusan should be retained. The propriety of this would be questionable, and could only be justified on the ground of necessity. Equally important alterations in the treaty would be—first, to insist on having an ambassador at Pekin; secondly, to allow our merchants to trade at any of the ports of the empire; and thirdly, to break down those absurd regulations regarding boundaries which are altogether unnecessary, and which only tend to give the native population a false idea of the character of foreigners. If foreigners break the laws, let them be seized by the Chinese authorities and punished, or delivered over to the nearest British consul. The latter proceeding would be necessary only in the southern districts, where the people are much prejudiced against us: in the north we have only to fear that the Chinese authorities would allow the criminals to escape altogether. These alterations would, I am convinced, place our relations with this vast empire upon a much more satisfactory basis.

native land. In the mornings the grass sparkles with dew, the air is cool and refreshing, the birds are singing in every bush, and flowers are hanging in graceful festoons from the trees and hedges.

The new plants of the island, some of which I had discovered in the preceding autumn, I now saw in flower for the first time. Early in spring the hill-sides were covered with a beautiful Daphne with lilac flowers (*Daphne Fortuni*, Lindl.); *Azalea ovata*, Lindl., certainly one of the finest and most distinct plants of this kind which I have introduced, also grows wild on the hills, and was in full bloom at this period. A fine new Buddlea (*B. Lindleyana*) had a most graceful appearance, as its long spikes of purple flowers hung in profusion from the hedges on the hill-sides, often side by side with the well-known *Glycine sinensis*. Another plant, certainly one of the most beautiful shrubs of Northern China, the *Weigela rosea*, was first discovered in the garden of a Chinese mandarin near the city of Tinghae on this island. This spring it was loaded with its noble rose-coloured flowers, and was the admiration of all who saw it, both English and Chinese. I have great pleasure in saying that all these plants, and many others, natives of Chusan, are now growing in our gardens in England.

Ning-po is about 40 miles west from Chusan, and is situated on the mainland. My visits to it at different times during this summer were attended with much less difficulty than in the preceding autumn. I was now beginning to speak a little Chinese, and was perfectly acquainted with the town, and the whole of the places where the different mandarins' gardens and nurseries were situated. The mandarins were particularly inquisitive at this time about everything which related to the movements of the English, or other foreigners who were likely to establish themselves at their port; and I soon perceived that, as we were able to keep up a conversation together in Chinese, my visits were very agreeable to them. The nurserymen, too, having found out that my money was as valuable to them as that which they received from their own countrymen, threw aside their shyness and were all anxiety to sell me any plants I wanted.

The gardens of the mandarins were extremely gay, particularly during the early months of the year: and, what was of more importance to me, contained a number of new plants of great beauty and interest. On entering one of the gardens on a fine morning in May I was struck with a mass of yellow flowers which completely covered a distant part of the wall. The colour was not a common yellow, but had something of buff in it, which gave the flowers a striking and uncommon appearance. I immediately ran up to the place, and, to my surprise and delight, found that it was a most beautiful *new double yellow climbing rose.* I have no doubt, from what I afterwards learned, that this rose is from the more northern districts of the empire, and will prove perfectly hardy in Europe. Another rose, which the Chinese call the "*five-coloured,*" was also found in one of these gardens at this time. It belongs to the section commonly called China roses in this country, but grows in a very strange and beautiful manner. Sometimes it produces self-coloured blooms—being either red or French white, and frequently having flowers of both on one plant at the same time—while at other times the flowers are striped with the two colours. This will also be as hardy as our common China rose.

We are generally led to believe that ladies of rank in this country are never seen by visitors. It is quite true that Chinese custom, in this respect, differs entirely from ours; and that the females here, like those of most half-civilised or barbarous nations, are kept in the background, and are not considered as on an equality with their husbands. For example, they do not sit at the same table; when a "sing-song" or theatrical performance is got up, they are put in a place out of view, where they can see all that is going on and yet remain unseen. But for all this they are not entirely secluded from society; at least they used frequently to honour me with their presence, and crowd round me with the greatest curiosity. At first they used to be extremely shy, and only took sly peeps at me from behind doors and through windows; by and by, however, their strong curiosity conquered their bashfulness, and then they used to stand and look on very composedly. They generally, however, kept at a little distance, and, whenever a movement was made towards where they stood, they pretended to be vastly frightened, and ran away; but they soon came back again.

During the summer which had now passed by I had had frequent opportunities of inspecting the tombs of the Chinese both in the northern and southern districts. In the south the natives form no regular cemeteries or churchyards, as we do in Europe, but the tombs of the dead are scattered all over the sides of the hills, the most pleasant situations being generally selected. The more wealthy individuals often convey their dead a considerable distance, and employ a kind of fortune-teller, whose duty it is to find out the most appropriate resting-place. This man goes with the corpse to the place appointed, and of course pretends to be very wise in the selection of the spot as well as in the choice of the soil with which the ashes of the dead are to mingle in after years; and upon trial, should the particular earth appear unsuitable, he immediately orders the procession off to some other place in the neighbourhood, where he expects to be more successful. I believe many of the Chinese have this important point settled before they die; for one day, when one of our principal merchants went to call on old Howqua, the late Hong-merchant at Canton, a tray was brought into the room with several kinds of earth upon it, which the old man examined with great care, and then fixed on the one in which he wished to be buried.

A situation on the hill-side is also considered of great importance, especially if it commands a view of a beautiful bay or lake. But I believe that of all places the one most coveted is where a winding stream, in its course, passes and then returns again to the foot of the hill where the grave is to be made. The director of the ceremonies, with a compass in his hand, settles the direction in which the body is to lie, which is another point of great importance. An intelligent Chinese with whom I was acquainted informed me that this fortune-teller of the dead is often very eloquent in his descrip-

A CHINESE

MARRIAGE PROCESSION.

tions of the future happiness of those who obey his directions: he informs them that they or their children, or some one in whom they are much interested, shall enjoy riches and honours in after life, as a reward for the attention and respect they have paid to the remains of their fathers; that, as the stream which they then behold when standing around their father's grave flows and returns again in its windings, so shall their path through life be smooth and pleasant until they sink into the tomb, hoary with years, respected, beloved, and mourned by their children.

These men are generally great rogues, and play upon the prejudices of the people. It frequently happens that after a corpse has been interred for some time they call upon the relatives, and inform them that, for some cause which they affect to explain, it is absolutely necessary to remove and re-inter it. Should the relations object to this, the answer is, "Very well, I don't care; but your children and relations will also be regardless of your remains when you die, and you will be miserable in your graves." The feelings of the poor deluded people are thus wrought upon, and a further sum of money is extracted for finding a more suitable grave.

The late Mr. Lay, during one of his rambles amongst the hills on the banks of the river Min, was present at one of these ceremonies, and the relatives of the deceased crowded round him and consulted him as to the site of the grave, under the impression that he was well versed in such matters. He remarks in his journal that "much good or much evil is thought to betide the survivors from a right or wrong position. Keangse practitioners in this '*te le*' and '*fung shwuy*,' or soothsaying from the influence of the earth's local modalities, get large moneys by the trade; but as they do not agree amongst themselves, the people are fain to ask counsel of a stranger."

In my travels in the south of China I often came upon graves in the most retired places amongst the hills; they were all more or less of the same form, namely, a half-circle cut out of the hill-side, having the body interred behind it. Sometimes, indeed generally, there were several of these half-circles with a succession of terraces in front of the grave; and in the burying-places of the more wealthy the semicircles were built of brick or stone, and on a more extensive scale. In the centre of the semicircle, and of course near the body, the grave-stone is placed with its inscription. M. Callery, an excellent Chinese scholar, informed me that these inscriptions are always of the most simple kind, merely stating the name of the deceased, that he died in such a dynasty, in such a year. This is the plain and unflattering tale which the Chinese tombstone tells. In some instances—I cannot tell if in all—after the body has decayed, the bones are dug up and carefully put into earthenware vessels, which are then placed on the hill-side above ground. These, as well as the graves, are visited at stated times by the relatives. They go first to the grave of the patriarch, or father of the tribe, and then to those of the other members of the family in rotation, where they perform their devotions, and offer incense. They afterwards dine together when the ceremonies are over.

I was once or twice in the wild mountain districts in the interior at the time when the natives visited the tombs. Even the most retired parts had their visitors, and it was both pleasing and affecting to see the little groups assembled round the graves, paying the tribute of affection to those whose memory they revered and loved. The widow was seen kneeling by the grave of her lost husband; children, often very young, shedding tears of sorrow for a father or mother; and sometimes an old man whose hair was white with age was there mourning the loss of those whom he had looked to as the support of his declining years. All were cutting the long grass and weeds which were growing round the tombs, and planting their favourite flowers to bloom and to decorate them.

Near Amoy this scattered mode of interring the dead has been departed from, and perhaps necessarily, in consequence of the large population; in the country, however, I sometimes found tombs in retired and inaccessible parts of the hills here, as well as in the more southern provinces; but these were evidently the property of the wealthy inhabitants.

As the traveller proceeds northward the circular form of the tombs is less common, and they become more varied in their appearance. In Chusan, Ning-po, and various other places in that district, a great number of the coffins are placed on the surface of the ground and merely thatched over with straw. I met with these coffins in all sorts of places,—on the sides of the public highway—on the banks of the rivers and canals—and in woods and other retired parts of the country. Sometimes the thatch was completely off, the wood rotten, and the remains of the Chinamen of former days exposed to view. On one hill-side on the island of Chusan skulls and bones are lying about in all directions, and more than once, when wandering through the long brushwood in this place, I have been entangled by getting my feet through the lid of a coffin.

Tombs on the Island of Chusan.

I believe that the wealthy in these districts generally bury their dead, and some of them build very chaste and beautiful tombs. There are three or four very fine ones in the island of Chusan, where the paving in front of the mound which contains the body is beautiful, and the carving elaborate; the whole of the stone-work is square, instead of circular as in the tombs in the south of China. Here, as at home—and I believe in every part of the world—trees of the pine tribe are generally planted in the burying-grounds. Lord Jocelyn, in his 'Campaign in China,' mentions such places in the following beautiful and appropriate language:—"Here and there, as if dropped at random upon the sides of the hills, were clumps of pine-trees, and, peeping through their thick foliage, the roofs of houses and temples diversified the scene. Amongst many of the beautiful groves of trees which here invite the wanderer to repose, spots are selected as the resting-places of mortality; and gazing on those tranquil scenes, where the sweet clematis and fragrant flowers help to decorate the last home of man, the most careless eye cannot fail to mark the beauties of the grave."

In the Shanghae district I have frequently visited large houses which seem to have been built by the rich expressly as mausoleums. In these houses I generally found a coffin in one of the principal rooms, and an altar, with all the trappings of idolatry, where incense on high days is burned to the memory of the deceased, and various other ceremonies are gone through by the relatives. These houses or temples are generally surrounded by a pine wood, and sometimes the body is buried out of doors—the altar and records only being kept in the temple, where a servant with his family is always placed to look after them.

When the English first established themselves at Shanghae, some of them had thoughts of taking houses in the country, that their families might enjoy retirement and fresh air. One day towards the end of 1843 I accompanied a gentleman of my acquaintance on an errand of this kind. When we had proceeded about six or eight miles from Shanghae we observed a good-looking house in a wood hard by, and determined to pay it a visit and see whether the occupant would be inclined to let it. As we drew near, all was still and quiet; not even our old enemies, the dogs, appeared to dispute our approach. When the Chinese—who always followed us in considerable numbers wherever we went—saw us approaching the house, they stood still at a little distance, watching our proceedings with a great degree of interest. We knocked at the door of the mansion, and then stood at one side, so that the porter might not see that his visitors were the *Hong-mou-jins*, or red-haired race, as they are pleased to call the English; for we well knew that, if we were seen, the door would not be opened. In a few seconds we heard the sounds of feet, and then a voice summoned us to know our business. We mumbled something in Chinese, and the poor man, quite unconscious of his danger, threw open the door. I shall never forget the look of mingled fear and astonishment which he gave us as we quietly walked into the court; at the same time the group of natives outside were indulging in hearty laughter at the way in which he had been entrapped.

The court-yard, where we now were, was neatly paved, and the whole of the house appeared to be in excellent repair. As we were led from room to room by our terrified guide, everything appeared quite suitable for a country residence, at least as good as one could expect in such an out-of-the-way place, and my friend remarked that it was the best he had yet seen, and that he should certainly make an effort to get possession of it. At last we came to what appeared the principal room: "Ah, this shall be my drawing-room," said my companion; "but what is that?" added he in the same breath. I looked in the direction in which he pointed, and a large massive coffin met my eye. We then discovered that we were in one of those places set apart for the remains of the dead.

During one of my journeys in the interior I met with a very curious tomb near the town of Sung-kiang-foo. It was placed on the side of a hill, in a wood, and evidently belonged to some very wealthy or important personage of that city. From the base of the hill to where the tomb stood, about halfway up, the visitor ascended by a broad flight of steps, on each side of which were placed a number of figures carved in stone. As far as I can recollect, the following was the order in which the figures were placed: first, a pair of goats or sheep, one on each side; second, two dogs; third, two cats; fourth, two horses saddled and bridled; and fifth, two most gigantic priests; the effect of the whole being most strange and imposing. There is another tomb of the same description near Ning-po, but on a much smaller scale.

The flowers which the Chinese plant on or among the tombs are simple and beautiful in their kind. No expensive camellias, moutans, or other of the finer ornaments of the garden, are chosen for this purpose.

Sometimes the conical mound of earth—when the grave is of this kind—is crowned with a large plant of fine, tall, waving grass. At Ning-po wild roses are planted, which soon spread themselves over the grave, and, when their flowers expand in spring, cover it with a sheet of pure white. At Shanghae a pretty bulbous plant, a species of *Lycoris*, covers the graves in autumn with masses of brilliant purple. When I first discovered the *Anemone Japonica*, it was in full flower amongst the graves of the natives, which are round the ramparts of Shanghae; it blooms in November, when other flowers have gone by, and is a most appropriate ornament to the last resting-places of the dead.

The poor, as well as the rich, often keep their dead in their dwelling-houses for a long time: I should imagine, from the numerous coffins which I met with in such circumstances, that many are thus kept for years. The coffins are remarkably thick and strong, and the joints so carefully cemented that no unpleasant smell is emitted during the decay of the body.

Much of the respect which is paid by the Chinese to the memory of their deceased relatives may doubtless be a mere matter of form, sanctioned and rendered necessary by the custom of ages, but I am inclined to think that a considerable portion springs from a higher and purer source, and I have no doubt that, when the Chinese periodically visit the tombs of their fathers to worship and pay respect to their memory, they indulge in the pleasing reflection that, when they themselves are no more, their graves will not be neglected or forgotten, but will also be visited by their children and grandchildren, in whose hearts and affections they will live for many, many years after their bodies have mouldered into dust.

Tomb of a Mandarin's Wife.

CHAPTER XVI.

Spring in the North of China — New Flowers — Journey through the Country — Motley Group of Fellow-Passengers — A Morning Scene in a Chinese Junk — Tartar City of Chapoo — Shops and Trade — Crowds of People — A Visit to the Mandarins — A Free Passage onward offered — Their Object in this — Means taken to thwart them — Leave Chapoo for Shanghae — Country and Town of Ping-hoo — Silk-Districts visited — Cultivation of the Mulberry — Management of the Silkworm — Arrival at Shanghae — Consul's Letter enclosing one from the Taoutae, or Head Mandarin — A most satisfactory Reply.

IT was the commencement of spring when I returned to the north of China, from Hong-kong and Manila, where I had been during the winter. In this season of the year no country can be more agreeable or healthy than this. The air is bracing, the sky generally clear, and the mornings are delightfully cool. Before long, vegetation progressed with wonderful rapidity, far surpassing anything of the kind I had ever witnessed in England. By the middle of April deciduous trees and shrubs were covered with leaves, barley was in full ear, and the oil-plant (*Brassica sinensis*) was seen forming masses of golden yellow, on the hill-sides and on the plains, where the air was perfumed with the fragrance of its blossoms.

My object during this summer was to make a complete collection of all my finest plants, for the purpose of taking them home under my own care. I lost no time, therefore, in visiting all my former acquaintances—mandarins, and nurserymen—and made my selections when the plants were in bloom.

The distance from Ning-po to Shanghae is about a hundred miles. I had completed my researches in the Ning-po district, and was very anxious to get to Shanghae as soon as possible, in order to see some Azaleas in bloom, which I was anxious to add to my collections. In another fortnight their flowers would have been all faded, and it would then have been impossible to identify the different varieties. There were two routes from Ning-po to Shanghae, one for the foreigners and the other for the natives. The *legal* road was to go across to Chusan, then garrisoned by the English, a distance of thirty or forty miles, nearly due east, and then take the chance of finding some vessel about to sail for Woosung or Shanghae. I knew that, if I took this line, in all probability I should have to wait for eight or ten days in Chusan before such an opportunity would occur, a delay which would have entirely defeated the object which I had in view. I determined, therefore, to go by the interdicted route, and take my chance of consequences.

The journey overland was a very interesting one. When I reached the town of Chinhae, at the mouth of the Ning-po river, I found that some small junks were to sail that evening for Chapoo, and I lost no time in securing a passage on board one of them. I was surprised at my success thus far, as I had anticipated my greatest if not my only difficulty would have been in making a start. I found afterwards that I was indebted for this to my Chinese servant, who happened to be a native of Chinhae and knew the captain of the junk. He persuaded him that there was no harm in my going by that route; and, at all events, that he could easily land me at Chapoo, and that nobody would know how I had come there.

In the evening, after many delays on account of wind and tide, and also with the view of securing more passengers and cargo, we lifted our anchor and set sail. In crossing the bay of Hangchow, the tide runs very rapidly, and the Chinese junks and boats never go across without a fair or leading wind. I shall never forget the strange and motley group of passengers who were my fellow-travellers in this little vessel. We were all huddled together in the centre cabin, and our beds were spread down on each side, merely leaving room for us to walk down the middle. Some of the passengers were respectable merchants, but even these had something filthy and disagreeable about them. Little insects whose names sound harsh to "ears polite" were charitably supported in great numbers amongst the warm folds of their dresses. The first thing I did when my bed was spread down was to surround it with my trunks, gun-case, and another box or two, to prevent, if possible, any visitors of this description from leaving their rightful lord and master, and taking up their quarters with me. With all my care it was next to impossible to keep myself apart from the Chinese, owing to the motion of the little vessel, which sometimes sent us rolling from one side to the other.

A great part of the night was spent by the Chinese in smoking opium and tobacco. When morning dawned, the scene which the cabin presented was a strange one. Nearly all the passengers were sound asleep. They were lying in heaps, here and there, as they had been tossed and wedged by the motion of the vessel during the night. Their features and appearance, as seen in the twilight of a summer morning, were striking to the eye of a foreigner. I almost fancied that I could read the characters of the different beings who lay stretched before me. There was the habitual opium-smoker—there was no mistaking him—his looks were pale and haggard, his breathing quick and disturbed, and so thin was he, that his cheek-bones seemed piercing the skin. Some seemed careworn with business, and others again apparently slept soundly with hearts light and joyous. All had the fore-part of their heads shaved, and their tails lay about in wild confusion.

We were now far on our way across the bay, having had a fair wind and tide during the greater part of the night, and the hills near Chapoo were already visible on the horizon to the northward. All hands were soon busily engaged in getting breakfast ready. A Chinese sea-breakfast consists chiefly of rice, fish, and vegetables. The proprietors of the junk provide food for the passengers, for which they charge a small sum from each, independent of the passage-money. If the passengers do not choose to have breakfast or dinner, they are not required to pay for it. When breakfast was ended, some began to smoke opium and others tobacco, after which most of them went to bed again and were soon fast asleep. The Chinese when travelling do little else than eat, smoke, and sleep. During the whole time I was travelling in the country I never remember seeing one Chinese engaged in reading.

About eleven in the forenoon we came to anchor in a muddy bay abreast of the city of Chapoo, where many of the junks are high and dry at low water. I had my luggage put into a small boat and rowed for the shore. "You had better take off your shoes and stockings, and draw up your trousers," said one of the Chinese boatmen as we were getting near the landing-place. The prudence and necessity of this advice were soon apparent; for when the boat touched the beach, I found that I had to walk a quarter of a mile up to the knees in mud before I could get on firm ground. Now came the critical part of my expedition. When I had got through the mud, I inquired for the nearest spring, and commenced my ablutions; making no attempt to disguise myself, as I was dressed in the common English garb. Long before I had finished washing I was surrounded by some hundreds of the natives, who seemed perfectly astonished at the sight of an Englishman, although this place had been attacked and taken during the late war. All sorts of inquiries were made regarding me; "where had I come from?" "where was I bound for?" "what were my objects?" and a hundred other questions were put to me, or to those who accompanied me. All were, however, quite civil, and did not attempt to annoy me in the slightest degree. I now walked to some hills near the city, and inspected their vegetation. On the way I visited some temples which had been battered down by our troops during the war, and which still remained in the same ruinous condition. Hundreds of people followed me to the hills, the view from which is one of the finest I ever saw in this country. Here it is that the hills of the south end, and the wide plain of the Yang-tse-kiang commences. On one side, looking towards the south and west, mountains are seen towering in all their grandeur; whilst on the northern side the eye rests on a rich and level plain, watered by its thousand canals, and dotted all over with towns and villages peopled with an immense number of industrious and happy human beings. Chapoo and the country which surrounds it may well be called the garden of China.

After inspecting the hills I went down into the Tartar city of Chapoo. The suburbs are large and populous, but the walled city itself is not very extensive. It is a square, and the circuit of the walls is not more than three miles; they seem very old, and are surrounded by a moat, which also serves the purpose of a canal. Here the Tartar troops and their families reside, living entirely apart from the Chinese inhabitants of the town.

The streets, houses, and shops are of the same kind as those which I have already described. Indeed, so like is one town in China to another, that, if a traveller well acquainted with the northern cities was set down blindfolded in one of them, he would have the greatest difficulty in saying whether it was Chapoo, Ning-po, or Shanghae. I observed in the shops a considerable quantity of Japanese goods, which are brought annually to this place by the junks which trade with Japan.

By the time I had examined all the chief objects of interest it was late in the afternoon, and I began to think of leaving the city, and taking the road for Shanghae. I had already taken measures by means of my servant to find the part of the canal from which the Shanghae boats started, and thither proceeded with the intention of engaging a boat. A numerous crowd had surrounded and accompanied me during the whole of the day; but now that I was on the eve of taking my departure it was greatly augnented. Every street, lane, window and house-top was crowded with human beings; all, however, perfectly harmless and civil. When I reached the canal and attempted to speak with one of the boatmen, the crowd pressed after me in such numbers, that the boat, had I got on board, would probably have been swamped. The poor boatmen were so frightened, that no reward which I could hold out would induce them to give me a passage. They begged and prayed me not to enter their boats, as some accident would happen from the number of persons whom nothing could prevent from crowding in after me.

I was now in a dilemma, and I scarcely knew how to get out of it. At last I determined, much against my inclination, to go to the mandarins. It is a bad plan to have anything to do with Chinese officials when it can be possibly avoided, but in this case there was no help for it; so, having inquired for the residence of the superintendent of boats, I set off to call upon him, followed, of course, by an immense mob. As we were going to his house, my servant came up to me and requested that I would not tell the mandarin that he was in my service, or that he had anything to do in bringing me there. As I could speak the language sufficiently well to make myself understood, I did not need him as an interpreter, and I was of course anxious not to bring him or his relations into any scrape on my account.

When we reached the mandarin's house, the doors were thrown open, and I walked boldly into the reception-room. It was a most difficult matter for the servants to keep out the crowd, but they accomplished the task partly by threats, and partly by whips, which they used rather more freely than we should approve of in England. This, however, is a common mode of punishing the rabble in China, and when they know they deserve it they take it very quietly.

"Tell your master I want to see him," said I to one of the attendants, who immediately went into an inner apartment and returned with the mandarin himself, clothed in his most imposing robes of office—hat, button, peacock-feather, and all. I made him several very low bows, which he most politely returned. "I am in a great hurry," said I, "to go on to Shanghae, and have been trying to engage a boat for that purpose, but cannot succeed without your assistance. Will you have the goodness to aid me?" After repeating after me what I had said, as is the invariable custom in Chinese conversation, he put the following question to me:—"How old are you?" This may seem strange, but it is considered complimentary by the Chinese, and is generally amongst the first questions they put. I thanked him for his inquiry, told him my age, and then asked his, and again proposed the question regarding the boat. Upon this he promised to send one of his servants to get one, and in the mean time invited me to take some cake and tea, which were immediately set before me. The gun which I had with me was an object of great curiosity to the old man, more particularly the locks and percussion-caps, which he told me he had never seen before. During the time I was discussing the cake and tea, he asked me a multiplicity of questions; such as—Where had I come from last?—Who had told me there was a road to Shanghae this way? &c. &c., some of which I answered, and some I found it convenient not to understand. At last, through some blunder on the part of my servant, it became known that he belonged to me; a circumstance which was immediately communicated to the mandarin, who sent for him and subjected him to a close and searching examination.

While this was going on the mandarin of the highest rank in the city arrived, having been sent for by his brother in office to hold a conference regarding me. These worthies, after a long consultation in a private room, came out and informed me, in the blandest manner, that they intended to give me a free passage across the country to Shanghae, in a boat belonging to themselves, and that, to add more to my comfort, they would send another boat to convey my servant and luggage. This seemed at first sight remarkably kind; but I had been long enough in the celestial empire to be aware of the necessity of looking narrowly into their motives, in order to counteract any evil designs they might think proper to hide under their assumed kindness and civility. In this instance their motives were perfectly plain to me, and were simply these:—According to the treaty of Nanking, if any Englishman was found beyond the boundaries which were to have been fixed at each of the five ports, he was liable to be seized by the authorities and brought to the nearest British Consul, who, in these circumstances, was obliged to impose a very heavy fine upon the transgressor; and therefore, if I had accepted their *kind* offers, I should have found, on my arrival at Shanghae, that I was a prisoner instead of a guest, and should, in all probability, have been handed over as such to the British Consul. On the other hand, if I hired my own boat, and went unaccompanied by any of the mandarin's people, I was perfectly safe, according to the strict letter of the treaty, even although a complaint were lodged against me on my arrival at Shanghae. Nothing would have been done in the matter by the British Consul unless I had been *bonâ fide* taken up beyond the boundaries, which was not likely to happen; as the Chinese officials are extremely cautious in all matters of this kind, in order to avoid getting themselves into trouble.

I immediately determined that I would not be outdone in politeness, and therefore, with many bows and reiterated thanks, I told them that I could not think of accepting so much gratuitous kindness, as I was able to pay my own expenses; and that all I required of them was simply permission to hire a small boat, with three or four men, which would enable me to get on to Shanghae. They still kept on pressing their offer upon me, which I continued as firmly to refuse. Another long private conference between them was now held, which, I suppose, ended in a determination to try what effect could be produced on my servant, who was accordingly sent for. He was desired to tell me that the distance between Chapoo and Shanghae was very great, and that the roads were infested with bands of robbers who were sure to attack us; and that they could not answer for the consequences unless another boat and some of their own soldiers went along with us for protection. "Tell them," said I, "that I have made up my mind to travel in my usual way, and that no arguments which can be used will induce me to change my opinion, and that the arms which I have shown them are quite sufficient to repel the attacks of any robbers whom I may meet on the road." As a last resource they sent an officer and his servant to me, who said that they were going to Shanghae, and would be extremely obliged if I would allow them to accompany me. I was obliged to meet even this *civil request* with a refusal; and the mandarins, finding that they must either use force or allow me to have my own way, finally gave up the contest.

A boatman now made his appearance, and announced that he was ready to proceed to Shanghae. When I rose to take my leave, I found that all the servants and retainers had been ordered out for the purpose of keeping off the crowd and seeing me safely into the boat. The two mandarins accompanied me, and we marched off to the canal in grand style. The crowd which had assembled was immense, but they were all perfectly quiet and civil. When we reached the landing-place I thanked my two friends for their kindness, and bade them adieu: then, stepping into the boat, she was pushed out into the stream, and we soon left the crowd and the Tartar city far behind us.

The country through which we passed was perfectly level, highly cultivated, and more richly wooded than any of the lowlands which I had visited before. It was getting dark when we reached a town of considerable size, named Ping-hoo, which is distant only a few miles from Chapoo, and I determined to remain there for the night. When the morning dawned I roused the Chinamen, and we proceeded on our journey. We now passed through an extensive silk-district, where the mulberry-tree was the principal object of cultivation. The natives at this time (May 18th) were busily employed in gathering the leaves and feeding the silk-worms with them.

The mulberry-trees are all grafted, and produce very fine thick leaves. I obtained a plant which is now alive in England, in order to determine the particular variety, and whether it is different from the kinds which are used for the purpose in Europe. It is not yet, however, in a sufficiently advanced state for this to be ascertained. One thing, however, is certain, that the silk produced in this district is considered as being amongst the finest in China; but whether this is owing to the particular variety of mulberry-tree used in feeding the worms, or to climate or soil, still remains to be ascertained. If the plant should prove a different species or variety from that which is cultivated in the south of Europe, it may be a matter of some importance to introduce it to the plantations of Italy, as Chinese silk is much heavier in the thread than the Italian, and is used in the manufacture of those fabrics requiring lustre and firmness.

The trees, or rather bushes, are planted in rows, the banks of the canals being a favourite situation; and they are not allowed to grow more than from four to six feet in height. The natives set to work with a pair of strong scissors, and cut all the young shoots off close by the stump; they are then either stripped of their leaves, or taken home in bundles and stripped afterwards. Before this operation takes place, the plants seem in a high state of health, producing vigorous shoots and fine large and thick shining leaves. After the leaves have been taken off, the bushes look like a collection of dead stumps, and in the middle of summer have a curious wintry appearance; but the rain, which falls copiously, and the fertility of the soil, soon revive a succulent plant like the mulberry. The Chinese seem very particular in stirring up the earth amongst the roots of the bushes immediately after the young branches and leaves have been taken off, and the plantations appear to have great attention paid to them.

The farms are small, and are generally worked by the family and relatives of the farmer; who not only plant, graft, and cultivate the mulberry, but also gather the leaves, feed the silkworms, and wind the silk off the cocoons.

During my progress through the silk-district I visited a great number of cottages where the worms were feeding. They are commonly kept in dark rooms, fitted up with shelves, placed one above another, from the ground to the roof of the house. The worms are kept and fed in round bamboo sieves, placed upon these shelves, so that any one of the sieves may be taken out and examined at pleasure. The poor natives were greatly surprised when they saw a foreigner coming amongst them, and generally supposed that I intended to rob them of their silkworms. In all the villages where I went to they uniformly denied that they had any feeding-rooms —although the leaves and stems of the mulberry about their doors told a different tale; and they never failed to direct me to go on to some other part of the country, where they assured me I should find them. Before we parted, however, they generally gained confidence, and showed me their collections of worms, as well as their mode of managing them.

After passing through the Hang-chow silk-district, and keeping on in an easterly direction, we reached, late in the evening, a large town named SUNG-KIANG-FOO, which is about 30 miles to the west of Shanghae, and stopped for the night under its ramparts. By daybreak the next morning we were again on our road, and reached Shanghae on the afternoon of the same day. Having taken up my abode in the house of my friend Mr. Mackenzie, I was surprised in going down stairs next morning to find one of my Chapoo acquaintances—the officer already mentioned—in close conversation with the Chinese servants; but I now cared very little about the matter, knowing perfectly how the business must end. There was no doubt that the whole affair had been reported to the Taoutae, or head mandarin of Shanghae, and that he would be obliged, for his own sake, to take some little notice of it.

A day or two afterwards I had the honour to receive the following letter from H. B. M. Consul, and a translation of a note which had been sent to him by the Taoutae:—

"H. B. M. Consulate,
"Shanghae, 21st May, 1845.

"Sir—The annexed translation of a note received this morning from the Taoutae is transmitted to you for an explanation, which I request may be afforded as soon as possible. I have the honour to be, Sir, yours, &c.

"G. BALFOUR,
"H. B. M. Consul for Shanghae."

The enclosed ran as follows:—

"I have just heard that a merchant of your honourable nation, Fortune, and his attendant, Linguist ye Mingchoo, were coming from Tinghae to Shanghae, and met with a breeze at sea, when the vessel drifted to Chapoo; that the local officers in Chekiang then protected and sent them on along the coast, and that they are living at the Ming-le Warehouse. I would, therefore, trouble the honourable Consul to make inquiry of what ship he is the merchant, and let me know. This is written wishing you daily happiness."

"(*True Translation.*) (Signed) W. H. MEDHURST,
"Interpreter."

When I perused this document I could not but admire

the cunning of the old man. He knew perfectly well that it did not contain one word of truth: that I was not coming from Tinghae, but from Ning-po; that I met with no breeze at sea except that which had quietly brought us to the desired port; and, lastly, that I had not been sent along the coast, but had had a very pleasant journey through the interior of the country. I saw at once that the object of the good old Taoutae was to allow me to deny the truth of his statements; and, upon the principle that no man is bound to criminate himself, I sent the following answer to Her Majesty's Consul, which was doubtless perfectly satisfactory to the Taoutae, and just what he wanted:—

"Sir—I have the honour to acknowledge the receipt of a letter from you of yesterday's date, to which is annexed a translation of a note you had received from the Taoutae of Shanghae, concerning which you request an explanation may be afforded as soon as possible. In answer to this, I beg to inform you that the circumstances noticed in the Taoutae's letter do not apply to me, and he is, therefore, mistaken, or has been misinformed. I have the honour to be, Sir, yours," &c.

I need scarcely say that I heard no more of the matter, and from this I concluded that my answer must have been considered highly satisfactory. I arrived in Shanghae in good time to transact the business I had in hand, and not a little pleased at having so successfully accomplished my "overland" journey.

CHAPTER XVII.

Sail for Foo-chow-foo on the River Min — Novel Mode of engaging a Pilot — Entrance to the River — Scenery on its Banks — Bridge of Foo-chow-foo — Chinese Chairmen — Insults received from the Natives — City and Suburbs — Native Trade — Fishing Cormorants — Bank Notes — Character of the Natives — The Ladies, and their Fondness for Flowers — Population — Remarks on Foo-chow-foo as a Place of foreign Trade — Government Spies — Deceit of the Mandarins — Leave Foo-chow-foo for the Tea-Hills — Mountain Scenery described — Black-Tea Districts — Agriculture of the District — Native Fruit.

When I had finished my business in Shanghae I left that city, and sailed for *Foo-chow-foo*, on the river Min. Foo-chow-foo is the capital of the province of Fokien, situated in 25° 30′ N. latitude, near the celebrated Bohea hills, and about half-way between Chusan and Canton. On approaching the entrance to the Min, we anchored under the lee of some islands named the White Dogs, for the purpose of procuring a fisherman who could pilot the vessel into the river, as the entrance is rather difficult for a stranger, having been until very lately but imperfectly surveyed. Going to the shore for that purpose in the ship's boat, we found a small fishing village inhabited by men and boys, most of whom had a piratical and forbidding appearance. It seems that these people only come here at certain periods of the year to fish; and when the season is past they move to more comfortable quarters on the main-land. No women are ever allowed to inhabit the island.

Having picked out the most weather-beaten man we could find, we asked him if he knew the passage to the Min, and if he could take a vessel in which drew three fathoms of water. He immediately answered in the affirmative; but when we wanted him to come on board, he altered his mind and hesitated, probably because he had not confidence in us; or, it might be, he was frightened at the consequences, not knowing how his conduct would be viewed by the authorities. Mr. Shaw, Captain Freeman, and myself, now held a conference as to what was to be done. A ship and a valuable cargo were at stake; the numerous and dangerous sand-banks near the mouth of the river were visible; and, as the man only refused us his service through fear and ignorance, we concluded that, as "necessity has no law," there could be no great harm in taking him against his will. We accordingly pulled alongside his little junk, and took him and it off to the ship, where he very soon got over all his fears.

The Chinese are certainly a strange and unaccountable race. Never in my life did I witness greater apathy than was shown by this boat's crew when we took them off to the ship. Their companions, too—for there were several boats in the little bay—scarcely even looked at us, or manifested the least surprise, when they saw our men board the boat, get her anchor up, and hoist her sail.

The next morning our pilot got the ship under weigh, and took us into the river Min by a passage not marked in our charts; he evinced the most perfect acquaintance with the depth of water at every part, and at last anchored us in safety abreast of a small temple, a few miles from the mouth of the river. Before we came to the most dangerous point, where we had to pass between two sand-banks, the captain very quietly informed him that, if he made any mistake and got the ship aground, he should have his tail cut off—a punishment very nearly the greatest which can be inflicted on a Chinaman. When told, he shrugged up his shoulders, gave a sly look, and said; "Very well, we shall see by and by." The anchorage being reached in safety, the old man thought it was now his time for a joke, and, turning triumphantly round with his tail in one of his hands, exclaimed, "Now, what about the tail? is it to be cut off or not; or are you satisfied?"

The passage by which we entered the river is called by the natives the *Woo-hoo-mun*, or "the five-tiger gate;" and here we saw a most singular rock, or island, which is cleft, as it were, into five pyramids, and is much revered by the Chinese sailor. In fact, he seems to look upon it as representing the gods of the ocean, and he fails not to offer up his thanks and his offerings every time he passes by it on returning from the sea. The Chinese are often taunted with their indifference to the religion which they profess; and yet the earnest and devout manner in which they burn incense, and worship at their holy places, would put to the blush many of the professors of a holier and purer faith.

The scenery at the mouth of the Min and towards Foo-chow-foo is striking and beautiful. The river itself varies much in width and depth, according to the district through which it flows. Near its mouth, and at some parts where the country between it and the hills is flat, it is not less than a mile in width; but at other parts, where the mountains come almost to the water's edge, the river is narrow, deep, and rapid. There are two or three such places between the mouth of the Min and the city of Foo-chow-foo. The whole of this district is hilly, many of the mountains being at least 3000 feet high; and at this season of the year, when thunder-storms were almost of daily occurrence, the effects produced by them amongst these mountains were grand and sublime.

It is evident that the Chinese greatly dreaded our visiting this place during the war. I observed that forts had been built on all the most commanding positions on the sides of the river; but most of them were now without guns, and had already become dilapidated.

The little town and fortress of *Mingan*, a few miles up the river, is beautifully situated on a hill sloping down to the water; and the position is so strong by nature, that, if manned with English troops, it could defend the pass against the strongest force.

A few miles below the city the river is blocked up, almost all the way across, with stones and old junks, which are covered at high water. I believe the *intended* plan of defence was to wreck all our vessels on this barrier, and destroy our men by batteries erected near it!

On the banks of the river are numerous temples, or joss-houses, built in the most romantic and beautiful situations. A fig-tree (*Ficus nitida*)—a kind of Banyan—is a great favourite with the priests, and is always found growing beside the temples, where its dark green leaves and wide-spreading branches afford an agreeable shade from the fierce rays of the sun. About nine miles below Foo-chow-foo a pretty little pagoda stands on an island on the left bank of the river; near this is the anchorage for large vessels which it would not be prudent to take up to the town. All the low hills are neatly terraced and cultivated with sweet potatoes and earth-nuts, and on the more fertile of the mountains cultivation is carried on at least 2500 feet above the level of the sea. But many of the mountains are quite barren; bare rocks of granite are showing themselves over their surface, from amongst which springs are almost always flowing; and when the water accumulates in the glens between the hills, it forms numerous beautiful cascades, as it tumbles down into the Min. Some parts of the region are well wooded, at least for China; and, viewing the scenery as a whole—the beautiful river, winding its way between mountains, its islands, its temples, its villages and fortresses—I think, although not the richest, it is the most romantic and beautiful part of the country which has come under my observation.

The city and suburbs of Foo-chow-foo stand in an opening amongst the hills, about twenty miles from the mouth of the Min. The river runs through the suburbs, which are connected by the celebrated bridge called the *Wan-show*, or "myriads of ages," which was always said to consist of one hundred arches. It is not an arched bridge at all; but is nevertheless a wonderful structure, being about two thousand feet in length, and having fifty strong pillars of stone, with large slabs of granite reaching from the one to the other, and forming the top of the bridge. During the rains the river rushes through these divisions with great rapidity; and as the bridge has evidently stood for many ages, it is a proof of the substantial manner in which it was originally built.

Leaving the ship at the mouth of the Min, Mr. Shaw, Captain Freeman, and myself started in a native boat to go up to the city. When we were getting into the boat, our old friend the pilot, who by this time had become quite at home amongst us, came and begged us to give him a passage as far up as the first town we were to pass on our way. We inquired why he did not go back again to his fishing at the White Dog island. His reply was, "I should get robbed by pirates of all the money you have given me for pilotage. I must first make sure of it by depositing it in the hands of a friend of mine in the town; after that is done I shall return to the island."

We were nearly two days in getting up to the city, owing to the rapidity of the stream, caused by the late heavy rains. We landed near the bridge already noticed, and immediately inquired for the house of the English Consul, who, we were informed, lived in a temple situated within the city, and about three miles from the landing-place. As nearly the whole of the streets in the suburbs were under water at the time, in some parts to the depth of four feet, it was impossible to walk this distance; nor was it necessary to make the attempt, for chairmen surrounded us in great numbers, and were as determined on putting us into their chairs as a London conductor is to have passengers for his omnibus. We willingly yielded to their solicitations, and got into chairs and set off for the consular residence. The people here had seen but few foreigners, and were particularly impertinent and annoying. Hundreds followed us and crowded round the chairs; "Quang-yanga, quang-yanga,"—their term for foreigners—was rung in our ears from all sides, and frequently other appellations of a much worse signification. Our Chinese servants, who walked by our side, were attacked and reviled for having any connection with us. In one of the streets the water was so deep that I was obliged to stand up on the seat of the chair, and even then it reached my feet. Here the crowd became very abusive, and commenced throwing water over us. At first our servants bore this treatment pretty well; but their patience was at last exhausted, and they turned upon the assailants. The scene was now both amusing and disagreeable. Luckily I happened to be a little in advance, and was therefore pretty well out of the mêlée; but Captain Freeman came in for his full share of it, and was completely soaked through. When we got within the city walls we were not molested further, owing, I suppose, to the greater strength of the police.

The city is walled and fortified upon the same plan as Ning-po and Shanghae, and is at least eight or nine miles in circumference. At various points on the walls, as well as above the gates, guard-houses are erected, each containing guns; some of which, according to the writings on them, were cast about the commencement of the last war. A small area between the south and north gates is not built upon; but the greater part of the space within the walls is densely covered with houses. There are two rather handsome pagodas, and some small hills on which temples are built, and where a good view of the town and suburbs may be obtained. On one of these hills the British Consul has his residence.

The streets in all Chinese cities have much the same appearance: some are a little wider than others, and have better and more attractive shops; but by far the greater part of them are narrow and dirty, and Foo-chow-foo certainly forms no exception to the general rule. A large trade appears to be carried on here in copper, judging from the number of shops filled with manufactured articles of that metal, particularly of gongs, of which I observed an immense number of all sizes. This copper is brought here principally in junks from Loo-choo. They also bring a considerable quantity of gold. Both metals are said to be originally the exports of Japan. I went on board two of these junks at the mouth of the Min, which were bound to Loo-choo, and were loaded with tea-oil, which they told me they had taken in exchange for their copper. A great quantity of iron is manufactured here, and wire-drawing is carried on extensively. The great export trade of the port, however, is in wood, which is floated down the Min in large quantities, and covers many acres in the suburbs near the river-side. Hundreds of junks from

Amoy, Ning-po, Chapoo, and some even from as far north as the province of Shan-tung and the bay of Pee-che-lee, are constantly employed in this trade. The wood is chiefly a sort of common pine, employed in the building of houses, and it is generally cut into lengths suited to that purpose before it is shipped. Good planks of fine hard wood can also be had in any quantity at this place. The wood-junks are loaded with great skill, a great part of their cargo being lashed to their sides, thus making them about three times their ordinary width.

Banking is carried on to a greater extent in Foo-chow-foo than in the other towns which I have visited. Paper notes are a common medium of exchange, in which the people have the greatest confidence, preferring them to dollars or "cash." Some of the notes are as low as four hundred cash—about eighteen pence English money; others are for very large sums.

The people here are generally much cleaner in their habits, and appear to be a more active race, than those in the northern towns. In fact, they approach more nearly to the natives of Canton than to any other in these respects. I was much surprised to find them consuming beef, and even milk, in considerable quantities; articles which are never used by the inhabitants of the other districts where I have been: indeed, everywhere else the Chinese were wont to express their astonishment when they saw the English using such articles of food.

The ladies of Foo-chow-foo are particularly fond of flowers—artificial as well as natural—for the decoration of their hair. The rustic cottage beauty employs the more large and gaudy, such as the red Hibiscus; while the refined damsels prefer the jasmine, tuberose, and others of that description: artificial flowers, however, are more in use than natural ones.

The population of Foo-chow-foo has been estimated at about half a million; and I have no doubt that, if the suburbs and numerous villages in the vicinity be taken into account, the number is not over-stated. Up to the time when I left China, little or nothing had been done here in the way of trade, and I cannot help thinking that its advantages in this respect have been greatly over-rated. It is never likely to be a place of as great importance to England as the more northerly port of Shanghae; and for this very simple reason—the physical nature of the country is against it. The whole of the surrounding region is mountainous; the rivers are rapid and in some places shallow, and are often liable to rain-floods. There are consequently many impediments in the way of a free transmission of goods into the interior of the country. Foo-chow-foo was supposed to possess great advantages, owing to its being near the Bohea or black-tea district; and it was thought at one time that it might form the great emporium for the export of this article to Europe and America. This opinion, however, has hitherto proved fallacious, and I believe it is now ascertained that the black teas can be brought more readily to Shanghae or Ning-po than to Foo-chow-foo.

In addition to all these disadvantages the natives seem a lawless and turbulent race, having all the characteristics of those in the Canton province, and, like them, being inveterate in their hatred of foreigners, and full of conceit as to their own importance and power. Several very serious disturbances have taken place at the port since it was opened to the British.

After paying our visit to the English Consul we returned to the suburbs to look out for a house where we could put up during our stay. When we got back to the river we found all our luggage and servants already safely lodged in the house of a person who had been ordered by the mandarins to lodge us and look after us. We were glad to get in-doors from the insulting crowd, and were consequently not very particular as to quarters. We soon found, however, that we were very strictly watched, and that we could not move anywhere without the fact being communicated to the mandarins.

The valley of the Min was still flooded in many parts, and travelling over it was a very serious matter. One morning I started for a place at a considerable distance in the country, accompanied by a guide and a coolie. I took the eoolie that he might carry me over those low flats which were known to be still flooded. We got on pretty well for some time; but the tide beginning to rise, I soon found that I must either retrace my steps or make up my mind to disregard the water, as the whole of the paths in our route were flooded. Unwilling to return, I went on, often wading up to my middle; the same thing occurred during several successive days, and this under a burning sun, with a temperature of at least 95° Fahr. in the shade. Few constitutions could stand this with impunity; and I suffered severely for it afterwards.

I was now anxious to proceed further into the country, particularly into the hilly black-tea district; but the mandarins, who were informed of all my movements by their spies, did everything in their power to dissuade me from making the attempt. They told the consul that their only reason for wishing to prevent my going into the interior was, that the natives were in a state which made it unsafe for a foreigner to trust himself amongst them; that by and by they would communicate with the magistrates in the district to which I wanted to go, and that after this was done I might proceed with safety. But I had had too much to do with the Chinese authorities in various parts of the country to place any reliance in what they said, more particularly when I knew that they had some end to gain. In the present instance their object was to procrastinate matters from day to day until I should be obliged to leave the district. When the Chinese have an end to gain, the only question with them is, whether they are most likely to succeed by telling the truth or telling lies; either method is resorted to as may best suit their purpose, with a slight preference, perhaps, for the latter.

When they found that, notwithstanding all their descriptions of the fierce and hostile disposition of the people, I was still determined to go, they declared that no tea was grown in this district; being fully persuaded that an Englishman could have no other object in exploring the country than to see the cultivation of his favourite beverage. Indeed, every Chinaman firmly believes we could not continue to exist as a nation were it not for the productions of the celestial empire. It has been stated that his celestial majesty the Emperor, himself, during the war recommended his subjects to use every means in their power to prevent the English from getting tea and rhubarb—the one being what they lived upon, and the other their medicine; without which, his majesty said, they could not continue to exist for any length of time; and consequently would be more easily conquered in this way than by the sword.

I told the mandarins that I did not care whether there were tea-farms on these hills or not; but that, to cut the matter short, I was determined to go and see.

Accordingly, on the following morning I started early, taking the road for the tea-hills. The flat country through which I passed, between the north side of the city and the mountains, is chiefly cultivated with rice, sugar-cane, ginger, and tobacco. On the sides of the little hills, and also for a considerable distance up the loftier ranges, large quantities of sweet potatoes and earth-nuts are grown during the summer season; but as we ascend, the mountains become more rugged, cultivation ceases, and plants indigenous to the country alone show themselves.

After toiling up one of the celebrated mountain passes, which is paved all the way, and has a house of refreshment about half way up, I reached the summit of the mountain—the highest land in this part of China. A glorious prospect was spread before me: the valley of the Min stretching far across to the other hills; the city of Foo-chow-foo, with its pagodas, temples, and watch-towers, standing in the centre of the plain; and the broad river winding smoothly along in its course to the sea; mountain towering above mountain, and the whole striking the mind with wonder and admiration.

Among these mountains, and at a height of 2000 and 3000 feet above the level of the sea, I found the black-tea district, which I was anxious to see, and the existence of which had been denied by my *affectionate* friends the mandarins. Having been in several green-tea countries further north, I was desirous to ascertain clearly whether the plant was the same species in both places, or whether, as generally believed, they were different. I was now fortunate enough not only to find an extensive tea-district, but also to be present when the natives were picking and preparing the leaves; and I not only procured specimens for my herbarium, but also a living plant, which I afterwards took to the green-tea hills of the north, and found, on minute comparison, that it was identical with the *Thea viridis.* In other words, the black and green teas which generally come to England from the northern provinces of China are made from the same species, and the difference of colour, flavour, &c., is solely the result of the different modes of preparation.

The natives amongst these hills were much surprised at the sight of a foreigner, and came crowding from all quarters to see me; they were, however, much more civil and respectful than their countrymen in the lowlands and at Foo-chow-foo.

On my return from this excursion I devoted most of my time to the examination of nurseries in the vicinity of the city. They contained some interesting plants. The celebrated *Fingered-Citron*, so common in the shops throughout China, seems to be cultivated in great perfection in this part of the country; in fact, it appears to be its natural locality. The district round Foo-chow-foo seems to be the great Camellia garden of China, and in no other part of the country did I ever see these plants in such perfect health, or so beautifully cultivated. The *Ixoras* and *Hydrangeas* are also particularly well grown and handsome, the latter invariably producing flowers of the deepest blue, much deeper than I have ever seen them in England. They are grown in a fine rich loam, which contains some chemical ingredient which is the cause of their deep colour.

Here, as well as further north, the farmer grows crops of wheat and green vegetables during the winter months. A great part of the low country, at least all that is capable of being flooded, is cultivated with rice during the summer and autumn. The first crop is ripe in July, and the second is planted between the rows of the former, in the same manner as in the northern provinces, and ripens in the autumn. Large quantities of tobacco are grown in the province. The farmers cultivate this plant with very great care, and take every means to have the leaves large and fine. For this purpose all the flowers are regularly picked off, and also all the small and useless leaves as soon as they are formed. Sugar and ginger are likewise grown to a greater extent in this part of China than in any other with which I am acquainted; and crops of sweet potatoes and earth-nuts abound on the sides of the hills.

Amongst fruits, the plums are good, but inferior to those we have in England; the peaches are curiously formed, but worthless. What may be more properly called Chinese fruits, such as leechees, longans, and wangpees, are, however, excellent, the climate suiting them admirably. When I was here (in July) the leechee-trees were covered with their fine red fruit, and were very beautiful, the fruit contrasted so well with the deep clear green foliage. Large quantities of oranges, citrons, and pumeloes are also found in the district of the Min; but none of them were ripe at this season. I saw for the first time the tree commonly called the Chinese olive, from the resemblance its fruit bears to the olive of Europe; also the Chinese date, which produces a fruit not unlike the date imported into England.

In the fields in the vicinity of Foo-chow-foo large quantities of the sweet-scented *Jasminum Sambac* are cultivated. It is used to decorate the hair of the ladies, and to garnish the tables of the wealthy. I believe that all the gardens, both in the north and south, are supplied with this favourite flower from the province of Fokien. Various other shrubs, such as *Murraya exotica*, *Aglaia odorata*, and *Chloranthus inconspicuus*, are grown for their blossoms, which are used for mixing with the tea.

During my stay here I received a great deal of kindness from Mr. Walker, of H. M. Consulate. The natives continued to the last troublesome and annoying; and I was very glad when my labours in the district were ended.

Pagoda Island, on the River Min.

CHAPTER XVIII.

Engage a Passage in a Junk — Leave the District of the Min — An Attack of Fever — Religious Ceremonies on board the Junk — Attacked by Pirates — Scene on board — Cowardice of the Chinese — Pirates beat off — Gratitude of the Crew — A safe Anchorage! — Another Fleet of Pirates — Attack and Results — Arrive at Chusan — Ingratitude of the Crew — Mode of making them keep their word — Kindness of foreign Residents at Shanghae — Large Peaches — Collections packed — Leave the North of China — Sail for England — Arrival in the Thames — Conclusion.

AT the time when I visited *Foo-chow-foo*, although it was open to the English as a place of trade and had a British consul, it was little known in a mercantile point of view. The entrance to the river Min was described as extremely difficult and dangerous, and consequently few foreign vessels ventured to touch at this port. When, therefore, my botanical researches were completed, and I was ready to return north to Shanghae, I was obliged to apply for a passage in a Chinese junk, a whole fleet of which were to sail in few days for Ning-po and Chapoo. Knowing the dislike and jealousy which most of the natives manifest towards foreigners, I had some doubt whether I should be able to induce them to take me as a passenger, and, in that event, I had determined to go down to the mouth of the river, and "*sans cérémonie,*" get on board whether they consented or not. I was therefore agreeably surprised when, on sending my servant to make inquiries as to the time when they were likely to sail, he returned bringing with him the captain and some of the sailors, who were all not only willing but most anxious that I should go with them.

The principal part of the cargo carried by the Ning-po and Chapoo junks is wood. This is stowed on deck, and also lashed firmly to the gunwales and sides with large ropes of bamboo which are of great strength. Several hundreds of these vessels may be seen loading at the port of Foo-chow-foo, particularly in the summer season, when the monsoon is fair for their voyage home. The mandarins are extremely jealous of so large a fleet, and will not allow them to carry guns, even for their own defence; evidently fearing that some day or other these might be turned against the government. The consequence of this regulation is, that these poor sailors, and all they possess on board, often fall an easy prey to the pirates who abound all along this coast.

When the cargo was completed the captain of the junk came to inform me that he was ready to start, and requested me to come on board. Whilst I was packing up my luggage, he began to examine my fire-arms very minutely, and said to me, "I hope your gun is a good one, and that you have plenty of powder and shot?" "What is your reason for putting this question?" said I: "I am sure we shall have nothing to shoot in our voyage up the coast." "Oh yes, you will," answered he; "we are very likely to be attacked by the *Jan-dous* who swarm outside amongst the islands." "Who are the *Jan-dous ?"* said I to my servant, never having heard the name before. "Oh! they are pirates," said he, "and we are all very much frightened at them." "Nonsense!" I exclaimed: "no pirates will attack us." At this time I had no idea that the coast was so infested with these lawless characters, and I put it all down to the cowardice of my informants.

As soon as I got on board we hove up the anchor and dropped down to the mouth of the Min. We here found a large fleet of junks—about one hundred and seventy sail—all like ourselves loaded with wood and ready to start for the northern parts of Ning-po and Chapoo. That evening a meeting of the captains was held on board of our vessel, and a deputation appointed to wait upon the mandarins to request them to send a convoy of war-junks to protect the fleet from the pirates. These negotiations were carried on for several days; but the demands of the mandarins were so exorbitant, that the junk people would not comply with them, and it was at last determined to sail without the convoy. Just as they came to this decision the wind changed and blew a gale from the north for three days, when it veered round to the south, and blew nearly as strong from that quarter, and for the same space of time. These vessels never go to sea in stormy weather, even if the wind is fair; and what with gales of wind and negotiations with mandarins, I was obliged to content myself with a junk life for a fortnight at the mouth of the river.

As long as I enjoyed health I got on well enough; but the exposure during the past summer, particularly at Foo-chow-foo, had gradually undermined my constitution; and the fever, which was probably kept off for a certain time by bodily exertion, now seized me, and compelled me to take to my cot, where I lay for a number of days insensible at intervals. At times, when consciousness returned, I certainly thought that my travels were drawing to a close, and that my grave would be a lonely one on the banks of the Min. It seemed hard for me to die in a land of strangers, without a friend or countryman to close my eyes, or follow me to my last resting-place.

The wind having been fair for several days, and the weather appearing settled, the captain of the junk came down to the place where I lay, and told me they intended to sail on the following morning. He again inquired if I had my gun and pistols in proper order and plenty of powder and ball. Still imagining that they were exaggerating the dangers of the voyage, I laughed and said, "Do not be afraid; I have everything in order, and I will undertake to beat off any pirates who may attack us;" nevertheless I clearly saw that both captain and sailors were really uneasy about the voyage, and would have been very glad of another gale to afford a pretext for deferring it a little longer. They had, however, no further excuse for delay, and it was settled that the whole fleet should sail early the next day.

The Chinese sailor never goes to sea without first presenting an offering to the gods, to propitiate them, in order that the voyage may be a speedy and successful one. Accordingly, on this day the cabin of our junk was set in order, and the tables covered with dishes of pork, mutton, fruits, and vegetables. Candles and incense were burned upon the tables for a short time, and the whole business had something solemn and imposing about it. The cook, who seemed to be the high priest, conducted all the ceremonies. On other days, as well as this, it was part of his duty to light the candles in the little temple where the gods were kept, as well as to burn incense and prostrate himself before them.

Early on the following morning the whole fleet was in motion, starting all at the same time, for the sake of mutual protection. The wind and tide were both fair, and we proceeded along the coast with great rapidity, and were soon out of sight of the Min and its beautiful and romantic scenery. The plan of mutual protection soon seemed to be abandoned, and the vessels separated into threes and fours, each getting on as well and as fast as it could. About four o'clock in the afternoon, and when we were some fifty or sixty miles from the Min, the captain and pilot came hurriedly down to my cabin and informed me that they saw a number of *Jan-dous* right ahead lying in wait for us. I ridiculed the idea, and told them that they imagined every junk they saw to be a pirate; but they still maintained that they were so, and I therefore considered it prudent to be prepared for the worst. I got out of bed, ill and feverish as I was, and carefully examined my fire-arms, clearing the nipples of my gun and pistols and putting on fresh caps. I also rammed down a ball upon the top of each charge of shot in my gun, put a pistol in each side pocket, and patiently waited for the result. By the aid of a small pocket telescope, I could see as the nearest junk approached that her deck was crowded with men;

I then had no longer any doubts regarding her intentions. The pilot, an intelligent old man, now came up to me, and said that he thought resistance was of no use; I might manage to beat off one junk, or even two, but that I had no chance with five of them. Being at that time in no mood to take advice or be dictated to by any one, I ordered him off to look after his own duty. I knew perfectly well that, if we were taken by the pirates, I had not the slightest chance of escape; for the first thing they would do would be to knock me on the head and throw me overboard, as they would deem it dangerous to themselves were I to get away. At the same time I must confess I had little hopes of being able to beat off such a number, and devoutly wished myself anywhere rather than where I was.

The scene around me was a strange one. The captain, pilot, and one or two native passengers were taking up the boards of the cabin-floor, and putting their money and other valuables out of sight amongst the ballast. The common sailors, too, had their copper cash or "*tsien*" to hide; and the whole place was in a state of bustle and confusion. When all their more valuable property was hidden, they began to make some preparations for defence. Baskets of small stones were brought up from the hold, and emptied out on the most convenient parts of the deck, and were intended to be used instead of fire-arms when the pirates came to close quarters. This is a common mode of defence in various parts of China, and is effectual enough when the enemy has only similar weapons to bring against them; but on the coast of Fokien, where we were now, all the pirate junks carried guns, and consequently a whole deck-load of stones could be of very little use against them.

During the general bustle I missed my own servant for a short time. When he returned to me he had made such a change in his appearance that I did not recognise him. He was literally clothed in rags which he had borrowed from the sailors, all of whom had also put on their very worst clothes. When I asked him the reason of this change in his outward man, he told me that the pirates only made those persons prisoners who had money and were likely to pay handsomely for their ransom; and that they would not think it worth their while to lay hold of a man in rags.

I was surrounded by several of the crew, who might well be called "Job's comforters," some suggesting one thing, and some another; and many proposed that we should bring the junk round and run back to the Min. The nearest pirate was now within 200 or 300 yards of us, and, putting her helm down, gave us a broadside from her guns. All was now dismay and consternation on board our junk, and every man ran below except two who were at the helm. I expected every moment that these also would leave their post; and then we should have been an easy prey to the pirates. "My gun is nearer you than those of the *Jan-dous*," said I to the two men; "and if you move from the helm, depend upon it I will shoot you." The poor fellows looked very uncomfortable, but I suppose thought they had better stand the fire of the pirates than mine, and kept at their post. Large boards, heaps of old clothes, mats, and things of that sort which were at hand, were thrown up to protect us from the shot; and as we had every stitch of sail set, and a fair wind, we were going through the water at the rate of seven or eight miles an hour.

The shot from the pirates fell considerably short of us, and I was therefore enabled to form an opinion of the range and power of their guns, which was of some use to me. Assistance from our cowardly crew was quite out of the question, for there was not a man amongst them brave enough to use the stones which had been brought on deck; and which perhaps might have been of some little use when the pirates came nearer. The fair wind and all the press of sail which we had crowded on the junk proved of no use; for our pursuers, who had much faster sailing vessels, were gaining rapidly upon us. Again the nearest pirate fired upon us. The shot this time fell just under our stern. I still remained quiet, as I had determined not to fire a single shot until I was quite certain my gun would take effect. The third shot which followed this came whizzing over our heads and through the sails, without, however, wounding either the men at the helm or myself.

The pirates now seemed quite sure of their prize, and came down upon us hooting and yelling like demons, at the same time loading their guns, and evidently determined not to spare their shot. This was a moment of intense interest. The plan which I had formed from the first was now about to be put to the proof; and if the pirates were not the cowards which I believed them to be, nothing could save us from falling into their hands. Their fearful yells seem to be ringing in my ears even now, after this lapse of time, and when I am on the other side of the globe.

The nearest junk was now within thirty yards of ours; their guns were now loaded, and I knew that the next discharge would completely rake our decks. "Now," said I to our helmsmen, "keep your eye fixed on me, and the moment you see me fall flat on the deck you must do the same, or you will be shot." I knew that the pirate, who was now on our stern, could not bring his guns to bear upon us without putting his helm down and bringing his gangway at right angles with our stern, as his guns were fired from the gangway. I therefore kept a sharp eye upon his helmsman, and the moment I saw him putting the helm down I ordered our steersmen to fall flat on their faces behind some wood, and at the same moment did so myself. We had scarcely done so when bang, bang, went their guns, and the shot came whizzing close over us, splintering the wood about us in all directions. Fortunately, none of us were struck. "Now, mandarin, now, they are quite close enough," cried out my companions, who did not wish to have another broadside like the last. I, being of the same opinion, raised myself above the high stern of our junk; and while the pirates were not more than twenty yards from us, hooting and yelling, I returned their fire, with shot and ball from my double-barrelled gun.

Had a thunderbolt fallen amongst them they could not have been more surprised; doubtless many were wounded, and probably some killed. At all events, the whole of the crew, not fewer than forty or fifty men, who a moment before crowded the deck, disappeared in a marvellous manner; sheltering themselves behind the bulwarks, or lying flat on their faces. They were so completely taken by surprise, that their junk was left without a helmsman, her sails flapped in the wind; and as we were still carrying all sail and keeping on our right course, they were soon left a considerable way astern.

Another was now bearing down upon us as boldly as his companion had done, and commenced firing in the same manner. Having been so successful with the first, I determined to follow the same plan with this one, and to pay no attention to his firing until he should come to close quarters. The plot now began to thicken; for the first junk had gathered way again and was following in our wake, although keeping at a respectful distance, and three others, although still farther distant, were making for the scene of action as fast as they could. In the mean time, the second was almost alongside, and continued raking our decks in a deadly manner with their guns. Watching their helm as before, we sheltered ourselves as well as we could; at the same time my poor fellows who were steering kept begging and praying that I would fire into our pursuers as soon as possible, or we should be all killed. As soon as they came within twenty or thirty yards of us I gave them the contents of both barrels as before. This time the helmsman fell, and doubtless several others were wounded. In a minute or two I could see nothing but boards and shields, which were held up by the pirates to protect themselves from my firing; their junk went up into the wind for want of a helmsman, and was soon left some distance behind us.

While I was watching this vessel our men called out to me that there was another close on our lee-bow, which I had not observed on account of our main-sail. Luckily, however, it proved to be a Ning-po wood-junk like ourselves, which the pirates had taken a short time before, but which, although manned by these rascals, could do us no harm, having no guns. The poor Ning-po crew, whom I could plainly see on board, seemed to be very much down-hearted and frightened. I was afterwards informed that, when a junk is captured, all the principal people, such as the captain, pilot, and passengers, are taken out of her, and a number of the pirates go on board and take her into some of their dens amongst the islands, and keep her there until a heavy ransom is paid, both for the junk and the people. Sometimes, when a ransom cannot be obtained, the masts and spars and everything else which is of any value are taken out of her and she is set on fire.

Two other piratical junks which had been following in our wake for some time, when they saw what had happened, would not venture any nearer; and at last, much to my satisfaction, the whole set of them bore away.

Now was the time for my heroical companions to come from their hiding-place, which they did with great alacrity, hooting and yelling as the pirates had done before, and in derision calling on them to come back and renew the fight. The stones, too, were now boldly seized and thrown after the retreating junks, reaching to almost a tenth part of the distance, and a stranger who had not seen these gentry before would have supposed them very brave indeed. Fortunately the pirates did not think proper to accept the challenge.

With the captain, pilot, crew, and passengers, I was now one of the greatest and best of men. They actually came and knelt before me, as to some superior being, and expressed their deep and lasting gratitude, which, however, did not last long. The sun was now setting in all his glory behind the hills of Fokien, and many of the more devout amongst the passengers and crew did not fail to bow low in adoration and thankfulness to this supposed deity for their escape out of the hands of the pirates. Shortly after nightfall we arrived at one of the safe anchorages, where the mandarins are too strong for the lawless bands which infest the other parts of the coast.

On the following morning we again got under way, and proceeded the whole day without molestation. In the evening we arrived at another safe anchorage, or place of rendezvous; but the security at this place consisted in the number and strength of the junks actually at anchor there, and not in the fear which the pirates entertained for the government. When we reached this place the night was fine, and, as it was nearly full moon, it was almost as light as day. The tide too was just turning in our favour; and as I was most anxious to proceed on our voyage, I did everything in my power to induce them to go on. It was of no use, however; for as soon as we reached the anchorage, and found a large fleet of junks, the anchor was dropped and they determined to stay there all night. I felt very much annoyed, but saw it was no use to grumble, and went quietly to bed. In less than an hour from this time, and before I had fallen asleep, hearing a stir upon deck, I inquired what was the cause, and found that we were getting under way. This was agreeable news; but as I could not imagine what had caused them to change their minds so soon, I went upon deck to see what was going on. Our people, it appeared, had gone to sleep the moment our anchor was down; shortly after this, the other junks, which, it turned out, were only waiting for the rise of the tide to enter some river in the vicinity, had all weighed anchor and gone off. All on board were now in great consternation, lest the pirates should come down upon us whilst at anchor, and no time was lost in getting it up and proceeding on our voyage, much, of course, to my satisfaction.

On the following day, late in the afternoon, when I was laid up in my bed with fever, the captain came hurriedly down, and informed me that another fleet of pirates were in sight, and evidently lying in wait for us. I was obliged to get up, ill as I was, and when I got on deck I could see by the aid of my telescope six junks coming out from amongst the islands under the main land, and evidently bearing down towards us. This time I was not so sceptical as the last. After having once seen these rascally vessels, there was no mistaking others of the same class, as they came sneaking out of the bays. Their clipper-built hulls, the cut of their sails, their raking masts, and the crowd of fellows who lined their decks, all told the business they were after. It was therefore evident that we must prepare for another encounter.

It now struck me that perhaps I might be able to deceive the pirates with regard to our strength, as I was afraid that I might not again be so successful with them, particularly if they found out that there was only one foreigner on board: knowing that they have a great dread of foreigners and their guns, my object was to make them believe that there were a number of us, and that we were well armed. For this purpose I got up all the spare clothes I had, and put them on the least Chinese-looking Chinamen on board. At the same time I desired them to collect all the short levers which they use for hoisting their sails, and which at a distance would look not unlike fire-arms, particularly if the deception was assisted by the report of a double-barrelled gun. Everything looked promising, and I thought my recruits were likely to be of some service to me; but when the nearest pirate, who had been coming fast down upon us, gave us a broadside, it was too much for my Chinamen, who were instantly panic-struck, threw down their *arms*, and ran below; and added to this I had again to threaten the men at the helm, who seemed half inclined to follow the example of the others.

The pirates came on, firing at intervals as the others had done, and I followed my former plan of watching their movements until they were near enough for my gun to tell upon them with fearful precision. Their shot was now flying about our ears and riddling our sails, and they came on in their usual noisy manner, perfectly unconscious of what I had in store for their reception. For the last time the helm of the nearest junk was put down, when we instantly fell flat on our faces and allowed the shot to pass over us. As soon as their last gun was fired, and before they had time to load again, I poured the contents of my gun amongst them fore and aft, as I had done before. This took them completely by surprise; and as we were still under a heavy press of sail, we were soon a considerable way ahead of them. Two others of the fleet came up and fired some shots at us, but the whole of them evidently imagined that a number of foreigners were on board of our junk, a belief which doubtless had a great deal to do with the success which attended my efforts. At length, darkness coming on, they gave up the pursuit and bore away from us, and in two hours more we arrived at a safe anchorage. The fever, which I had scarcely felt during all this excitement, now returned with greater violence, and I was heartily glad to go below and turn into my bed.

During the night I heard a great noise on board, but was too feverish and weak to make any inquiries as to the cause. In the morning my servant informed me that it was occasioned by the arrival of three junks during the night, which had been chased to the entrance of the harbour by the pirates; there had, he said, originally been four in company, but one of them had been taken.

The sailors on board these junks had not been so fortunate as we had been, for several of them were severely wounded, and I was now asked to extract the balls. The wounds were large and ragged, owing to the iron shot which the Chinese use in their guns; I advised the wounded men to hurry on to Chusan, where they would get good medical advice.

Up to nine o'clock in the morning, although the wind and tide were both favourable, there were no signs of the junks getting under way; I therefore sent for the captain and inquired if it was not his intention to proceed. He told me that he had had a meeting with the captains of the other vessels, and that they had determined to get a convoy of war-junks from the mandarin before they went on. Being now within eighty or ninety miles of Chusan, I could easily hire a small boat for that distance, and therefore said to the captain, "Very well; then I shall leave you here, as I am very unwell, and anxious to get to Chusan as soon as possible." "Go," said I, turning to my servant, "and engage a boat to take me on to Chusan, and bring it here as soon as you can." When he was about to leave the vessel, several of the crew gathered round him and attempted to persuade him not to go; anxious to serve his countrymen, although at my expense, he loitered about for a little while and then came back and informed me that it was no use going on shore, as I should not be able to engage a boat to take me so far. As I had been informed by one of the shore people who had come on board that plenty of boats were to be had on hire, I felt annoyed at his deceit, and threatened to punish him if he did not start immediately and bring a boat off. When he saw that I was determined, he turned sulkily away, jumped into a sand-pan, and procured a boat without the slightest difficulty. The captain and crew now crowded round me, begging me not to leave them, and offering to get up their anchor and proceed at once. Although my destination was Chusan, I had taken my passage for Ning-po, as all the wood-junks were bound either for that port or Chapoo; on their now begging me to stay, I told them that, unless they would sail into Chusan harbour and leave me there as they passed, I would proceed in the small boat, as I was anxious to get there as soon as possible, in order to obtain medicine and advice. "Oh," said they, "if you will only go with us, we will run into Chusan harbour and leave you there before we cross over to Ning-po." Upon this assurance I agreed to accompany them.

The captains of the other junks now came to me and asked me if I would undertake to protect them all from the attacks of the pirates; as, if so, they would get under weigh and go with us also. Upon my telling them that I could not undertake to do this, they told me that they must wait until some arrangement could be made with the mandarins, as they were afraid to proceed alone. We therefore left them at anchor, and proceeded on our voyage. During the day we frequently saw suspicious-looking craft, which were pronounced by the crew to be *Jan-dous;* but none of them were near enough to attack us. Late in the afternoon, as we approached Keto-point—a promontory of the main land near Chusan—we met a large fleet of merchant-junks sailing together for mutual protection on their way down. Some of them came alongside us, and made anxious inquiries regarding the *Jan-dous*, and how many of them they might expect to meet with. Our people did not fail to give them an exaggerated account of the number we had seen and fought with, and the news did not appear greatly to delight them. During the night the tide turned against us; and as the wind, although fair, was light, we were obliged to anchor until morning.

When I went on deck at daylight the following morning, I found we were just under Keto-point, and only a few miles from Chusan harbour. The land was well known to me, having been frequently there before. It was the most welcome sight which had met my eyes for many a long day; and I was thankful indeed to the Almighty for my escape from the pirates.

Whilst the men were heaving up the anchor, my old friends the captain and pilot came below, bolder and in much better spirits than heretofore, and informed me, with the greatest coolness, that they had changed their minds about going into the harbour of Chusan; and that I must go over with them to Ning-po, from whence I could easily return in a small boat for Chusan. I felt very much nettled at this conduct, which, considering that I had saved their junk from being taken by the pirates on two different occasions, was most ungrateful. I reproached them with this ingratitude, telling them that, as they were now safe from the *Jan-dous*, they imagined that they could do with me just as they pleased. "But you never deceived yourselves more," added I; "you may show as much ingratitude as you please; but I shall take care that you fulfil the promise you made to me yesterday, and take me into the harbour of Chusan, before you go over to Ning-po. Look here: you see this gun and these pistols; they are all loaded: you know what effects they produced upon the *Jan-dous;* take care they are not turned against yourselves. Englishmen never allow promises which have been made to them to be broken with impunity. I know the way into Chusan harbour as well as you do, and when the anchor is up I shall stand at the helm; and if the pilot attempts to steer for Ning-go, he must take the consequence." This threat had the desired effect, and the trembling varlets landed me safely at Chusan in the course of the forenoon.

What with the fever and the excitement of the last few days, I was in a most deplorable condition when I reached Chusan; but as the greater part of my collections were in the country near Shanghae, I was most anxious to ascertain in what state they were; and, finding an English vessel about to sail for the Yang-tse-kiang, I immediately crawled on board, and, having a fair wind, we soon reached our destination. I was kindly received by my friend Mr. Mackenzie, and, under the skilful treatment of Dr. Kirk, the fever gradually left me, and I was soon enabled to attend to my collections.

Amongst the more important of the acquisitions which I made in the vicinity of Shanghae, I must not forget to mention a fine and large variety of peach, which comes into the markets there about the middle of August, and remains in perfection for about ten days. It is grown in the peach-orchards a few miles to the south of the city; and it is quite a usual thing to see peaches of this variety eleven inches in circumference and twelve ounces in weight. This is, probably, what some writers call the Peking peach, about which such exaggerated stories have been told. Trees of the Shanghae variety are now in the garden of the Horticultural Society of London.

The whole of my plants from the districts of Foo-chow-foo, Chusan, and Ning-po, being brought together at Shanghae, I got them packed, and, on the 10th of October, left the north of China for Hong-kong and ENGLAND. As I went down the river I could not but look around me with pride and satisfaction; for in this part of the country I had found the finest plants in my collections. It is only the patient botanical collector, the object of whose unintermitted labour is the introduction of the more valuable trees and shrubs of other countries into his own, who can appreciate what I then felt.

When we arrived at Hong-kong I divided my collections and despatched eight glazed cases of living plants for England: the duplicates of these and many others I reserved to take home under my own care. I then went up to Canton and took my passage for London in the ship "John Cooper." Eighteen glazed cases, filled with the most beautiful plants of northern China, were placed upon the poop of the ship, and we sailed on the 22nd of December. After a long but favourable voyage we anchored in the Thames on the 6th of May, 1846. The plants arrived in excellent order, and were immediately conveyed to the garden of the Horticultural Society at Chiswick. Since then they have been propagated in large quantities, and are now common in our parks and gardens.

Anemone on the Tombs.

END OF VOL. I.

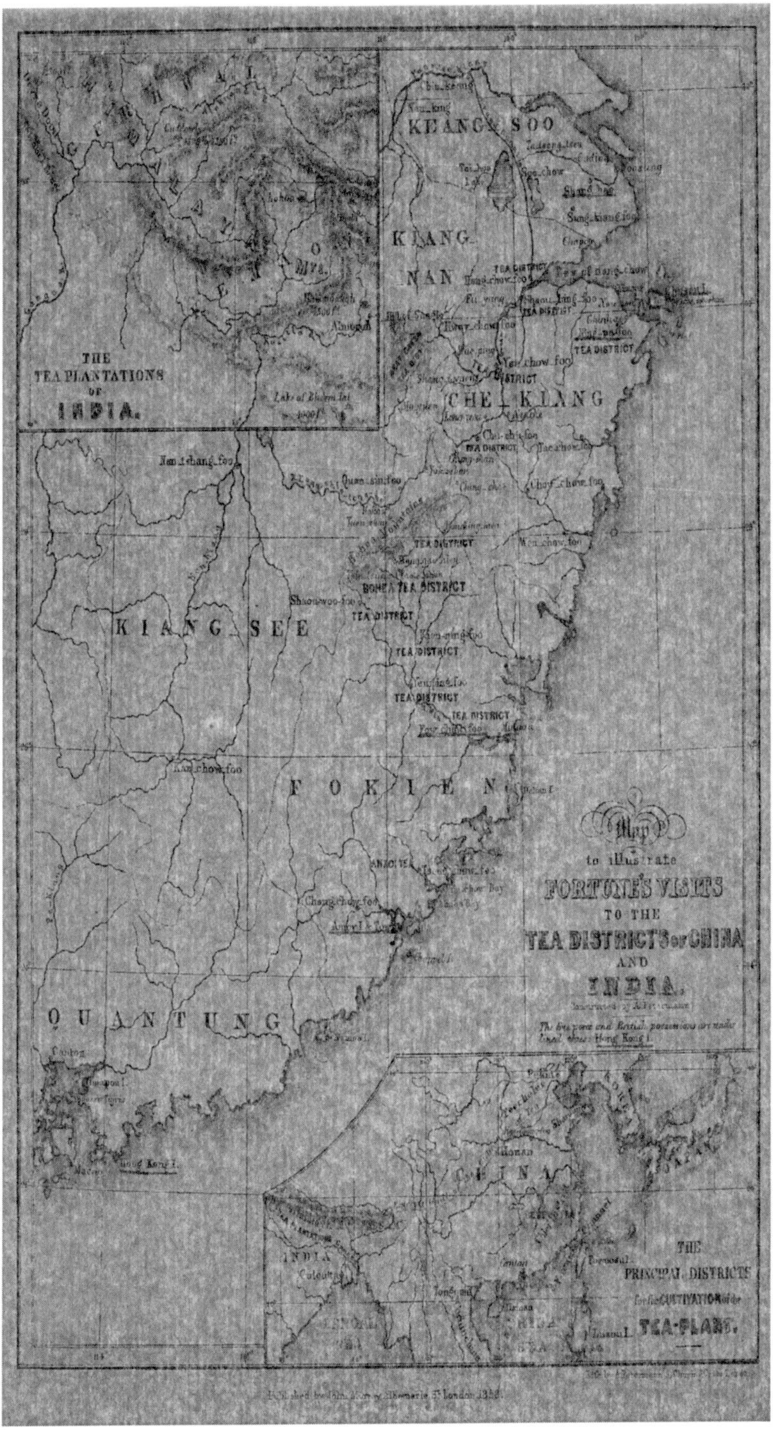

THE TEA PLANTATIONS OF INDIA.
KEANG SOO
KIANG NAN
CHE KIANG
KIANG SEE
FOKIEN
QUANTUNG
TEA DISTRICT
BOHEA TEA DISTRICT
Nan_tchang_foo
Kan_chow_foo
Shaou-woo-foo
Wen_chow_foo
Sung_kiang_foo
Canton
Map to illustrate FORTUNE'S VISITS TO THE TEA DISTRICTS of CHINA AND INDIA.
CHINA
INDIA
JAPAN
THE PRINCIPAL DISTRICTS for the CULTIVATION of the TEA-PLANT.